028.9
B65L

70604

DATE DUE			
GAYLORD M-2			PRINTED IN U.S.A.

A LIBRARIAN'S OPEN SHELF

ESSAYS ON VARIOUS SUBJECTS

A LIBRARIAN'S OPEN SHELF

ESSAYS ON VARIOUS SUBJECTS

ARTHUR E. BOSTWICK

Essay Index Reprint Series

BOOKS FOR LIBRARIES PRESS
FREEPORT, NEW YORK

First Published 1920
First Reprinting in this Series 1967
Second Reprinting 1969

STANDARD BOOK NUMBER:
8369-0226-2

LIBRARY OF CONGRESS CATALOG CARD NUMBER:
67-23182

PRINTED IN THE UNITED STATES OF AMERICA

PREFACE

The papers here gathered together represent the activities of a librarian in directions outside the boundaries of his professional career, although the influences of it may be detected in them here and there. Except for those influences they have little connection and the transition of thought and treatment from one to another may occasionally seem violent. It may, however, serve to protect the reader from the assaults of monotony. A. E. B.

CONTENTS

DO READERS READ?

Those who are interested in the proper use of our libraries are asking continually, "What do readers read?" and the tables of class-percentages in the annual reports of those institutions show that librarians are at least making an attempt to satisfy these queries. But a question that is still more fundamental and quite as vital is: Do readers read at all? This is not a paradox, but a common-sense question, as the following suggestive little incident will show. The librarian-in-charge of a crowded branch circulating-library in New York City had occasion to talk, not long ago, to one of her "star" borrowers, a youth who had taken out his two good books a week regularly for nearly a year and whom she had looked upon as a model—so much so that she had never thought it necessary to advise with him regarding his reading. In response to a question this lad made answer somewhat as follows: "Yes, ma'am, I'm doing pretty well with my reading. I think I should get on nicely if I could only once manage to read a book through; but somehow I can't seem to do it." This boy had actually taken to his home nearly a hundred books, returning each regularly and borrowing another, without reading to the end of a single one of them.

That this case is not isolated and abnormal, but is typical of the way in which a large class of readers treat books, there is, as we shall see, only too much reason to believe.

The facts are peculiarly hard to get at. At first sight there would seem to be no way to find out whether the books that our libraries circulate have been read through from cover to cover, or only half through, or not at all. To be sure, each borrower might be questioned on the subject as he returned his book, but this method would be resented as inquisitorial, and after all there would be no certainty that the data so gathered were true. By counting the stamps on the library book-card or dating-slip we can tell how many times a book has been borrowed, but this gives us no information about whether it has or has not been read. Fortunately for our present purpose, however, many works are published in a series of volumes, each of which is charged separately, and an examination of the different slips will tell us whether or not the whole work has been read through by all those who borrowed it. If, for instance in a two-volume work each volume has gone out twenty times, twenty borrowers either have read it through or have stopped somewhere in the second volume, while if the first volume is charged twenty times and the second only fourteen, it is certain that six of those who took out the first volume did not get as far as the second. In works of more than two volumes we can tell with still greater accuracy at what point the reader's interest was insufficient to carry him further.

Such an investigation has been made of all works in more than one volume contained in seven branches of the Brooklyn Public Library, and with very few exceptions it has been found that each successive volume in a series has been read by fewer persons than the one immediately preceding. What is true of books in more than one volume is presumably also true, although perhaps in a less degree, of one-volume works, although we have no means of showing it directly. Among the readers of every book, then, there are generally some who, for one reason or other, do not read it to the end. Our question, "Do readers read?" is thus answered in the negative for a large number of cases. The supplementary question, "Why do not readers read?" occurs at once, but an attempt to answer it would take us rather too deeply into psychology. Whether this tendency to leave the latter part of books unread is increasing or not we can tell only by repeating the present investigation at intervals of a year or more. The probability is that it is due to pure lack of interest. For some reason or other, many persons begin to read books that fail to hold their attention. In a large number of cases this is doubtless due to a feeling that one "ought to read" certain books and certain classes of books. A sense of duty carries the reader part way through his task, but he weakens before he has finished it.

This shows how necessary it is to stimulate one's general interest in a subject before advising him to read a book that is not itself calculated to arouse and sustain that interest. Possibly the modern newspaper habit, with its encouragement of slipshod reading, may play its part in producing the general result, and doubtless a careful detailed investigation would reveal still other partial causes, but the chief and determining cause must be lack of interest. And it is to be feared that instead of taking measures to arouse a permanent interest in good literature, which would in itself lead to the reading of standard works and would sustain the reader until he had finished his task, we have often tried to replace such an interest by a fictitious and temporary stimulus, due to appeals to duty, or to that vague and confused idea that one should "improve one's mind," unaccompanied by any definite plan of ways and means. There is no more powerful moral motor than duty, but it loses its force when we try to apply it to cases that lie without the province of ethics. The man who has no permanent interest in historical literature, and who is impelled to begin a six-volume history because he conceives it to be his "duty" to read it, is apt to conclude, before he has finished the second volume, that his is a case where inclination (or in this instance disinclination) is the proper guide.

As a matter of fact, the formation of a cultivated and permanent taste for good reading is generally a matter of lifelong education. It must be begun when the child reads his first book. An encouraging sign for the future is the care that is now taken in all good libraries to supervise the reading of children and to provide for them special quarters and facilities. A somewhat disheartening circumstance, on the other hand, is the multiplication of annotated and abbreviated children's editions of all sorts of works that were read by the last generation of children without any such treatment. This kind of boned chicken may be very well for the mental invalid, but the ordinary child prefers to separate his meat from the "drumstick" by his own unaided effort, and there is no doubt that it is better for him to do so.

In the following table, the average circulation of first volumes, second volumes, etc., is given for each of seven classes of works. The falling off from volume to volume is noticeable in each class. It is most marked in science, and least so, as might be expected, in fiction. Yet it is remarkable that there should be any falling off at all in fiction. The record shows that the proportion of readers who cannot even read to the end of a novel is relatively large. These are doubtless the good people who speak of Dickens as "solid reading" and who regard Thackeray with as remote an eye as they do Gibbon. For such "The Duchess" furnishes good mental pabulum, and Miss Corelli provides flights into the loftier regions of philosophy.

CLASS	Vol. I.	Vol. II.	Vol. III.	Vol. IV.	Vol. V.	Vol. VI.	Vol. VII.	Vol. VIII.	Vol. IX.	Vol. X.	Vol. XI.	Vol. XII.
History	10.1	6.9	4.9	4.4	4.6	4.3	2.5	2.8	1.0	0.5	1.0	3.0
Biography	7.2	5.1	3.0	2.3	1.6	1.0	1.6	1.2	1.0	2.		
Travel	9.2	7.9										
Literature	7.3	5.9	3.5	3.8	5.3	6.6	19.0	15.0	21.0			
Arts	4.7	3.7	3.0									
Sciences	5.2	2.7	1.5									
Fiction	22.0	18.9	15.8	16.	26.	16.						

The figures in the table, as has been stated, are averages, and the number of cases averaged decreases rapidly as we reach the later volumes, because, of course, the number of works that run beyond four or five volumes is relatively small. Hence the figures for the higher volumes are irregular. Any volume may have been withdrawn separately for reference without any intention of reading its companions. Among the earlier volumes such use counts for little, owing to the large number of volumes averaged, while it may and does make the figures for the later volumes irregular. Thus, under History the high number in the twelfth column represents one-twelfth volume of Froude, which was taken out three times, evidently for separate reference, as the eleventh was withdrawn but once. Furthermore, apart from this irregularity, the figures for the later volumes are relatively large, for a work in many volumes is apt to be a standard, and although its use falls rapidly from start to finish enough readers persevere to the

end to make the final averages compare unduly well
with the initial ones where the high use of the same
work is averaged in with smaller use of dozens of
other first and second volumes. That the falling off
from beginning to end in such long works is much
more striking than would appear from the averages
alone may be seen from the following records of separate works in numerous volumes:

History	Vol. I.	Vol. II.	Vol. III.	Vol. IV.	Vol. V.	Vol. VI.	Vol. VII.	Vol. VIII.	Vol. IX.	Vol. X.
Grote, "Greece"	11	6	5	2	1	0	1	1	1	0
Bancroft, "United States"	22	10	6	8	10	8				
Hume, "England"	24	7	5	2	1	1				
Gibbon, "Rome"	38	12	7	3	4	6				
Motley, "United Netherlands"	7	1	1	1						
Prescott, "Ferdinand and Isabella"	20	4	2							
Carlyle, "French Revolution"	18	10	8							
McCarthy, "Our Own Times"	27	8	11							

BIOGRAPHY

Bourienne, "Memoirs of Napoleon"	19	18	9	7						
Longfellow's "Life"	6	4	2							
Nicolay and Hay, "Lincoln"	6	3	3	2	2	2	2	1	1	2
Carlyle, "Frederick the Great"	7	3	2	2	2					

FICTION

Dumas, "Vicomte de Bragelonne"	31	30	24	22	21	16
Dumas, "Monte Cristo"	27	17	18			
Dickens, "Our Mutual Friend"	5	4	1	0		
Stowe, "Uncle Tom's Cabin"	37	24				

Of course, these could be multiplied indefinitely.
They are sufficiently interesting apart from all comment. One would hardly believe without direct evidence that of thirty-one persons who began one of
Dumas's romances scarcely half would read it to the
end, or that not one of five persons who essayed
Dickens's "Mutual Friend" would succeed in getting
through it.

Those who think that there can be no pathos in
statistics are invited to ponder this table deeply.

Can anyone think unmoved of those two dozen readers who, feeling impelled by desire for an intellectual stimulant to take up Hume, found therein a soporific instead and fell by the wayside? A curious fact is that the tendency to attempt to "begin at the beginning" is so strong that it sometimes extends to collected works in which there is no sequence from volume to volume. Thus we have the following:

	Vol. I.	Vol. II.	Vol. III	Vol. IV.	Vol. V.	Vol. VI.
Chaucer, "Poetical Works"	38	9	5			
Milton, "Poetical Works"	19	8				
Longfellow, "Poetical Works"	14	15	2	10	3	3
Emerson, "Essays"	48	13				
Ward, "English Poets"	13	2	6			

There are of course exceptions to the rule that circulation decreases steadily from volume to volume. Here are a few:

	Vol. I.	Vol. II.	Vol. III.	Vol. IV.
Fiske, "Old Virginia"	26	24		
Spears, "History of the Navy"	44	39	36	36
Andrews, "Last Quarter Century"	8	8		
Kennan, "Siberia"	15	13		

In the case of the two-volume works the interest-sustaining power may not always be as great as would appear, because when the reader desires it, two volumes are given out as one; but the stamps on the dating-slips show that this fact counted for little in the present instances.

I would not assume that the inferences in the present article are of any special value. The statistical facts are the thing. So far as I know, no one has called attention to them before, and they are certainly worthy of all interest and attention.

WHAT MAKES PEOPLE READ?

Does the reading public read because it has a literary taste or for some other reason? In the case of the public library, for instance, does a man start with an overwhelming desire to read or study books and is he impelled thereby to seek out the place where he may most easily and best obtain them? Or is he primarily attracted to the library by some other consideration, his love for books and reading acting only in a secondary manner? The New York Public Library, for instance, carries on the registry books of its circulating department nearly 400,000 names, and in the course of a year nearly 35,000 new applications are made for the use of its branch libraries, scattered over different parts of the city. What brings these people to the library? This is no idle question. The number of library users, large as it is, represents too small a fraction of our population. If it is a good thing to provide free reading matter for our people—and every large city in the country has committed itself to the truth of this proposition—we should certainly try to see that what we furnish is used by all who need it. Hence an examination into the motives that induce people to make their first use of a free public library may bring out information that is not only interesting but useful. To this end several hundred regular users of the branches of the New York Public Library were recently asked this question directly, and the answers are tabulated and discussed below. In each of sixteen branch libraries the persons interrogated numbered forty—ten each of men, women, boys and girls. Thirty answers have been thrown out for irrelevancy or defectiveness. The others are classified in the following table:

	Sent or Told by Teacher	Sent or Told by Friend	Sent or Told by Relative	Sent or Told by Clergyman	Sent or Told by Library Assistant	Through Reading Room	Saw Building	Saw Sign	Saw Library Books	Saw Bulletin	Saw Article in Paper	Sought Library	Totals
Men	6	64	10	..	..	..	37	20	3	1	9	4	154
Boys	38	63	28	..	4	3	9	6	5	..	..	3	159
Women	12	67	14	4	..	..	20	21	2	1	2	5	148
Girls	33	69	34	..	..	..	5	3	3	..	..	2	149
Total ...	89	263	86	4	4	3	71	50	13	2	11	14	610

It will be seen that the vast majority of those questioned were led to the library by some circumstance other than the simple desire to find a place where books could be obtained. Of more than six hundred persons whose answers are here recorded only fourteen found the library as the result of a direct search for it prompted by a desire to read. In a majority of the other cases, of course, perhaps in all of them, the desire to read had its part, but this desire was awakened by hearing a mention of the library or by seeing it or something connected with it. These determining circumstances fall into two classes, those that worked through the ear and those that operated through the eye.

Those who *heard* of the library in some way numbered 449, while those who *saw* it or something connected with it were only 147—an interesting fact, especially as we are told by psychologists that apprehension and memory through sight are of a higher type than the same functions where exercised through hearing. Probably, however, this difference was dependent on the fact that the thing heard was in most cases a direct injunction or a piece of advice, while the thing seen did not act with similar urgency. There are some surprises in the table. For instance, only four persons were sent directly to libraries by persons employed therein. Doubtless the average library assistant wishes to get as far from "shop" as possible in her leisure hours, but it is still disappointing to find that those who are employed in our libraries exercise so little influence in bringing persons to use them. The same thing is true of the influence of reading rooms. In many of the branch libraries in New York there are separate reading rooms to which others than card-holders in the library are admitted, and one of the chief arguments for this has been that the user of such a room, having become accustomed to resort to the library building, would be apt to use the books. Apparently, however, such persons are in the minority. No less disappointing is the slight influence of the clergy. Only four persons report this as a determining influence and these were all women connected with a branch which was formerly the parish library of a New York church.

The influence of the press, too, seems to amount to little, in spite of the fact that the newspapers in New York have freely commented on the valuable work of the branch libraries and have called attention to it both in the news and editorial columns whenever occasion offered. Do the readers of library books in New York shun the public press, or do they pay scant heed to what they read therein?

Another somewhat noteworthy fact is that of the 449 persons who sought the library by advice of some one, only 89 were sent by teachers. But perhaps this is unfair. Of 265 boys and girls who thus came to the library, only 71 were sent by teachers. This is a larger percentage, but it is still not so large as we might expect.

The difference between adults and children comes out quite strikingly in a few instances. We should have foreseen this of course in the case of advice by teachers, which was reported by 71 children and only 18 adults as a reason for visiting the library. Here we should not have expected this reason to be given by adults at all. Doubtless these were chiefly young men and women who had used the library since their school-days. In like manner the advice or injunction of relatives was more patent with children than with adults, the proportion here being 62 to 24. This probably illustrates the power of parental injunction. In another case the difference comes out in a wholly unexpected way. Of the 71 persons who reported that they were attracted to the library by seeing the buildings, 57 were adults and only 14 children. The same is true of those who were led in by seeing a sign, who numbered 41 adults to only 9 children. This seems to show either that adults are more observant or that children are more diffident in following out an impulse of this kind. It completely negatives the ordinary impression among librarians, at least in New York, where it has been believed that the sight of a library building, especially where the work going on inside is visible from the street, is a potent attraction to the young. Some of the new branch buildings in New York have even been planned with a special view to the exercise of this kind of attraction.

The small number of persons who were attracted by printed matter, in library or general publications, were entirely adults. The one instance where age seems to exercise no particular influence is that of the advice of friends, by which old and young alike seem to have profited.

The influence of sex does not appear clearly, although among those who followed the injunction of relatives the women and girls are slightly in the majority, and the four who were sent by clergymen were all women. Of those who were attracted by the buildings 46 were male and 25 female, which may mean that men are somewhat more observant or less diffident than women.

A few of those questioned relate their experiences at some length. Says one boy: "A boy friend of mine said he belonged to this library and he found some very good books here. He asked me if I wanted to join; I said yes. He told me I would have to get a reference. I got one, and joined this library." Another one reports: "I saw a boy in the street and asked him where he was going. He said he was going to the library. I asked him what the library was and he told me; so I came up here and have been coming ever since."

Critical judgment is shown by some of the young people. One boy says: "I heard all the other boys saying it was a good library and that the books were better kept than in a majority of libraries." A girl says that friends "told her what nice books were in this library." In one case a boy's brother "told him he could get the best books here for his needs."

The combination of man and book seems to be very attractive. One child "saw a boy in school with a book, telling what a boy should know about electricity; I wanted to read that book and joined the library." Others "followed a crowd of little boys with books"; "saw children taking books out of the building and asked them about joining"; "saw a boy carrying books and asked if there was a library in the neighborhood." A woman "saw a child with a library book in the park and asked her for the address of the library." Sometimes the book alone does the work, as shown by the following laconic report: "Found a book in the park; took it to the library; joined it." A cause of sorrow to many librarians who have decided ideas regarding literature for children will be the report of a boy who exclaimed: "Horatio Alger did it!" On being asked to explain, he said that a friend had brought one of Alger's books to his house and that he was thereby attracted to the library.

Among those who were brought in by relatives are children who were first carried by their mothers to the library as infants and so grew naturally into its use. Sometimes the influence works upward instead of downward, for several adults report that their children brought them to the library or induced them to visit it. One man reports that he "got married and his wife induced him to come."

Some of the reasons given are curious. A few are unconnected with the use of books. One girl came to the library because "it was a very handy library"; another, because she "saw it was a nice place to come to on a rainy day." Still another frankly avows that "it was the fad among the boys and girls of our neighborhood; we used to meet at the library." A postman reported that he entered the library first in the line of his duty, but was attracted by it and began to take out books. A clergyman had his attention called to the library by requests from choir-boys that he should sign their application blanks; afterwards thinking that he might find books there for his own reading, he became a regular user. One user came first to the library to see an exhibition of pictures of old New York. A recent importation says: "When I came from Paris I found all my cousins speaking English; 'well,' they said, 'go to the library and take books'"—a process that doubtless did its share toward making an American of the new arrival. In another case, the Americanizing process has not yet reached the stage where the user's English is altogether intelligible. He says: "Because I like to read the book. I ask the bakery lady to my reference and I sing my neam" [sign my name?].

Here are some examples of recently acquired elegance in diction that are almost baboo-like in their hopelessness: "Because it interest about the countries that are far away. It gives knowledge to many of the people in this country." "So as to obtain knowledge from them and by reading books find out how the great men were in their former days and all about them and the world and its people." It will be seen that the last two writers were among those who misunderstood our questions and told why they read books rather than how they were first led to the use of a library.

These reports are far from possessing merely a passing interest for the curious. For the public librarian, whose wish it is to reach as large a proportion of the public as possible, they are full of valuable hints. They emphasize, for instance, the urgent necessity of winning the good will of the public, and they forcibly remind us that this is of more value in gaining a foothold for the library than columns of notices in the papers or thousands of circulars or cards distributed in the neighborhood. It is even more potent than a beautiful building. Attractive as this is, its value as an influence to secure new readers is vastly less than a reputation for hospitality and helpfulness.

In looking over the figures one rather disquieting thought cannot be kept down. If the good will of the public is so potent in increasing the use of the library, the ill will of the same public must be equally potent in the opposite direction. Some of those who are satisfied with us and our work are here put on record. How about the dissatisfied? A record of these might be even more interesting, for it would point out weaknesses to be strengthened and errors to be avoided—but that, as Kipling says, "is another story."

THE PASSING OF THE POSSESSIVE: A STUDY OF BOOK-TITLES

If there is one particular advantage possessed by the Teutonic over the Romance languages in idiomatic clearness and precision it is that conferred by their ownership of a possessive case, almost the sole remaining monument to the fact that our ancestors spoke an inflected tongue. That we should still be able to speak of "the baker's wife's dog" instead of "the dog of the wife of the baker" certainly should be regarded by English-speaking people as a precious birthright. Yet, there are increasing evidences of a tendency to discard this only remaining case-ending and to replace its powerful backbone with the comparatively limp and cartilaginous preposition. This tendency has not yet appeared so much in our spoken as in our written language, and even here only in the most formal parts of it. It is especially noticeable in the diction of the purely formal title and heading.

That the reader may have something beyond an unsupported assertion that this is the case, I purpose to offer in evidence the titles of some recent works of fiction, and to make a brief statistical study of them.

The titles were taken from the adult fiction lists in the Monthly Bulletins of the New York Free Circulating Library from November, 1895, to March, 1897, inclusive, and are all such titles as contain a possessive, whether expressed by the possessive case or by the preposition "of" with the objective. Some titles are included in which the grammatical relation is slightly different, but all admit the alternative of the case-ending "'s" or "of" followed by the objective case.

Of the 101 titles thus selected, 41 use the possessive case and 60 the objective with the preposition. This proportion is in itself sufficiently suggestive, but it becomes still more so by comparing it with the corresponding proportion among a different set of titles. For this purpose 101 fiction titles were selected, just as they appeared in alphabetical order, from a library catalogue bearing the date 1889; only those being taken, as before, that contain a possessive. Of these 101, 71 use the possessive case and 30 the objective with "of." In other words, where eight years ago nearly three-quarters of such titles used the possessive case, now only two-fifths use it, a proportionate reduction of nearly one-half.

The change appears still more striking when we study the titles a little more closely. Of those in the earlier series there is not one that is not good, idiomatic English as it stands, whichever form is used; we may even say that there is not one that would not be made less idiomatic by a change to the alternative form. Among the recent titles, however, while the forms using the possessive case are all better as they are, of the 60 titles that use the objective with "of" only 22 would be injured by a change, and the reason why 8 of these are better as they are is simply that change would destroy euphony. Among these eight are

    "The Indiscretion of the Duchess,"
    "The Flight of a Shadow,"
    "The Secret of Narcisse," etc.,

where the more idiomatic forms,
    "The Duchess's Indiscretion,"
    "Narcisse's Secret,"
    "A Shadow's Flight," etc.,
are certainly not euphonic.

Of the others, 8 would not be injured by a change, and no less than 30 would be improved from the standpoint of idiomatic English. It may be well to quote these thirty titles. They are:

"The Shadow of Hilton Fernbrook,"
"The Statement of Stella Maberly,"
"The Shadow of John Wallace,"
"The Banishment of Jessop Blythe,"
"The Desire of the Moth,"
"The Island of Dr. Moreau,"
"The Damnation of Theron Ware,"
"The Courtship of Morrice Buckler,"
"The Daughter of a Stoic,"
"The Lament of Dives,"
"The Heart of Princess Osra,"
"The Death of the Lion,"
"The Vengeance of James Vansittart,"
"The Wife of a Vain Man,"
"The Crime of Henry Vane,"
"The Son of Old Harry,"
"The Honour of Savelli,"
"The Life of Nancy,"
"The Story of Lawrence Garthe,"
"The Marriage of Esther,"
"The House of Martha,"
"Tales of an Engineer,"
"Love-letters of a Worldly Woman,"
"The Way of a Maid,"
"The Soul of Pierre,"
"The Day of Their Wedding,"
"The Exploits of Brigadier Gerard,"
"The Hand of Ethelberta,"
"The Failure of Sibyl Fletcher,"
"The Love-affairs of an Old Maid,"

Of course, in such a division as this, much must depend on individual judgment and bias. Probably no two persons would divide the list in just the same way, but it is my belief that the general result in each case would be much the same. To me the pos-

sessive in every one of the above-quoted titles would
have been more idiomatic, thus:

"Hilton Fernbrook's Shadow,"
"Stella Maberly's Statement,"
"John Wallace's Shadow,"
"Morrice Buckler's Courtship,"
"A Stoic's Daughter,"
"Henry Vane's Crime," etc., etc.

In one case, at least, this fact has been recognized by a publisher, for "The Vengeance of James
Vansittart," whose title is included in the list given
above, has appeared in a later edition as "James Vansittart's Vengeance"—a palpable improvement.

I shall not discuss the cause of this change in the
use of the possessive, though it seems to me an evident Gallicism, nor shall I open the question of
whether it is a mere passing fad or the beginning of
an actual alteration in the language. However this
may be, it seems undeniable that there is an actual
and considerable difference in the use of the possessive to-day and its use ten years ago, at least in
formal titles and headings. I have confined myself
to book-titles, because that is the department where
the tendency presents itself to me most clearly; but
it may be seen on street signs, in advertisements, and
in newspaper headings. It is not to be found yet in
the spoken language, at least it is not noticeable
there, but it would be decidedly unsafe to prophesy
that it will never appear there. Ten years from now
we may hear about "the breaking of the arm of John
Smith" and "the hat of Tom," without a thought
that these phrases have not been part of our idiomatic speech since Shakespeare's time.

SELECTIVE EDUCATION *

Since Darwin called attention to the role of what he named "natural selection" in the genesis and preservation of species, and since his successors, both followers and opponents, have added to this many other kinds of selection that are continually operative, it has become increasingly evident that from one standpoint we may look on the sum of natural processes, organic and inorganic, as a vast selective system, as the result of which things are as they are, whether the results are the positions of celestial bodies or the relative places of human beings in the intellectual or social scale. The exact constitution of the present population of New York is the result of a great number of selective acts, some regular, others more or less haphazard. Selection is no less selection because it occurs by what we call chance— for chance is only our name for the totality of trivial and unconsidered causes. When, however, we count man and man's efforts in the sum of natural objects and forces, we have to reckon with his intelligence in these selective processes. I desire to call attention to the place that they play in educative systems and in particular to the way in which they may be furthered or made more effective by books, especially by public collections of books.

When we think of any kind of training as it affects the individual, we most naturally regard it as changing that individual, as making him more fit, either for life in general or for some special form of life's activities. But when we think of it as af-

* Read before the Schoolmen of New York.

fecting a whole community or a whole nation, we may regard it as essentially a selective process. In a given community it is not only desirable that a certain number of men should be trained to do a specified kind of work, but it is even more desirable that these should be the men that are best fitted to do this work. When Mr. Luther Burbank brings into play the selection by means of which he achieves his remarkable results in plant breeding he gets rid of the unfit by destruction, and as all are unfit for the moment that do not advance the special end that he has in view, he burns up plants—new and interesting varieties perhaps—by the hundred thousand. We cannot destroy the unfit, nor do we desire to do so, for from the educational point of view unfitness is merely bad adjustment. There is a place for every man in the world and it is the educator's business to see that he reaches it, if not by formative, then by selective processes. This selection is badly made in our present state of civilization. It depends to a large extent upon circumstances remote from the training itself—upon caprice, either that of the person to be trained or of his parents, upon accidents of birth or situation, upon a thousand irrelevant things; but in every case there are elements present in the training itself that aid in determining it. A young man begins to study medicine, and he finds that his physical repulsion for work in the dissecting-room can not be overcome. He abandons the study and by doing so eliminates an unfit person. A boy who has no head for figures enters a business college. He can not get his diploma, and the community is spared one bad bookkeeper. Certainly in some instances, possibly in all, technical and professional schools that are noted for the excellence of their product are superior not so much because they have better methods of training, but because their material is of better quality, owing to selection exercised either purposely, or automatically, or perhaps by some chance. The same is true of colleges. Of two institutions with the same curriculum and equally able instructors, the one with the widest reputation will turn out the best graduates because it attracts abler men from a wider field. This is true even in such a department as athletics. To him that hath shall be given. This is purely an automatic selective effect.

It would appear desirable to dwell more upon selective features in educational training, to ascertain what they are in each case and how they work, and to control and dispose them with more systematic care. Different minds will always attach different degrees of importance to natural and acquired fitness, but probably all will agree that training bestowed upon the absolutely unfit is worse than useless, and that there are persons whose natural aptitudes are so great that upon them a minimum of training will produce a maximum effect. Such selective features as our present educational processes possess, the examination, for instance, are mostly exclusive; they aim to bar out the unfit rather than to attract the fit. Here is a feature on which some attention may well be fixt.

How do these considerations affect the subject of general education? Are we to affirm that arithmetic is only for the born mathematician and Latin for the born linguist, and endeavor to ascertain who these may be? Not so; for here we are training not experts but citizens. Discrimination here must be not in the quality but in the quantity of training. We may divide the members of any community into classes according as their formal education—their school and college training—has lasted one, two, three, four, or more years. There has been a selection here, but it has operated, in general, even more imperfectly than in the case of special training. Persons who are mentally qualified to continue their schooling to the end of a college course, and who by so doing would become more useful members of the community, are obliged to be content with two or three years in the lower grades, while others, who are unfitted for the university, are kept at it until they take, or fail to take, the bachelor's degree. An ideal state of things, of course, would be to give each person the amount of general education for which he is fitted and then stop. This would be difficult of realization even if financial considerations did not so often interfere. But at least we may keep in view the desirability of preventing too many misfits and of insisting, so far as possible, on any selective features that we may discover in present systems.

For instance, a powerful selective feature is the attractiveness of a given course of study to those who are desired to pursue it. If we can find a way, for example, to make our high school courses attractive to those who are qualified to take them, while at the same time rendering them very distasteful to those who are not so qualified, we shall evidently have taken a step in the right direction. It is clear that both parts of this prescription must be taken together or there is no true selection. Much has been done of late years toward making educational courses of all kinds interesting and attractive, but it is to be feared that their attractiveness has been such as to appeal to the unfit as well as to the fit. If we sugar-coat our pills indiscriminately and mix them with candy, many will partake who need another kind of medicine altogether. We must so arrange things that the fit will like while the unfit dislike, and for this purpose the less sugar-coating the better. This is no easy problem and it is intended merely to indicate it here, not to propose a general solution. The one thing to which attention should be directed is the role that may be and is played by the printed book in selective education. There is more or less effort to discredit books as educative tools and to lay emphasis on oral instruction and manual training. We need not decry these, but, it must be remembered that after all the book contains the record of man's progress; we may tell how to do a thing, and show how to do it, but we shall never do it in a better way or explain the why and wherefore, and surely transmit that ability and that explanation to posterity, without the aid of a stable record of some kind. If we are sure that our students could and would pick out only what they needed, as a wild animal picks his food in the woods, we might go far toward solving our problem, by simply turning them loose in a collection of books. Some people have minds that qualify them to profit by such "browsing," and some of these have practically educated themselves in a library. Even in the more common cases where formal training is absolutely necessary, access to other books than text-books is an aid to selection both qualitative and quantitative. Books may serve as samples. To take an extreme case, a boy who had no knowledge whatever of the nature of law or medicine would certainly not be competent to choose between them in selecting a profession, and a month spent in a library where there were books on both subjects would certainly operate to lessen his incompetence. Probably it would not be rash to assert that with free access to books, under proper guidance, both before and during a course of training, the persons who begin that course will include more of the fit and those who finish it will include less of the unfit, than without such access.

Let us consider one or two concrete examples. A college boy has the choice of several different courses. He knows little of them, but thinks that one will meet his needs. He elects it and finds too late that he is wasting his time. Another boy, whose general reading has been sufficient to give him some superficial knowledge of the subject-matter in all the courses, sees clearly which will benefit him, and profits by that knowledge.

Again, a boy, full of the possibilities that would lead him to appreciate the best in literature, has gained his knowledge of it from a teacher who looks upon a literary masterpiece only as something to be dissected. The student has been disgusted instead of inspired, and his whole life has been deprived of one of the purest and most uplifting of all influences. Had he been brought up in a library where he could make literary friends and develop literary enthusiasms, his course with the dryasdust teacher would have been only an unpleasant incident, instead of the wrecking of a part of his intellectual life.

Still again, a boy on a farm has vague aspirations. He knows that he wants a broader horizon, to get away from his cramped environment—that is about all. How many boys, impelled by such feelings, have gone out into the world with no clear idea of what they are fitted to do, or even what they really desire! To how many others has the companionship of a few books meant the opening of a peephole, thru which, dimly perhaps, but none the less really, have been descried definite possibilities, needs, and opportunities!

To all of these youths books have been selective

aids merely—they have added little or nothing to the actual training whose extent and character they have served to point out. Such cases, which it would be easy to multiply, illustrate the value of books in the selective functions of training. To assert that they exercise such a function is only another way of saying that a mind orients itself by the widest contact with other minds. There are other ways of assuring this contact, and these should not be neglected; but only thru books can it approach universality both in space and in time. How else could we know exactly what Homer and St. Augustine and Descartes thought and what Tolstoi and Lord Kelvin and William James, we will say, are even now thinking?

It has scarcely been necessary to say all this to convince you of the value of books as aids to education; but it is certainly interesting to find that in an examination of the selective processes in education, we meet with our old friends in such an important role.

A general collection of books, then, constitutes an important factor in the selective part of an education. Where shall we place this collection? I venture to say that altho every school must have a library to aid in the formative part of its training, the library as a selective aid should be large and central and should preferably be at the disposal of the student not only during the period of his formal training, but before and after it. This points to the public library, and to close cooperation between it and the school, rather than to the expansion of the classroom library. This is, perhaps, not the place to dispute the wisdom of our Board of Education in developing classroom libraries, but it may be proper to put in a plea for confining them to books that bear more particularly on the subjects of instruction. The general collection of books should be outside of the school, because the boy is destined to spend most of his life outside of the school. His education by no means ends with his graduation. The agents that operate to develop and change him will be at work so long as he lives, and it is desirable that the book should be one of these. If he says good-by to the book when he leaves school, that part of his training is likely to be at an end. If he uses, in connection with, and parallel to, his formal education a general collection of books outside of the school, he will continue to use it after he leaves school. And even so far as the special classroom library is concerned, it must be evident that a large general collection of books that may be drawn upon freely is a useful supplement. For the teacher's professional use, the larger the collection at his disposal the better. A sum of money spent by the city in improving and making adequate the pedagogical section of its public library, particularly in the department of circulation, will be expended to greater advantage than many times the amount devoted to a large number of small collections on the same subjects in schools.

These are the considerations that have governed the New York Public Library in its effort to be of assistance to the teachers and pupils in the public schools of the city. Stated formally, these efforts manifest themselves in the following directions:

(1) The making of library use continuous from the earliest possible age, thru school life and afterwards;

(2) Cooperation with the teacher in guiding and limiting the child's reading during the school period;

(3) Aid within the library in the preparation of school work;

(4) The supplementing of classroom libraries by the loan of books in quantity;

(5) The cultivation of personal relations between library assistants and teachers in their immediate neighborhood;

(6) The furnishing of accurate and up-to-date information to schools regarding the library's resources and its willingness to place them at the school's disposal;

(7) The increase of the library's circulation collection along lines suggested and desired by teachers;

(8) The granting of special privileges to teachers and special students who use the library for purposes of study.

Toward the realization of these aims three departments are now cooperating, each of them in charge of an expert in his or her special line of work.

(1) The children's rooms in the various libraries, now under the direction of an expert supervisor.

(2) The traveling library office.

(3) The division of school work, with an assistant in each branch, under skilled headquarters superintendence.

When our plans, which are already in good working order, are completely carried out, we shall be able to guarantee to every child guidance in his reading up to and thru his school course, with direction in a line of influence that will make him a user of books thruout his life and create in him a feeling of attachment to the public library as the home and dispenser of books and as a permanent intellectual refuge from care, trouble, and material things in general, as well as a mine of information on all subjects that may benefit or interest him.

Some of the obstacles to the immediate realization of our plans in full may be briefly stated as follows:

(1) Lack of sufficient funds. With more money

we could buy more books, pay higher salaries, and
employ more persons. The assistants in charge of
children's rooms should be women of the highest culture and ability, and it is difficult to secure proper
persons at our present salaries. Assistants in charge
of school work must be persons of tact and quick-
ness of perception, and they should have no other
work to do; whereas at present we are obliged to
give this work to library assistants in addition to
their ordinary routine duties, to avoid increasing
our staff by about forty assistants, which our appropriation does not permit.

(2) Misunderstanding on the part of the public,
and also to some extent on the part of teachers, of
our aims, ability, and attitude. This I am glad to
say is continually lessening. We can scarcely expect that each of our five hundred assistants should
be thoroly imbued with the spirit of helpfulness
toward the schools or even that they should perfectly understand what we desire and aim to do. Nor
can we expect that our wish to aid should be appreciated by every one of fifty thousand teachers or a
million parents. This will come in time.

(3) A low standard of honesty on the part of certain users of the library. It is somewhat disheartening to those who are laboring to do a public service
to find that some of those whom they are striving to
benefit, look upon them merely as easy game. To
prevent this and at the same time to withstand those
who urge that such misuse of the library should be
met by the withdrawal of present privileges and facilities uses up energy that might otherwise be directed toward the improvement of our service. Now,
like the intoxicated man, we sometimes refuse invita-
tions to advance because it is "all we can do to stay
where we are." Here is an opportunity for all the
selective influences that we may bring to bear, and

unfortunately the library can have but little part in these.

Have I wandered too far from my theme? The good that a public library may do, the influence that it may exert, and the position that it may assume in a community, depend very largely on the ability and tact with which it is administered and the resources at its disposal. Its public services may be various, but probably there is no place in which it may be of more value than side by side with the public school; and I venture to think that this is the case largely because education to be complete must select as well as train, must compel the fit to step forward and the unfit to retire, and must do this, not only at the outset of a course of training but continuously thruout its duration. We speak of a student being "put thru the mill," and we must not forget that a mill not only grinds and stamps into shape but also sifts and selects. A finished product of a given grade is always such not only by virtue of formation and adaptation but also by virtue of selection. In human training one of the most potent of these selective agencies is the individual will, and to train that will and make it effective in the right direction there is nothing better than constant association with the records of past aims and past achievements. This must be my excuse for saying so much of libraries in general, and of one library in particular, in an address on what I have ventured to give the name of Selective Education.

THE USES OF FICTION *

Literature is becoming daily more of a dynamic and less of a static phenomenon. In other days the great body of written records remained more or less stable and with its attendant body of tradition did its work by a sort of quiet pressure on that portion of the community just beneath it—on a special class peculiarly subject to its influence. To-day we have added to this effect that of a moving multitude of more or less ephemeral books, which appear, do their work, and pass on out of sight. They are light, but they make up for their lack of weight by the speed and ease with which they move. Owing to them the use of books is becoming less and less limited to a class, and more and more familiar to the masses. The book nowadays is in motion. Even the classics, the favorites of other days, have left their musty shelves and are moving out among the people. Where one man knew and loved Shakespeare a century ago, a thousand know and love him to-day. The literary blood is circulating and in so doing is giving life to the body politic. In thus wearing itself out the book is creating a public appreciation that makes itself felt in a demand for reprinting, hence worthy books are surer of perpetuation in this swirling current than they were in the old time reservoir. But besides these books whose literary life is continuous, though their paper and binding may wear out, there are other books that vanish utterly. By the time that the material part of them needs renewing, the book

* Read before the American Library Association, Asheville Conference, May 28, 1907.

itself has done its work. Its value at that moment is not enough, or is not sufficiently appreciated, to warrant reprinting. It drops out of sight and its place is taken by another, fresh from the press. This part of our moving literature is what is called ephemeral, and properly so; but no stigma necessarily attaches to the name. In the first place, it is impossible to draw a line between the ephemeral and the durable. "One storm in the world's history has never cleared off," said the wit—"the one we are having now." Yet the conditions of to-day, literary as well as meteorological, are not necessarily lasting.

We are accustomed to regard what we call standard literature as necessarily the standard of innumerable centuries to come, forgetful of the fact that other so-called standards have "had their day and ceased to be." Some literature lasts a century, some a year, some a week; where shall we draw the line below which all must be condemned as ephemeral? Is it not possible that all literary work that quickly achieves a useful purpose and having achieved it passes at once out of sight, may really count for as much as one that takes the course of years to produce its slow results? The most ephemeral of all our literary productions—the daily paper—is incalculably the most influential, and its influence largely depends on this dynamic quality that has been noted—the penetrative power of a thing of light weight moving at a high speed. And this penetrative power effective literature must have to-day on account of the vastly increased mass of modern readers.

Reading is no longer confined to a class, it is wellnigh universal, in our own country, at least. And the habit of mind of the thoughtful and intent reader is not an affair of one generation but of many.

New readers are young readers, and they have the characteristics of intellectual youth.

Narrative—the recapitulation of one's own or someone else's experience, the telling of a story—is the earliest form in which artistic effort of any kind is appreciated. The pictorial art that appeals to the young or the ignorant is the kind that tells a story— perhaps historical painting on enormous canvasses, perhaps the small genre picture, possibly something symbolic or mythological; but at any rate it must embody a narrative, whether it is that of the signing of a treaty, a charge of dragoons, a declaration of love or the feeding of chickens. The same is true of music. The popular song tells something, almost without exception. Even in instrumental music, outside of dance rhythms, whose suggestion of the delights of bodily motion is a reason of their popularity, the beginner likes program music of some kind, or at least its suggestion. So it is in literature. With those who are intellectually young, whether young in years or not, the narrative form of expression is all in all. It is, of course, in all the arts, a most important mode, even in advanced stages of development. We shall never be able to do without narrative in painting, sculpture, music and poetry; but wherever, in a given community, the preference for this form of expression in any art is excessive, we may be sure that appreciation of that form of art is newly aroused. This is an interesting symptom and a good sign. To be sure, apparent intellectual youth may be the result of intellectual decadence; there is a second as well as a first childhood, but it is not difficult to distinguish between them. In general, if a large proportion of those in a community who like to look at pictures, prefer such as "tell a story," this fact, if the number of the appreciative is at the same time increasing, means a newly stimulated interest in art. And similarly, if a large proportion of those persons who enjoy reading prefer the narrative forms of literature, while at the same time their total numbers are on the increase, this surely indicates a newly aroused interest in books. And this is precisely the situation in which we find ourselves to-day. A very large proportion of the literature that we circulate is in narrative form—how large a proportion I daresay few of us realize. Not only all the fiction, adult and juvenile, but all the history, biography and travel, a large proportion of literature and periodicals, some of the sciences, including all reports of original research, and a lesser proportion of the arts, philosophy and religion, are in this form. It may be interesting to estimate the percentage of narrative circulated by a large public library, and I have attempted this in the case of the New York public library for the year ending July 1, 1906.

Class	Per cent.	Estimated per cent. of narrative
Fiction		
Juvenile 26		
Adult 32	58	58
History	6	6
Biography	3	3
Travel	3	3
Literature	7	3
Periodicals	4	2
Sciences	9	3
Arts	3	1
Philos. & Relig.	2	1
Foreign	5	4
	100	84

In other words, if my estimates are not too much out of the way—and I have tried to be conservative —only 16 per cent. of our whole circulation, and 38 per cent. of our non-fiction, is non-narrative, despite the fact that our total fiction percentage is low.

I attach little importance in this regard to any distinction between true and fictitious narrative. People who read novels do not enjoy them simply because the subject matter is untrue. They enjoy the books because they are interesting. In fact, in most good fiction, little beside the actual sequence of the events in the plot and the names of the characters is untrue. The delineation of character, the descriptions of places and events and the statements of fact are intended to be true, and the further they depart from truth the less enjoyable they are. Indeed, when one looks closely into the matter, the dividing line between what we call truth and fiction in narrative grows more and more hazy.

In pictorial art we do not attempt to make it at all. Our museums do not classify their pictures into true and imaginary. Our novels contain so much truth and our other narrative works so much fiction, that it is almost as difficult to draw the line in the the literary as it is in the pictorial arts. And in any case objections to a work of fiction, as well as commendations, must be based on considerations apart from this classification.

To represent a fictitious story as real or an imaginary portrait as a true one is, of course, a fault, but the story and the portrait may both be of the highest excellence when the subjects are wholly imaginary. It should be noted that the crime of false representation, when committed with success, removes a work from library classification as fiction and places it in one of the other classes. Indeed, it is probable that much more lasting harm is done by false non-fiction than by fiction. The reader, provided he uses literature temperately, has much less need to beware of the novel, which he reads frankly for entertainment, than of the history full of "things that are not so," of the biased biography, of science "popularized" out of all likeness to nature, of absurd theories in sociology or cosmology, of silly and crude ideas masquerading as philosophy, of the out-and-out falsehood of fake travellers and pseudo-naturalists.

In what has gone before it has been assumed that the reader is temperate. One may read to excess either in fiction or non-fiction, and the result is the same; mental over-stimulation, with the resulting reaction. One may thus intoxicate himself with history, psychology or mathematics—the mathematics-drunkard is the worst of all literary debauchees when he does exist—and the only reason why fiction-drunkenness is more prevalent is that fiction is more attractive to the average man. We do not have to warn the reader against over-indulgence in biography or art-criticism, any more than we have to put away the vichy bottle when a bibulous friend appears, or forbid the children to eat too many shredded-wheat biscuits. Fiction has the fatal gift of being too entertaining. The novel-writer must be interesting or he fails; the historian or the psychologist does not often regard it as necessary—unless he happens to be a Frenchman.

But with this danger of literary surfeit or over-stimulation, I submit that the librarian has nothing to do; it is beyond his sphere, at least in so far as he deals with the adult reader. We furnish parks and playgrounds for our people; we police them and see that they contain nothing harmful, but we cannot guarantee that they will not be used to excess—that a man may not, for example, be so enraptured with the trees and the squirrels that he will give up to their contemplation time that should be spent in supporting his family. So in the library we may and do see that harmful literature is excluded, but we cannot be expected to see that books which are not in themselves injurious are not sometimes used to excess.

I venture to suggest that very much of our feeling of disquietude about the large use of fiction in the public library and elsewhere arises from our misapprehension of something that must always force itself upon the attention in a state of society where public education and public taste are on the increase. In this case the growth will necessarily be uneven in different departments of knowledge and taste, and in different localities; so that discrepancies frequently present themselves. We may observe, for instance, a quietly and tastefully dressed woman reading, we will say, Laura Jean Libbey. We are disconcerted, and the effect is depressing. But the discrepancy may arise in either of two ways. If we have here a person formerly possessing good taste both in dress and reading, whose taste in the latter regard has deteriorated, we certainly have cause for sadness; but if, as is much more likely, we have one who had formerly bad taste of both kinds and whose taste in dress has improved, we should rather rejoice. The argument is the same whether the change has taken place in the same generation or in more than one. Our masses are moving upward and the progress along the more material lines is often more rapid than in matters of the intellect. Or, on the contrary, intellectual progress may be in advance of manners. Such discrepancies are frequently commented upon by foreign travelers in the United States, who almost invariably misinterpret them in the same way. Can we blame them, when we make the same mistake ourselves? M. Jules Huret, in his recent interesting book "En Amerique,"

notes frequently the lapses in manners and taste of
educated persons among us. He describes, for instance, the bad table-manners of a certain clergyman. His thought is evidently, "How shocking that
a clergyman should act in this way!" But we might
also put it: "How admirable that professional education in this country is so easily obtained that one
of a class in which such manners prevail can secure
it! How encouraging that he should desire to enter
the ministry and succeed in doing so!" These are
extreme standpoints; we need of course endorse
neither of them. But when I find that on the upper
west side of New York, where the patrons of our
branch libraries are largely the wives and daughters
of business men with good salaries, whose general
scale of living is high, the percentage of fiction circulated is unduly great, I do not say, as I am tempted to do "How surprising and how discouraging that
persons of such apparent cultivation should read
nothing but fiction, and that not of the highest
grade!" I say rather: "What an evidence it is of our
great material prosperity that persons in an early
stage of mental development, as evidenced by undue
preference for narrative in literature, are living in
such comfort or even luxury!"

Is not this the right way to look at it? I confess
that I can see no reason for despairing of the American people because it reads more fiction than it used
to read, so long as this is for the same reason that
a ten year old boy reads more stories than a baby.
Intellectual youth is at least an advance over mental
infancy so long as it is first childhood—not second.
It is undoubtedly our duty, as it is our pleasure, to
help these people to grow, but we cannot force them,
and should not try. Complete growth may take several generations. And even when full stature has

been obtained, literature in its narrative modes, though not so exclusively as now, will still be loved and read. Romance will always serve as the dessert in the feast of reason—and we should recollect that sugar is now highly regarded as a food. It is a producer of energy in easily available form, and, thinking on some such novels as "Uncle Tom," "Die Waffen nieder" and shall we say "The jungle"? we realize that this thing is a parable, which the despiser of fiction may well read as he runs.

THE VALUE OF ASSOCIATION *

Man is a gregarious animal; he cannot think, act, or even exist except in certain relations to others of his kind. For a complete description of those relations we must go to a treatise on sociology; our present subject is a very brief consideration of certain groups of individuals, natural or voluntary, and the application of the laws that govern such groups to the voluntary associations with which we are all familiar in library work. Men have joined together to effect certain things that they could not accomplish singly, ever since two savages found that they could lift a heavy log or stone together, when neither one could manage it alone. Until recently the psychology of human groups has received little study. Le Bon, in his book on "The Crowd," gives the modern treatment of it. A group of persons does not think and act precisely as each of its component individuals would think or act. The very act of association, loose as it may be, introduces a new factor. Even the two savages lifting the log do not work together precisely as either would have worked singly. Their co-operation affects their activity; and both thought and action may likewise be affected in larger groupings even by the mere proximity of the individuals of the group, where there is no stronger bond.

But although the spirit that collectively animates a group of men cannot be calculated by taking an arithmetical sum, it does depend on that possessed

* An address delivered before the Library Associations of Iowa, Nebraska, Kansas, Missouri, Indiana and Ohio, October 9-18, 1907.

by each individual in the group, and more particularly on what is common to them all and on the nature of the bonds that connect them. Even a chance group of persons previously unconnected and unrelated is bound together by feelings common to all humanity and may be appealed to collectively on such grounds. The haphazard street crowd thrills with horror at the sight of a baby toddling in front of a trolley-car and shouts with joy when the motorman stops just in time. But the same crowd, if composed of newly-arrived Poles, Hungarians and Slovaks, would fail utterly to respond to some patriotic appeal that might move an American crowd profoundly. You may sway a Methodist congregation with a tale of John Wesley that would leave Presbyterians or Episcopalians cold. Try a Yale mob with "Boola" and then play the same tune at Princeton, and watch the effect.

Thus, the more carefully our group is selected the more particular and definite are the motives that we can bring to bear in it, and the more powerful will its activities be along its own special lines. The mob in the street may be roused by working on elemental passions—so roused it will kill or burn, but you cannot excite in it enthusiasm for Dante's Inferno, or induce it to contribute money or labor toward the preparation of a new annotated edition. To get such enthusiasm and stimulate such action you must work upon a body of men selected and brought together for this very purpose.

Besides this, we must draw a distinction between natural and artificial groups. The group brought together by natural causes and not by man's contriving is generally lower in the scale of civilization when it acts collectively than any one of its components. This is the case with a mob, a tribe, even a municipal group. But an artificial or selected group, where the grouping is for a purpose and has been specially effected with that end in view may act more intelligently, and be, so far as its special activities are concerned, more advanced in the scale of progress than its components as individuals. There is the same difference as between a man's hand and a delicate tool. The former is the result of physical evolution only; the latter of evolution into which the brain of man has entered as a factor. The tool is not as good for "all round" use as the hand; but to accomplish its particular object it is immeasurably superior.

If, then, we are to accomplish anything by taking advantage of the very peculiar crowd or group psychology—owing to which a collected body of men may feel as a group and act as a group, differently from the way in which any one of its components would feel or act—we must see that our group is properly selected and constituted. This does not mean that we are to go about and choose individuals, one by one, by the exercise of personal judgment. Such a method is generally inferior and unnecessary. If we desire to separate the fine from the coarse grains in a sand-pile we do not set to work with a microscope to measure them, grain by grain; we use a sieve. The sieve will not do to separate iron filings from copper filings of exactly the same size, but here a magnet will do the business. And so separation or selection can almost always be accomplished by choosing an agency adapted to the conditions; and such agencies often act automatically without the intervention of the human will. In a voluntary association formed to accomplish a definite purpose we have a self-selected group. Such a body may be freely open to the public, as all our library clubs and associations practically are; yet it is still selective, for no one would care to join it who is not in some way interested in its objects. On the other hand, the qualifications for membership may be numerous and rigid, in which case the selection is more limited. The ideal of efficiency in an association is probably reached when the body is formed for a single definite purpose and the terms of admission are so arranged that each of its members is eager above all things to achieve its end and is specially competent to work for it, the purpose of the grouping being merely to attain the object more surely, thoroughly and rapidly. A good example is a thoroughly trained military organization, all of whose members are enthusiastic in the cause for which the body is fighting—a band of patriots, we will say—or perhaps a band of brigands, for what we have been saying applies to evil as well as to good associations. The most efficient of such bodies may be very temporary, as when three persons, meeting by chance, unite to help each other over a wall that none of them could scale by himself, and, having reached the other side, separate again. The more clearly cut and definite the purpose the less the necessity of retaining the association after its accomplishment. The more efficient the association the sooner its aims are accomplished and the sooner it is disbanded. Such groups or bodies, by their very nature are affairs of small detail and not of large and comprehensive purpose. As they broaden out into catholicity they necessarily lose in efficiency. And even when they are accomplishing their aims satisfactorily the very largeness of those aims, the absence of sharp outline and clear definition, frequently gives rise to complaint. I know of clubs and associations that are doing an immense amount of

good, in some cases altering for the better the whole
intellectual or moral tone of a community, but that
are the objects of criticism because they do not act
in matters of detail.

"Why don't they do something?" is the constant
cry. And "doing something," as you may presently
discover, is carrying on some small definite, relatively unimportant activity that is capable of clear description and easily fixes the attention, while the
greater services, to the public and to the individual,
of the association's quiet influences pass unnoticed.
The church that has driven out of business one cor-
ner-saloon gets more praise than the one that has
made better men and women of a whole generation
in one neighborhood; the police force that catches
one sensational murderer is more applauded than the
one that has made life and property safe for years
in its community by quiet, firm pressure.

There is no reason, of course, why the broader
and the more definite activities may not be united,
to some degree, in one organization. Either smaller
groups with related aims may federate for the larger
purpose, or the larger may itself be the primary
group, and may subdivide into sections each with
its specified object. Both these plans or a combination of the two may be seen in many of our large organizations, and it is this combination that seems
finally to have been selected as the proper form of
union for the libraries and the librarians of the
United States. We have a large organization which,
as it has grown more and more unwieldy, has been
subdivided into smaller specialized sections without
losing its continuity for its broader and perhaps
vaguer work. At the same time, specialized bodies
with related aims have been partially or wholly absorbed, until, by processes partly of subdivision and

partly of accretion, we have a body capable of dealing alike with the general and the special problems of library work. It should not be forgotten, however, that its success in dealing with both kinds of problems is still conditioned by the laws already laid down. The general association, as it grows larger, will be marked less and less by the enthusiasm of the specialist, will be less and less efficient, will move more slowly, will deliver its opinions with reticence and will hesitate to act upon them. The smaller constituent bodies will be affected by none of these drawbacks, but their purposes appeal to the few and their actions, though more energetic, will often seem to the majority of the larger group devoid of meaning. This is, of course, the case with the National Educational Association, the American Association for the Advancement of Science, and hosts of similar bodies here and abroad. To state the difficulty is merely to confess that all attempts hitherto have failed to form a group that is at once comprehensive, powerful and efficient, both in the larger matters with which it deals and in details.

Probably the most successful attempt of this kind is formulated in the Constitution of the United States itself and is being carried on in our country from day to day, yet successful as it is, our history is witness, and the daily press testifies, that the combination of general and local governments has its weak points and is dependent for its smooth working on the cordial consent and forbearance of the governed. This is true also of smaller combinations. In our own organization it is easy to find fault, it is easy to discover points of friction; only by the cordial effort of every member to minimize these points can such an organization begin to accomplish its aims. Failure is much more apt to be due to lack of appreciation of this fact than to any defect in the machinery of organization. This being the case we are thrown back upon consideration of the membership of our institution. How should it be selected and how constituted?

The constitution of the association says that "Any person or institution engaged in library work may become a member by paying the annual dues, and others after election by the executive board." We have thus two classes of members, those by their own choice and those by election. The annual lists of members do not record the distinction, but among those in the latest list we find 24 booksellers, 17 publishers, 5 editors, 9 school and college officials, 8 government employees not in libraries, and 24 wives and relatives of other members, while in the case of 132 persons no qualification is stated in the list. We have or have had as our associates, settlement workers, lawyers, lecturers, indexers, binders, and so on almost indefinitely. Our membership is thus freely open to librarians, interpreting this word very broadly, and to any others that we may desire to have with us, which means, practically, any who have sufficient interest in library work to come to the meetings. We must, therefore, be classed with what may be called the "open" as opposed to the "closed" professional or technical associations. The difference may be emphasized by a reference to two well-known New York clubs, the Players and the Authors. These organizations would appear by their names to be composed respectively of actors and writers. The former, however, admits also to membership persons interested in the drama, which may mean little or much, while the Authors Club, despite repeated efforts to broaden it out in the same way, has insisted on admitting none but *bona fide* authors. In advo-

cacy of the first plan it may be said that by adopting
it the Players has secured larger membership, embracing many men of means. Its financial standing
is better and it is enabled to own a fine club house.
On the other hand, the Authors has a small membership, and owns practically no property, but makes
up in *esprit de corps* what it lacks in these other respects. It is another phase of the question of spe-
cialization that we have already considered. The
larger and broader body has certain advantages, the
smaller and more compact, certain others. We
have, doubtless been right in deciding, or rather in
accepting what circumstances seem to have decided
for us, that our own association shall be of the larger
and less closely knit type, following the analogy of
the National Educational Association and the various associations for the advancement of science,
American, British and French, rather than that of
the Society of Civil Engineers, for instance, or the
various learned academies. Our body has thus greater general but less special influence, just as on a
question of general scientific policy a petition from
the American association might carry greater
weight, whereas on a question of engineering it
would be incomparably inferior to an opinion of the
civil engineers. There is in this country, it is true,
a general scientific body of limited membership—the
National Academy of Sciences, which speaks both
on general and special questions with expert authority. In the formation of the American Library Institute it was sought to creat some such special body
of librarians; but it is too soon to say whether or
not that expectation is to be fulfilled. The fact remains that in the American Library Association we
are committed to very nearly the broadest plan of
organization and work that is possible. We are

united only by our connection with library work or our interest in its success, and are thus limited in our discussions and actions as a body to the most general problems that may arise in this connection, leaving the special work to our sections and affiliated societies, which are themselves somewhat hampered by our size in the treatment of the particular subjects that come before them, inasmuch as they are not separate groups whose freedom of action no one can call in question.

In illustration of the limitations of a general body of the size and scope of our Association, I may perhaps be allowed to adduce the recent disagreement among librarians regarding the copyright question, or rather regarding the proper course to be followed in connection with the conference on that question called by the Librarian of Congress. It will be remembered that this conference was semi-official and was due to the desire of members of Congress to frame a bill that should be satisfactory to the large number of conflicting interests involved. To this conference our Association was invited to send, and did send, delegates. It is obvious that if these and all the other delegates to the conference had simply held out for the provisions most favorable to themselves no agreement would have been possible and the objects of the conference would have been defeated. Recognizing this, all the bodies and interests represented worked from the beginning to secure an agreement, striving only that it should be such as would represent a minimum of concession on all sides. This view was shared by the delegates of this Association. The law as it stood was, it is true, most favorable to libraries in its provisions regarding importation, and the retention of these provisions might have been facilitated by withdrawal from the conference and subsequent opposition to whatever new bill might have been framed. But the delegates assumed that they were appointed to confer, not to withdraw, and that if the Association had desired to hold aloof from the conference that result would have been best attained by appointing no delegates at all. The Association's delegates accordingly joined with their fellows in the spirit of compromise to agree on such a bill as might be least unacceptable to all, and the result was a measure slightly, but only slightly, less favorable to libraries than the existing law. With the presentation of this bill to the proper committees of Congress, and a formal statement that they approved it on behalf of the Association, the duties of the delegates ended. And here begins to appear the applicability of this chapter from library history to what has preceded. The action of the delegates was officially that of the Association. But it was disapproved by very many members of the Association on the ground that it seemed likely to result in lessening the importation privilege of libraries. Whether these dissidents were in a majority or not it seemed impossible to say. The Association's legislative body, the Council, twice refused to disapprove or instruct the delegates, thus tacitly approving their action, but the dissidents asserted that the Council, in this respect, did not rightly reflect the opinion of the Association. The whole situation was an instructive illustration of the difficulty of getting a large body of general scope to act on a definite, circumscribed question, or even of ascertaining its opinion or its wishes regarding such action. Recognizing this, the dissidents properly and wisely formed a separate association with a single end in view—the retention of present library importation privileges, and especially the defeat of the part of the bill affecting such privileges as drafted in the conference. The efforts of this body have been crowned with success in that the bill as reported by the committee contains a modified provision acceptable to the dissidents. Thus a relatively small body formed for a definite purpose has quickly accomplished that purpose, while the objects of the larger body have been expressed but vaguely, and so far as they have been definitely formulated have failed of accomplishment. There is a lesson in this both for our own association and for others.

It must not be assumed, however, that limitation of action along the lines I have indicated means weakness of organization. On the contrary, foreign observers have generally testified to the exceptional strength and efficiency of societies and groups of all kinds in this country. It may be interesting to quote here what a recent French writer on the United States has to say of the part played by associations of all kinds in our national life. And, in passing, he who is proud of his country nowadays should read what is said of her by French and German, and even English writers. The muck-raking is all on this side of the water. The writer from whom I quote, M. Paul de Rousiers, author of "La Vie Américaine," does not commend without discrimination, which makes what he has to say of more value. He notes at the outset that "the spirit of free association is widely extended in the United States, and it produces results of surprising efficiency." There are two motives for association, he thinks, the consciousness of weakness, which is generally operative abroad, and the consciousness of strength, which is our motive here. He says:

The need of association comes generally from the conscience of one's own feebleness or indolence. . . . When such people join they add together their incapacities; hence the failure of many societies formed with great eclat. On the contrary, when men accustomed to help themselves without depending on their neighbors form an association, it is because they really find themselves facing a common difficulty . . . such persons add their capacities; they form a powerful union of capables, the only one that has force. Hence the general success of American associations.

The radical difference in the motives for association here and in the old world was noted long ago by De Tocqueville, who says:

European societies are naturally led to introduce into their midst military customs and formulas. . . . The members of such associations respond to a word of command like soldiers in a campaign; they profess the dogma of passive obedience, or rather, by uniting, they sacrifice entirely, at a single stroke, their judgment and free will. . . . In American associations, on the other hand, individual independence finds its part; as in society every man moves at the same time toward the same goal, but all are not forced to go by the same road. No one sacrifices his will or his reason, but applies them both toward the success of the common enterprise.

Commenting on this, De Rousiers goes on:

This is not to say that the discipline necessary to the pursuit of the common end is less exact than with us. As far as I can judge, the members of an American association, on the contrary, take their obligations more seriously than we, and precisely because they have undertaken them very freely, without being forced into them by environment or fashion, and also because the heads of the association have not sought to make it serve their own interests. In fine, their discipline is strong, but it is applied only to one precise object; it may thus subsist intact and without tyranny, despite the most serious divergences of view among the members regarding objects foreign to its aim. These happy conditions—this large and concrete mind, joined to the effective activity of the Americans, have given rise to a multitude of groups that are rendering the greatest service.

De Rousiers enlarges on this point at great length and gives many illustrations. He returns to it even when he appears to have gone on to other subjects. In an account of a visit to a militia encampment in Massachusetts, where he was inclined at the outset to scoff at the lack of formal military training, but finally became enthusiastic over the indi-

vidual efficiency and interest of the militiamen, he
ends by saying:

> What I have seen here resembles what I have seen everywhere
> throughout the United States; each organism, each individual, pre-
> serves all its freedom, as far as it can; hence the limited and
> special character of the public authorities, to whom little is left to
> do. This doubtless detracts from the massed effects that we are in
> the habit of producing; we are apt to think that this kind of liberty
> is only disorder; but individual efforts are more energetic and
> when they converge toward a single end, by spontaneous choice of
> each will, their power is incalculable. This it is that makes the
> strength of America.

An interesting and satisfactory summary. There
is, however, another way of looking at it. A well-
known scientific man recently expressed to me his
conviction that an "American" association of any
kind is destined to failure, whether it be of scientific men, commercial travellers or plumbers. By
"American" here he meant continental in extent.
There may thus be, according to this view, a successful Maine hotel-keeper's association, a New York bar
association, or a Pennsylvania academy of fine arts,
but no such body truly representative of the whole
United States. Many such organizations are "American" or "National" in name only; for instance, the
"American" Academy of Sciences, which is a Boston
institution, or the "National" Academy of Fine Arts,
which belongs to New York City. Many bodies have
attempted to obviate this trouble by the creation of
local sections in different parts of the country, and
the newly-formed Society of Illuminating Engineers
has, I understand, in mind the organization of perfectly co-ordinate bodies in various parts of the
country, without any attempt to create a central
body having headquarters at a definite place. This
is somewhat as if the American Library Association
should consist of the federated state associations,
perhaps with a council consisting of a single repre-

sentative from each. It would seem to be a workable and rather attractive plan. We may remind ourselves again that the United States itself is the classic example of an American association, and that it has been fairly successful by adopting this very system. Our recognition of the necessity of local divisions in our own association and of close affiliation with the various state bodies is shown by the recent resolution of the council providing for sectional meetings and by the presence at this and several other state meetings in the present month of an official representative of the American Library Association, That these, or similar means of making our national body continental in something more than name are necessary we may freely admit. Possibly it may take some years of experimentation, ending perhaps in appropriate constitutional revision, to hit upon the best arrangement. Too much centralization is bad; but there must be some centralization. We must have our capital and our legislative and administrative machinery, as the United States has at Washington. For legislative purposes our Washington is a shifting one. It is wherever the Association may hold its annual meeting and wherever the Council may convene in the interim. For such administrative and executive purposes as require a fixed location, our Washington is for the present in Boston. Next year it may be elsewhere; but whether it shall remain there or move to some other place would seem to be a matter of small importance. Wherever it may be, it will be inaccessible to a large majority of American librarians. If immediate accessibility is a requisite, therefore, some of its functions may and should be divided. It may not be too much to look forward to a sectional headquarters in every state in the Union, related perhaps to the general headquarters somewhat as branch libraries to a central library, or, perhaps, carried on under the auspices of the state associations. At any rate, it is encouraging to reflect that we are not insensible to the obstacles in the way of making our own, or any other association truly American in scope, and are experimenting toward obviating them.

All these considerations appear to me to lead to one conclusion—the duty of every librarian to become and remain a member of the American Library Association. I do not desire to dwell on the direct advantages that membership offers—these are not few, and they are sufficiently obvious. Possibly most of those who are likely to be affected by them are already members of the Association. I would recommend for consideration higher grounds than these. Instead of asking the question, "What is there in it for me?" I should inquire, "What is there in it for other people?" How will it benefit the general status of library work, the general standing of librarians in the community, the influence of libraries on those who use or ought to use them—these and a hundred other elements of progress that are closely bound up with the success of library effort, but that may not add to the welfare of any one individual.

There seems to be no doubt that the answers to these questions all point toward increased member· ship. As we have chosen to work along the broader lines and by the energy of mass rather than that of velocity—with the sledge-hammer rather than the rifle bullet—it is surely our duty to make that mass as efficient and as impressive as possible, which means that it must be swelled to the largest possible proportions. Large membership may be efficient in two ways, by united weight and by pervasiveness. An army is powerful in the first way. Ten thou·

sand men concentrated in one spot may strike a
sledge-hammer blow and carry all before them. Yet
the same ten thousand men may police a great city
without even seeing one another. Scattered about
on different beats they are everywhere. Every block
or two one meets a patrol and the sense of security
that they give is overwhelming. It is in this way, it
seems to me, that large membership in the American
Library Association may be effective. We meet together but once a year, and even then we do not
bring out our full force. We have no intention of
marching on Washington *en masse* to secure legislation or even of forcing our trustees to raise salaries
by a general library strike. But if we can make it
an unusual thing for a librarian not to be a member
of the American Library Association; if wherever
one goes he meets our members and recognizes what
they stand for, then, it seems to me, public opinion
of librarians and librarianship is sure to rise. Our
two savages, who band together for a few moments
to lift a log, become by that act of association marked
men among their fellows; the mere fact that they
have intelligence enough to work together for any
purpose raises them above the general level. It is
not alone that increasing numbers, strength, and influence make for the glory of the Association itself;
the most successful bodies of this kind are those that
exalt, not themselves but the professions, localities
or ideals that they represent. It is because increasing our numbers and scattering our membership
throughout the land will increase the influence of
the library and strengthen the hands of those who
work in it that I believe such increase a worthy object of our effort. Associations and societies come
and go, form and disband; they are no more immortal than the men and women that compose them.

Yet an association, like a man, should seek to do the work that lies before it with all its strength, and to keep that strength at its maximum of efficiency. So doing, it may rest content that, be its accomplishment large or small, its place in the history of human endeavor is worthy and secure.

MODERN EDUCATIONAL METHODS

Those who complain that the average of general education has been lowered are both right and wrong —right literally and wrong in the general impression that they give. It is undoubtedly true that among young persons with whom an educated adult comes intellectually in contact the average of culture is lower than it was twenty years ago. This is not, however, because the class of persons who were well educated then are to-day less well trained, but rather because the class has been recruited from the ignorant classes, by the addition of persons who were not educated at all then, or educated very slightly, and who are now receiving a higher, though still inadequate degree of training. In other words the average of education among all persons in the community is higher, but the average among educated persons is lower, because the educated class has been enlarged by the addition of large numbers of slightly educated persons.

This phenomenon is common to all stages of progress in all sorts of things. It is true, for instance, in the general advance of the world in civilization. The average degree of appreciation of art among persons who know anything of art at all is less, for instance, than in the days of ancient Greece, because the class of art-lovers throughout the world is vastly larger and includes a very large number of persons whose appreciation of art is slight and crude. There is, nevertheless, a greater total amount of love for art, and a higher average of art education, taking into account the world's entire population, than there was then. Let us state the case mathematically: If, of one thousand persons, ten have a hundred dollars each and the rest nothing, a gift of five dollars each to five hundred others will raise the average amount owned by each of the thousand, but will greatly lower the average amount held by the property owners in the group, who will now number 510, instead of ten.

"How do you demonstrate all this?" will probably be asked. I do not know of any statistical data that will enable it to be proved directly, but it is certain that education is becoming more general, which must increase the number of partly educated persons having an imperfect educational background— a lack of ancestral training and home influence. Thus, among the persons with whom the educated adult comes in contact, he necessarily meets a larger number of individuals than formerly who betray lack of education in speech, writing or taste; and he wrongly concludes that the schools are not doing their work properly. If the schools were not doing their work properly, we should have direct statistical evidence of it, and all the direct evidence I have seen goes to show that the schools are accomplishing more to-day and accomplishing it by better methods, than ever before.

Similarly, I believe that the totality of teaching ability in the profession has increased. The conspicuous failures are persons who are unfit to be teachers and who have been drafted into service because of our sudden increase in educational plant. The result in some cases has been a curious aberration in disciplinary methods—a freakishness that is inseparable from any sudden advance such as we are making.

Our schools can and will advance much further in personnel, methods and results; but they are by no means on the downward path now. One way in which they may do better work is by greater appreciation of their selective as well as their training function.

Suppose we have twenty bushels of raspberries and the same quantity of potatoes to be prepared for food. Our present educational methods are a good deal like those of a cook who should try to make the whole into either jam or Saratoga chips, or should divide the lot in some arbitrary way unrelated to their fitness for one or the other operation. We are giving in our educational institutions many degrees and many kinds of training without proper selection of the persons to whom the training is to be applied. Selection must be and is made, of course, but it is made on arbitrary lines, or for reasons unrelated to fitness. One boy's education lasts ten years, and another's two, not because the former is fitted to profit by a longer period of training, but because his father happens to have money and inclination to give it to him. One young man studies medicine and another goes into business, not because these are the careers for which they are specially fitted, but because one thinks that the prefix "Doctor" would look well in front of his name and the other has a maternal uncle in the dry-goods trade.

I am not so foolish as to think that selection of this kind could ever be made with unerring accuracy, but I do assert that an effort should be made to effect it in a greater degree through our regular educational institutions and to leave it less to chance. Our present methods are like those of wild nature, which scatters seeds broadcast in the hope that some may settle on favoring soil, rather than those of the skilled cultivator, who sees that seed and soil are fitted for each other.

In this and other particulars I look for great improvement in our educational methods; but I do not think that, except in local and unessential particulars, here and there, they are now retrograding.

SOME ECONOMIC FEATURES OF LIBRARIES*

Of the three great divisions of economics—production, distribution and consumption—the library has to do chiefly with the second, and it is as a distributor of literature that I desire to speak of it, although it has its share both in the production and consumption of books—more briefly, in the writing and reading of them. Much writing of books is done wholly in libraries and by their aid, and much reading is done therein. These functions I pass by with this brief notice.

A library distributes books. So does a bookseller. The functions of these two distributors, however, should differ somewhat as do those of the two producers of books—the author and the publisher. The author creates the soul of the book and the publisher gives it a body. The former produces the immaterial, possibly the eternal, part and the latter merely the material part. Likewise, in our distribution we librarians should lay stress upon what is in the book, upon the production of the author rather than on that of the publisher, though we may not neglect the latter. We are, however, eminently distributors of ideas rather than of mere merchandise, and in so far as we lay stress on the material side of the book—important as this is—and neglect what is in it, we are but traders in books and not librarians.

Among many of the great distributors of ideas—the magazine, the newspaper, the school—it is be-

* Read at the opening of the Chestnut Hill Branch, Philadelphia Free Library, January 22, 1909.

coming increasingly difficult to find any that do not feel what I may call an anti-civic tendency. They have come to be supported largely by other agencies than the public, and they are naturally controlled by those agencies. As for the public, it has become accustomed to paying less than cost for what it gets along these lines, and is thus becoming intellectually pauperized. It is no more possible to distribute ideas at a profit, as a commercial venture, nowadays, than it would have been to run a circus, with an admission fee, in Imperial Rome. Thus a literary magazine is possible only because it is owned by some publisher who uses it as an advertising medium. He can afford to sell it to the public for less than cost; the public would leave a publication sold at a fair profit severely alone, hence such a venture is impossible. A scientific magazine in like manner must have some one to back it—a firm of patent-office brokers or a scientific society. The daily papers depend almost wholly on their advertisements; the public would not buy a simple compilation of the day's news at a fair profit. Even our great institutions of higher education give their students more than the latter pay for; the student is getting part of his tuition for nothing. A college that depends wholly on tuition fees for its support is soon left without students. Thus all these disseminators of ideas are not dependent on the persons to whom they distribute those ideas, for whose interest it is that the ideas shall be good and true and selected with discrimination. They depend rather for support on outside bodies of various kinds and so tend to be controlled by them—bodies whose interests do not necessarily coincide with those of the public. This is not true of material things. Their distributors still strive to please the public, for it is by the public that they are supported. If the public wants raspberry jam, raspberry jam it gets; and if, being aroused, it demands that this shall be made out of raspberries instead of apples, dock-seeds and aniline, it ultimately has its way. But if the department store were controlled by some outside agency, benevolent or otherwise, which partly supported it and enabled it to sell its wares below cost, then if this controlling agency willed that we should eat dock-seeds and aniline—dock-seeds and aniline we should doubtless eat.

Not that the controlling powers in all these instances are necessarily malevolent. The publisher who owns a literary magazine may honestly desire that it shall be fearlessly impartial. The learned body that runs a scientific periodical may be willing to admit to its pages a defense of a thesis that it has condemned in one of its meetings; the page-advertiser in a great daily may be able to see his pet policy attacked in its editorial columns without yielding to the temptation to bring pressure to bear; the creator of an endowed university may view with equanimity an attack by one of its professors on the methods by which he amassed his wealth. All these things may be; we know in fact that they have been and that they are. But unfortunately we all know of cases where the effect of outside control has been quite the contrary. The government of a benevolent despot, we are told, would be ideal; but alas! rules for making a despot benevolent and for ensuring that he and his successors shall remain so, are not yet formulated. We have fallen back on the plan of fighting off the despot—good though he may possibly be; would that we could also abolish the non-civic control of the disseminators of ideas!

Are there, then, no disseminators of ideas free

from interference? Yes, thank heaven, there are at
least two—the public school and the public library.
Of these, the value of academic freedom to the public
school is slight, because the training of the very
young is of its nature subject little to the influences
of which we have spoken. There is little opportunity, during a grammar school or high school course,
to influence the mind in favor of particular government policies and particular theories in science or
literature or art. This opportunity comes later.
And it is later that the public library does its best
work. Supported by the public it has no impulse
and no desire to please anyone else. No suspicion of
outside control hangs over it. It receives gifts; but
they are gifts to the public, held by the public, not
by outsiders. It is tax-supported, and the public
pays cost price for what it gets—no more and no
less. The community has the power of abolishing
the whole system in the twinkling of an eye. The library's power in an American municipality lies in
the affections of those who use and profit by it. It
holds its position by love. No publisher may say to
it: "Buy my books, not those of my rival"; no scientist may forbid it to give his opponent a hearing;
no religious body may dictate to it; no commercial
influence may throw a blight over it. It is untram-
meled.

How long is it to remain thus? That is for its
owners, the public, to say. I confess that I feel un-
easy when I realize how little the influence of the
public library is understood by those who might try
to wield that influence, either for good or for evil.
Occasionally an individual tries to use it sporadical-
ly—the poet who tries to secure undying fame by
distributing free copies of his verses to the libraries,
the manufacturer who gives us an advertisement of

his product in the guise of a book, the enthusiast who runs over our shelf list to see whether the library is well stocked with works on his fad—socialism or Swedenborgianism, or the "new thought." But, so far, there has been no concerted, systematic effort on the part of classes or bodies of men to capture the public library, to dictate its policy, to utilize its great opportunities for influencing the public mind. When this ever comes, as it may, we must look out!

So far as my observation goes, the situation— even the faintest glimmering of it—is far from dawning on most of these bodies. Most individuals, when the policy of the library suits them not, exhaust their efforts in an angry kick or an epistolary curse; they never even think of trying to change that policy, even by argument. Most of them would rather write a letter to a newspaper, complaining of a book's absence, than to ask the librarian to buy it. Organizations—civil, religious, scientific, political, artistic—have usually let us severely alone, where their influence, if they should come into touch with the library, would surely be for good—would be exerted along the line of morality, of more careful book selection, of judicial mindedness instead of one-sidedness.

Let us trust that influences along this line—if we are to have influences at all—may gain a foothold before the opposite forces—those of sordid commercialism, of absurdities, of falsities, of all kinds of self-seeking—find out that we are worth their exploitation.

When it comes, as I expect it will some day— this general realization of what only a few now understand—that the public library is worth trying to influence and to exploit, our trouble will be that we shall be without any machinery at all to receive it, to take care of it, to direct the good into proper channels and to withstand the evil. We are occasionally annoyed and disconcerted now by the infinitesimal amount of it that we see; we wish people would mind their own business; we detest meddlers; we should be able to do more work if it were not for the bores—and so on. But what—what in heaven's name shall we do with the deluge when it comes? With what dam shall we withstand it; through what sluices shall we lead it; into what useful turbines shall we direct it? These things are worth pondering.

For the present then, this independence of the library as a distributor may be regarded as one of its chief economic advantages. Another is its power as a leveler, and hence as an adjunct of democracy. Democracy is a result, not a cause, of equality. It is natural in a community whose members resemble each other in ability, modes of thought and mental development, just as it is unthinkable where great natural differences racial or otherwise, exist. If we wish to preserve democracy, therefore, we must first maintain our community on something like a level. And we must level it up, not down; for although a form of democracy may exist temporarily among individuals equally ignorant or degraded, the advent of a single person more advanced in the scale of ability, quickly transforms it into absolutism. Similar inequalities may result in an aristocratic régime. The reason why England, with its ancient aristocracy, on the whole, is so democratic, is that its commoners are constantly recruited by the younger sons of its nobility, so that the whole body politic is continually stirred and kept more homogeneous than on the continent, where all of a noble's sons and daughter's are themselves noble. This stirring or levelling process may be effected in many ways and along many lines, but in no way better than by popular education, as we have well understood in this country. This is why our educational system is a bulwark of our form of government, and this is why the public library—the only continuous feature of that system, exercising its influence from earliest childhood to most advanced age—is worth to the community whatever it may cost in its most improved form. There are enough influences at work to segregate classes in our country, and they come to us ready-made from other countries; we may be thankful that the public library is helping to make Americans of our immigrants and to make uniformly cultivated and well-informed Americans of us all.

Another interesting light on the functions of the printed page, and hence of the library, is shown by the recent biological theory that connects the phenomena of heredity with those of habit and memory. The inheritance of ancestral characteristics, according to this view, may be described as racial memory. To illustrate, we may take an interesting study of a family of Danish athletes, recently made and published in France. The members of this family, adults and children, men and women, have all been gymnasts for over three hundred years—no one of them would think of adopting any other means of gaining a livelihood. It seems certain to the scientific men who have been conducting the investigation, that not only the physical ability to become an acrobat, but also the mental qualities that contribute so much to success in this occupation—pride in the acrobatic pre-eminence of the family, courage, love of applause, and so on—have been handed down from one generation to another, and that it has cost each generation less time and effort to acquire its skill than than its predecessor. In other words, we are told, members of this family are born with certain predispositions—latent ancestral memories, we may say, of the occupations of previous generations. To make these effective, it is necessary only to awaken them, and this may be done simply by the sight of other persons performing gymnastic feats. These they learn in weeks, where others, without such ancestral memories, would require months or years.

Evidently this may be applied much more widely than to mere physical skill. Few of us can boast of gymnastic ancestry, but all of us have inherited predispositions and have ancestral memories that make it easier for us to learn certain things and to choose certain courses than we should find it without them. Some of these are good; some bad. Some are useful; some injurious. It is necessary only to awaken them to set going a train of consequences; if not awakened, they may remain permanently dormant. How important, therefore, are the suggestions that may serve as such awakeners; how necessary to bring forward the useful, and to banish the injurious ones!

Now of all possible agencies that may bring these predispositions into play—that may awaken our ancestral memories, if you choose to adopt this theory —I submit that the book stands at the very head. For it is itself a racial record; it may contain, in the form best suited to awaken our predispositions, the very material which, long ages ago, was instrumental in handing those predispositions down to us. It is in tune with our latent memories, and it may set them vibrating more vigorously than any merely contemporary agency.

Does this not place in a new and interesting light the library and the books of which it is composed?

We have learned to respect them as the records of
the race and to recognize their value as teachers and
their power as energizers; in addition we now see
that they may act as fingers on invisible mental trig-
gers. A slight impulse—altogether trivial compared
with its effect—and off goes the gun. The discharge
may carry a line to a wrecked ship, or it may sink
her with all on board.

We frequently hear it said of some book whose
tendency is bad: "Well, it can't hurt me, anyway;
I'm immune." Are you quite sure? Have you gone
quite to the bottom of those ancestral memories of
yours, and are you certain that there are none that
such a book may rouse, to your harm?

On the other hand, does this not explain much
that has always interested the librarian; for instance, the vast popularity of fairy tales, especially
those that date back to our racial infancy? I need
dwell no further on the economic importance of the
book as viewed from this standpoint.

But it has also a function almost diametrically
opposed to that which we have just considered; besides harking back to what is oldest it looks forward
to what is newest. It may stir us by awakening dim
racial recollections; but it may also thrill us by adding to the store of what is already in the mind. In
fact, we like to assimilate new ideas, to think new
thoughts, to do new acts; we like to read or hear
something that we could not have produced ourselves. When we are young and ignorant, therefore,
we like music or art or literature that appears trivial
to us as we grow older and have developed our own
creative powers. A poem that is no better than one
a man might dash off himself he likes no longer; he
prefers to be confronted with something that is above
and beyond his own powers, though not above his

comprehension. Thus, as he grows, his zone of enjoyment shifts upward, and the library covers the whole moving field. When Solomon John Peterkin, pen in hand, sat down to write a book, he discovered that he hadn't anything to say. Happy lad! He had before him all literature as a field of enjoyment, for all, apparently, was beyond his creative efforts.

Do those of you who are musicians remember when you first apprehended the relations between the tonic and the dominant chords? I have heard a small boy at a piano play these alternately for hours. Such a performance is torture to you and me; it is the sweetest harmony to him, because it is new and has just come into his sphere of creative power. When he is thoroughly satisfied that he can produce the effect at will, he abandons it for something newer and a little higher. The boy who discovers, without being told, that the dominant chord, followed by the tonic, produces a certain musical effect, is doing something that for him is on a par with Wagner's searching the piano for those marvellous effects of his that are often beyond technical explanation.

The child who reads what you think is a trivial book, re-reads it, and reads others like it, is doing this same thing in the domain of literature—he is **following the natural course that will bring him out at the top after a while.**

When we distribute books, then, we distribute ideas, not only actual, but potential. A book has in it not only the ideas that lie on its surface, but millions of others that are tied to these by invisible chords, of which we have touched on but a few—the invisible ancestral memories of centuries ago, the foretastes of future thoughts in our older selves and our posterity of centuries hence. When we think of it, it is hard to realize that a book has not a soul.

Gerald Stanley Lee, in his latest book, a collection of essays on millionaires, sneers at the efforts of the rich mill owners to improve their employees by means of libraries. Life in a modern mill, he thinks, is so mechanical as to dull all the higher faculties. "Andrew Carnegie," he says (and he apparently uses the name merely as that of a type), "has been taking men's souls away and giving them paper books."

Now the mills may be soul-deadening—possibly they are, though it is hard to benumb a soul—but I will venture to say that for every soul that Mr. Carnegie, or anyone else, has taken away, he has created, awakened and stimulated a thousand by contact with that almost soul—that near-soul—that resides in books. Mr. Lee's books may be merely paper; mine have paper and ink only for their outer garb; their inner warp and woof is of the texture of spirit.

This is why I rejoice when a new library is opened. I thank God for its generous donor. I clasp hands with the far-reaching municipality that accepts and supports it. I wish good luck to the librarians who are to care for it and give it dynamic force; I congratulate the public whose privilege it is to use it and to profit by it.

SIMON NEWCOMB: AMERICA'S FOREMOST ASTRONOMER

Among those in all parts of the world whose good opinion is worth having, Simon Newcomb was one of the best known of America's great men. Astronomer, mathematician, economist, novelist, he had well-nigh boxed the compass of human knowledge, attaining eminence such as is given to few to reach, at more than one of its points. His fame was of the far-reaching kind,—penetrating to remote regions, while that of some others has only created a noisy disturbance within a narrow radius.

Best and most widely known as an astronomer, his achievements in that science were not suited for sensational exploitation. He discovered no apple-orchards on the moon, neither did he dispute regarding the railways on the planet Venus. His aim was to make still more exact our knowledge of the motions of the bodies constituting what we call the solar system, and his labors toward this end, begun more than thirty years ago, he continued almost until the day of his death. Conscious that his span of life was measured by months and in the grip of what he knew to be a fatal disease, he yet exerted himself with all his remaining energy to complete his monumental work on the motion of the moon, and succeeded in bringing it to an end before the final summons came. His last days thus had in them a cast of the heroic, not less than if, as the commander of a torpedoed battleship, he had gone down with her, or than if he had fallen charging at the head of a forlorn hope. It is pleasant to think that such a man was laid to rest with military honors. The accident that he was a retired professor in the United States Navy may have been the immediate cause of this, but its appropriateness lies deeper.

Newcomb saw the light not under the Stars and Stripes, but in Nova Scotia, where he was born, at the town of Wallace on March 12, 1835. His father, a teacher, was of American descent, his ancestors having settled in Canada in 1761. After studying with his father and teaching for some little time in his native province he came to the United States while yet a boy of eighteen, and while teaching in Maryland in 1854-'56 was so fortunate as to attract, by his mathematical ability, the attention of two eminent American scientific men, Joseph Henry and Julius Hilgard, who secured him an appointment as computer on the Nautical Almanac. The date of this was 1857, and Newcomb had thus, at his death, been in Government employ for fifty-two years. As the work of the almanac was then carried on in Cambridge, Mass., he was enabled to enter the Lawrence Scientific School of Harvard University, where he graduated in 1858 and where he pursued graduate studies for three years longer. On their completion in 1861 he was appointed a professor of mathematics in the United States Navy, which office he held till his death. This appointment, made when he was twenty-six years old,—scarcely more than a boy,—is a striking testimony to his remarkable ability as a mathematician, for of practical astronomy he still knew little.

One of his first duties at Washington was to supervise the construction of the great 26-inch equatorial just authorized by Congress and to plan for mounting and housing it. In 1877 he became senior professor of mathematics in the navy, and from that time until his retirement as a Rear Admiral in 1897 he had charge of the Nautical Almanac office, with its large corps of naval and civilian assistants, in Washington and elsewhere. In 1884 he also assumed the chair of mathematics and astronomy in Johns Hopkins University, Baltimore, and he had much to to do, in an advisory capacity, with the equipment of the Lick Observatory and with testing and mounting its great telescope, at that time the largest in the world.

To enumerate his degrees, scientific honors, and medals would tire the reader. Among them were the degree of LL.D. from all the foremost universities, the gold medal of the Royal Astronomical Society of London in 1874, the great gold Huygens medal of the University of Leyden, awarded only once in twenty years, in 1878, and the Schubert gold medal of the Imperial Academy of St. Petersburg. The collection of portraits of famous astronomers at the Observatory of Pulkowa contains his picture, painted by order of the Russian Government in 1887. He was, of course, a member of many scientific societies, at home and abroad, and was elected in 1869 to our own National Academy of Sciences, becoming its vice-president in 1883. In 1893 he was chosen one of the eight foreign associates of the Institute of France,—the first native American since Benjamin Franklin to be so chosen. Newcomb's most famous work as an astronomer,—that which gained him world-wide fame among his brother astronomers,— was, as has been said, too mathematical and technical to appeal to the general public among his countrymen, who have had to take his greatness, in this regard, on trust. They have known him at first hand chiefly as author or editor of popular works such as his "Popular Astronomy" (1877); of his text-books on astronomy, algebra, geometry, trigonometry, and calculus; of his books on political economy, which science he was accustomed to call his "recreation"; and of magazine articles on all sorts of subjects not omitting "psychical research," which was one of the numerous by-paths into which he strayed. He held at one time the presidency of the American Society for Psychical Research.

The technical nature of his work in mathematical astronomy,—his "profession," as he called it, in distinction to his "recreations" and minor scientific amusements,—may be seen from the titles of one or two of his papers: "On the Secular Variations and Mutual Relations of the Orbits of the Asteroids" (1860); "Investigation of the Orbit of Neptune, with General Tables of Its Motion" (1867); "Researches on the Motion of the Moon" (1876); and so on. Of this work Professor Newcomb himself says, in his "Reminiscences of an Astronomer" (Boston, 1903), that it all tended toward one result,—the solution of what he calls "the great problem of exact astronomy," the theoretical explanation of the observed motions of the heavenly bodies.

If the universe consisted of but two bodies,—say, the sun and a planet,—the motion would be simplicity itself; the planet would describe an exact ellipse about the sun, and this orbit would never change in form, size, or position. With the addition of only one more body, the problem at once becomes so much more difficult as to be practically insoluble; indeed, the "problem of the three bodies" has been attacked by astronomers for years without the discovery of any general formula to express the resulting motions. For the actually existing system of many planets with their satellites and countless asteroids, only an approximation is possible. The actual mo-

tions as observed and measured from year to year
are most complex. Can these be completely account-
ed for by the mutual attractions of the bodies, according to the law of gravitation as enunciated by
Sir Isaac Newton? In Newcomb's words, "Does any
world move otherwise than as it is attracted by other
worlds?" Of course, Newcomb has not been the only
astronomer at work on this problem, but it has been
his life-work and his contributions to its solution
have been very noteworthy.

It is difficult to make the ordinary reader understand the obstacles in the way of such a determination as this. Its two elements are, of course, the
mapping out of the lines in which the bodies concerned actually do move and the calculations of the
orbits in which they ought to move, if the accepted
laws of planetary motion are true. The first involves
the study of thousands of observations made during
long years by different men in far distant lands, the
discussion of their probable errors, and their reduction to a common standard. The latter requires the
use of the most refined methods of mathematical
analysis; it is, as Newcomb says, "of a complexity
beyond the powers of ordinary conception." In
works on celestial mechanics a single formula may
fill a whole chapter.

This problem first attracted Newcomb's attention
when a young man at Cambridge, when by analysis
of the motions of the asteroids he showed that the
orbits of these minor planets had not, for several
hundred thousand years past, intersected at a single
point, and that they could not, therefore, have resulted, during that period, from the explosion of a
single large body, as had been supposed.

Later, when Newcomb's investigations along this
line had extended to the major planets and their

satellites, a curious anomaly in the moon's motion made it necessary for him to look for possible observations made long before those hitherto recorded. The accepted tables were based on observations extending back as far as 1750, but Newcomb, by searching the archives of European observatories, succeeded in discovering data taken as early as 1660, not, of course, with such an investigation as this in view, but chiefly out of pure scientific curiosity. The reduction of such observations, especially as the old French astronomers used apparent time, which was frequently in error by quarter of an hour or so, was a matter of great difficulty. The ancient observer, having no idea of the use that was to be made of his work, had supplied no facilities for interpreting it, and "much comparison and examination was necessary to find out what sort of an instrument was used, how the observations were made, and how they should be utilized for the required purpose." The result was a vastly more accurate lunar theory than had formerly been obtained.

During the period when Newcomb was working among the old papers of the Paris Observatory, the city, then in possession of the Communists, was beset by the national forces, and his studies were made within hearing of the heavy siege guns, whose flash he could even see by glancing through his window.

Newcomb's appointment as head of the Nautical Almanac office greatly facilitated his work on the various phases of this problem of planetary motions. Their solution was here a legitimate part of the routine work of the office, and he had the aid of able assistants,—such men as G. W. Hill, who worked out a large part of the theory of Jupiter and Saturn, and Cleveland Keith, who died in 1896, just as the final results of his work were being combined. In connection with this work Professor Newcomb strongly advocated the unification of the world's time by the adoption of an international meridian, and also international agreement upon a uniform system of data for all computations relating to the fixed stars. The former still hangs fire, owing to mistaken "patriotism"; the latter was adopted at an international conference held in Paris in 1896, but after it had been carried into effect in our own Nautical Almanac, professional jealousies brought about a modification of the plan that relegated the improved and modernized data to an appendix.

Professor Newcomb's retirement from active service made the continuance of his great work on an adequate scale somewhat problematical, and his data on the moon's motion were laid aside for a time until a grant from the newly organized Carnegie Institution in 1903 enabled him to employ the necessary assistance, and the work has since gone forward to completion.

What is the value of such work, and why should fame be the reward of him who pursues it successfully? Professor Newcomb himself raises this question in his "Reminiscences," and without attempting to answer it directly he notes that every civilized nation supports an observatory at great annual expense to carry on such research, besides which many others are supported by private or corporate contributions. Evidently the consensus of public opinion must be that the results are worth at least a part of what they cost. The question is included in the broader one of the value of all research in pure science. Speaking generally, the object of this is solely to add to the sum of human knowledge, although not seldom some application to man's physical needs springs unexpectedly from the resulting discoveries, as in the case of the dynamo or that of wireless telegraphy. Possibly a more accurate description of the moon's motion is unlikely to bring forth any such application, but those who applaud the achievements of our experts in mathematical astronomy would be quick to deny that their fame rests on any such possibility.

Passing now to Professor Newcomb's "recreation," as he called it,—political economy, we may note that his contributions to it were really voluminous, consisting of papers, popular articles and several books, including "The A B C of Finance" (1877) and "Principles of Political Economy" (1886). Authorities in the science never really took these as seriously as they deserved, possibly because they regarded Professor Newcomb as scarcely orthodox. Some of his distinctions, however, are of undoubted value and will live; for instance, that between the fund and the flux of wealth, on which he insists in his treatises on finance. As to Professor Newcomb's single excursion into fiction, a romance entitled "His Wisdom the Defender," it is perhaps sufficient to say that, like everything he attempted, it is at least worth notice. It is a sort of cross between Jules Verne and Bulwer Lytton's "Coming Race."

Professor Newcomb's mind was comprehensive in its activity. One might have thought that an intellect occupied to the last in carrying out one of the most stupendous tasks ever attempted by a mathematical astronomer would have had little time or little energy left for other things; but Newcomb took his rest and pleasure in popular articles and interviews. Only a short time before his death he published an essay on aeronautics that attracted wide attention, drawing the conclusions that the aeroplane can never be of much use either as a passenger-carrier or in war, but that the dirigible balloon may accomplish something within certain lines, although it will never put the railways and steamships out of business. In particular, he treated with unsparing ridicule the panic fear of an aerial invasion that so lately seized upon our transatlantic cousins.

Personally, Newcomb was an agreeable companion and a faithful friend. His success was due largely to his tenacity of purpose. The writer's only personal contact with him came through the "Standard Dictionary,"—of whose definitions in physical science Newcomb had general oversight. On one occasion he came into the office greatly dissatisfied with the definition that we had framed for the word "magnet."—a conception almost impossible to define in any logical way. We had simply enumerated the properties of the thing,—a course which in the absence of authoritative knowledge of their causes was the only rational procedure. But Newcomb's mind demanded a logical treatment, and though he must have seen from the outset that this was a forlorn hope, his tenacity of purpose kept him, pencil in hand, writing and erasing alternately for an hour or more. Finally he confessed that he could do no better than the following pair of definitions,—"*Magnet,* a body capable of exerting magnetic force," and "*Magnetic Force,* the force exerted by a magnet." With a hearty laugh at this beautiful *circulus in definiendo* he threw down his pencil, and the imperfect and illogical office definition was accepted.

Logical as he was, however, he was in no sense bound by convention. His economics, as has been said, was often unorthodox, and even in his mathematical text-books he occasionally shocked the hidebound. I well remember an interesting discussion among members of the Yale mathematical faculty just after the appearance of Newcomb's text-book of geometry, in which he was unsparingly condemned by some because he assumed in certain elementary demonstrations that geometrical figures could be removed from the paper, turned over and laid down again,—the so-called "method of superposition," now generally regarded as quite allowable. Of course, a figure can be treated in this way only in imagination and for this season, probably, the method was not employed by Euclid. Its use, however, leads always to true results, as anyone may see; and it was quite characteristic of Professor Newcomb that he should have taken it up, not having the fear of the Greek geometers before him.

Such was Newcomb; it will be long before American science sees his equal. Mathematical genius is like an automobile,—it is looked upon in two opposing fashions as one has it or has it not. A noted educator not long ago announced his belief that the possession of a taste for mathematics is an exact index of the general intellectual powers. Not much later, another eminent teacher asserted that mathematical ability is an exotic,—that one may, and often does, possess it who is in other respects practically an imbecile. This is scarcely a subject in which a single illustration decides, but surely Newcomb's career justifies the former opinion rather than the latter; the amount and kind of his mental abilities along all lines seemed to run parallel to his mathematical genius, to resemble it in quantity and in kind.

The great volumes of astronomical tables without which no astronomer may now venture upon a computation are his best monument; yet the general reader will longer remember, perhaps, the lucid expositor, the genial essayist, the writer of one of the most readable autobiographies of our day.

THE COMPANIONSHIP OF BOOKS *

Are books fitted to be our companions? That depends. You and I read them with pleasure; others do not care for them; to some the reading of any book at all is as impossible as the perusal of a volume in Old Slavonic would be to most of us. These people simply do not read at all. To a suggestion that he supplement his usual vacation sports by reading a novel, a New York police captain—a man with a common-school education—replied, " Well, I've never read a book yet, and I don't think I'll begin now." Here was a man who had never read a book, who had no use for books, and who could get along perfectly well without them. He is not a unique type. Hundreds of thousands of our fellow citizens might as well be quite illiterate, so far as the use that they make of their ability to read is concerned. These persons are not all uneducated; they possess and are still acquiring much knowledge, but since leaving school they have acquired it chiefly by personal experience and by word of mouth. Is it possible that they are right? May it be that to read books is unnecessary and superfluous?

There has been some effort of late to depreciate the book—to insist on its inadequacy and on the impracticality of the knowledge that it conveys. "Book-learning" has always been derided more or less by so-called "practical men". A recent series of comic pictures in the newspapers makes this clear. It is about "Book-taught Bilkins". Bilkins tries to do

* Read before the Pacific Northwest Library Association, June, 1910.

everything by a book. He raises vegetables, builds furniture, runs a chicken farm, all by the directions contained in books, and meets with ignominious failure. He makes himself, in fact, very ridiculous in every instance and thousands of readers laugh at him and his absurd books. They inwardly resolve, doubtless, that they will be practical and will pay no attention to books. Are they right? Is the information contained in books always useless and absurd, while that obtained by experience or by talking to one's neighbor is always correct and valuable?

Many of our foremost educators are displeased with the book. They are throwing it aside for the lecture, for laboratory work, for personal research and experiment. Does this mean that the book, as a tool of the teacher, will have to go?

What it all certainly does mean is that we ought to pause a minute and think about the book, about what it does and what it can not do. This means that we ought to consider a little the whole subject of written as distinguished from spoken language. Why should we have two languages—as we practically do—one to be interpreted by the ear and the other by the eye? Could we or should we abandon either? What are the advantages and what the limitations of each? We are so accustomed to looking upon the printed page, to reading newspapers, books, and advertisements, to sending and receiving letters, written or typewritten, that we are apt to forget that all this is not part of the natural order, except in the sense that all inventions and creations of the human brain are natural. Written language is a conscious invention of man; spoken language is a development, shaped by his needs and controlled by his sense of what is fitting, but not at the outset consciously devised.

We are apt to think of written language as simply a means of representing spoken language to the eye; but it is more than this; originally, at least in many cases, it was not this at all. The written signs represented not sounds, but ideas themselves; if they were intended to correspond directly with anything, it was with the rude gestures that signified ideas and had nothing to do with their vocal expression. It was not until later that these written symbols came to correspond to vocal sounds and even to-day they do so imperfectly; languages that are largely phonetic are the exception. The result is, as I have said, that we have two languages—a spoken and a written. What we call reading aloud is translation from the written to the spoken tongue; while writing from dictation is translation from the spoken to the written. When we read, as we say, "to ourselves," we sometimes, if we are not skilful, pronounce the spoken words under our breath, or at least form them with our vocal organs. You all remember the story of how the Irishman who could not read made his friend stop up his ears while reading a letter aloud, so that he might not hear it. This anecdote, like all good comic stories, has something in it to think about. The skilful reader does not even imagine the spoken words as he goes. He forgets, for the moment, the spoken tongue and translates the written words and phrases directly into the ideas for which they stand. A skilful reader thus takes in the meaning of a phrase, a sentence, even of a paragraph, at a glance. Likewise the writer who sets his own thoughts down on paper need not voice them, even in imagination; he may also forget all about the spoken tongue and spread his ideas on the page at first hand. This is not so common because one writes slower than he speaks, whereas he reads very much faster. The swift reader could not imagine that he was speaking the words, even if he would; the pace is too incredibly fast.

Our written tongue, then, has come to be something of a language by itself. In some countries it has grown so out of touch with the spoken tongue that the two have little to do with each other. Where only the learned know how to read and write, the written language takes on a learned tinge; the popular spoken tongue has nothing to keep it steady and changes rapidly and unsystematically. Where nearly all who speak the language also read and write it, as in our own country, the written tongue, even in its highest literary forms, is apt to be much more familiar and colloquial, but at the same time the written and the spoken tongue keep closer together. Still, they never accurately correspond. When a man "talks like a book," or in other words, uses such language that it could be printed word for word and appear in good literary form, we recognize that he is not talking ordinary colloquial English—not using the normal spoken language. On the other hand, when the speech of a southern negro or a down-east Yankee is set down in print, as it so often is in the modern "dialect story," we recognize at once that although for the occasion this is written language, it is not normal literary English. It is most desirable that the two forms of speech shall closely correspond, for then the written speech gets life from the spoken and the spoken has the written for its governor and controller; but it is also desirable that each should retain more or less individuality, and fortunately it is almost impossible that they should not do so.

We must not forget, therefore, that our written speech is not merely a way of setting down our

spoken speech in print. This is exactly what our
friends the spelling reformers appear to have forgotten. The name that they have given to what they
propose to do, indicates this clearly. When a word
as written and as spoken have drifted apart, it is
usually the spoken word that has changed. Reform,
therefore, would be accomplished by restoring the
old spoken form. Instead of this, it is proposed to
change the written form. In other words, the two
languages are to be forced together by altering that
one of them that is by its essence the most immut-
able. Where the written word has been corrupted
as in spelling "guild" for "gild," the adoption of the
simpler spelling is a reform; otherwise, not.

Now is the possession of two languages, a spoken
and a written, an advantage or not? With regard to
the spoken tongue, the question answers itself. If
we were all deaf and dumb, we could still live and
carry on business, but we should be badly handi-
capped. On the other hand, if we could neither read
nor write, we should simply be in the position of our
remote forefathers or even of many in our own day
and our own land. What then is the reasons for a
separate written language, beyond the variety thereby secured, by the use of two senses, hearing and
sight, instead of only one?

Evidently the chief reason is that written speech
is eminently fitted for preservation. Without the
transmittal of ideas from one generation to another,
intellectual progress is impossible. Such transmittal, before the invention of writing, was effected solely by memory. The father spoke to the son, and he,
remembering what was said, told it, in turn, to the
grandson. This is tradition, sometimes marvellous-
ly accurate, but often untrustworthy. And as it is
without check, there is no way of telling whether a

given fact, so transmitted, is or is not handed down faithfully. Now we have the phonograph for preserving and accurately reproducing spoken language. If this had been invented before the introduction of written language, we might never have had the latter; as it is, the device comes on the field too late to be a competitor with the book in more than a very limited field. For preserving particular voices, such as those of great men, or for recording intonation and pronunciation, it fills a want that writing and printing could never supply.

For the long preservation of ideas and their conveyance to a human mind, written speech is now the indispensable vehicle. And, as has been said, this is how man makes progress. We learn in two ways: by undergoing and reflecting on our own experiences and by reading and reflecting on those of others. Neither of these ways is sufficient in itself. A child bound hand and foot and confined in a dark room would not be a fit subject for instruction, but neither would he reach a high level if placed on a desert island far from his kind and forced to rely solely on his own experiences. The experiences of our forebears, read in the light of our own; the experiences of our forebears, used as a starting-point from which we may move forward to fresh fields—these we must know and appreciate if we are to make progress. This means the book and its use.

Books may be used in three ways—for information, for recreation, for inspiration. There are some who feel inclined to rely implicitly on the information that is to be found in books—to believe that a book can not lie. This is an unfortunate state of mind. The word of an author set down in print is worth no more than when he gives it to us in spoken language—no more and no less. There was, to be sure, a time when the printed word implied at least care and thoughtfulness. It is still true that the book implies somewhat more of this than the newspaper, but the difference between the two is becoming unfortunately less. Now a wrong record, if it purports to be a record of facts, is worse than none at all. The man who desires to know the distance between two towns in Texas and is unable to find it in any book of reference may obtain it at the cost of some time and trouble; but if he finds it wrongly recorded, he accepts the result and goes away believing a lie. If we are to use books for information, therefore, it is of the utmost consequence that we know whether the information is correct or not. A general critical evaluation of all literature, even on this score alone, without going into the question of literary merit, is probably beyond the possibilities, although it has been seriously proposed. Some partial lists we have, and a few lists of those lists, so that we may know where to get at them. There are many books about books, especially in certain departments of history, technology, or art, but no one place to which a man may go, before he begins to read his book, to find out whether he may believe what he reads in it. This is a serious lack, especially as there is more than one point of view. Books that are of high excellence as literature may not be at all accurate. How shall the boy who hears enthusiastic praise of Prescott's histories and who is spellbound when he reads them know that the results of recent investigation prove that those histories give a totally incorrect idea of Mexico and Peru? How is the future reader of Dr. Cook's interesting account of the ascent of Mount McKinley to know that it has been discredited? And how is he to know whether other interesting and well-written histories and books of travel have not been similarly proved inaccurate? At present, there is no way except to go to one who knows the literature of the subject, or to read as many other books on the subject as can be obtained, weighing one against the other and coming to one's own conclusions. Possibly the public library may be able to help. Mr. Charles F. Lummis of the Los Angeles library advocates labelling books with what he calls "Poison Labels" to warn the reader when they are inaccurate or untrustworthy. Most librarians have hesitated a little to take so radical a step as this, not so much from unwillingness to assume the duty of warning the public, as from a feeling that they were not competent to undertake the critical evaluation of the whole of the literature of special subjects. The librarian may know that this or that book is out of date or not to be depended on, but there are others about which he is not certain or regarding which he must rely on what others tell him. And he knows that expert testimony is notoriously one-sided. It is this fear of acting as an advocate instead of as a judge that has generally deterred the librarian from labelling his books with notes of advice or warning.

There is, however, no reason why the librarian should take sides in the matter. He may simply point out to the reader that there are other books on the same subject, written from different points of view, and he may direct attention to these, letting the reader draw his own conclusions. There is probability that the public library in the future will furnish information and guidance of this kind about books, more than it has done in the past.

And here it may be noted in passing that the library is coming out of its shell. It no longer holds itself aloof, taking good care of its books and taking

little care of the public that uses them. It is coming
to realize that the man and the book are complementary, that neither is much without the other, and
that to bring them together is its duty. It realizes
also that a book is valuable, not because it is so much
paper and ink and thread and leather, but because
it records and preserves somebody's ideas. It is the
projection of a human mind across space and across
time and where it touches another human mind those
minds have come into contact just as truly and with
as valuable results as if the bodies that held them
stood face to face in actual converse. This is the
miracle of written speech—a miracle renewed daily
in millions of places with millions of readers.

We have, in the modern library, the very best way
of perpetuating such relations as this and of ensuring that such as are preserved shall be worth preserving. When the ancients desired to make an idea
carry as far as possible, they saw to the toughness
and strength of the material object constituting the
record; they cut it in stone or cast it in metal, forgetting that all matter is in a state of continual flux
and change; it is the idea only that endures. Stone
and metal will both one day pass away and unless
some one sees fit to copy the inscription on a fresh
block or tablet, the record will be lost. It is, then,
only by continual renewal of its material basis that
a record in written language can be made to last,
and there is no reason why this renewal should not
take place every few years, as well as every few centuries. There is even an advantage in frequent renewal; for this ensures that the value of the record
shall be more frequently passed upon and prevents
the preservation of records that are not worth keeping. This preservation by frequent renewal is just
what is taking place with books; we make them of

perishable materials; if we want to keep them, we reprint them; otherwise they decay and are forgotten.

We should not forget that by this plan the reader is usually made the judge of whether a book is worth keeping. Why do we preserve by continual reprinting Shakespeare and Scott and Tennyson and Hawthorne? The reprinting is done by publishers as a money-making scheme. It is profitable to them because there is a demand for those authors. If we cease to care for them and prefer unworthy writers, Shakespeare and Scott will decay and be forgotten and the unworthy ones will be preserved. Thus a great responsibility is thrown upon readers; so far they have judged pretty well.

Just now, however, we are confining ourselves to the use of books for information; and here there is less preservation than elsewhere. Especially in science, statements and facts quickly become out of date; here it is not the old but the new that we want —the new based on the accurate and enduring part of the old.

Before we leave this part of the subject it may be noted that many persons have no idea of the kinds of information that may be obtained from books. Even those who would unhesitatingly seek a book for data in history, art, or mathematics would not think of going to books for facts on plumbing, weaving, or shoe-making, for methods of shop-window decoration or of display-advertising, for special forms of bookkeeping suitable for factories or for stock-farms— for a host of facts relating to trades, occupations, and business in general. Yet there are books about all these things—not books perhaps to read for an idle hour, but books full of meat for them who want just this kind of food. If Book-taught Bilkins fails, after trying to utilize what such books have taught him, it is doubtless because he has previously failed to realize that books plus experience, or, to put it differently, the recorded experience of others plus our own is better than either could be separately. And the same is true of information that calls for no physical action to supplement it. Books plus thought—the thoughts of others plus our own—are more effective in combination than either could be by itself. Reading should provoke thought; thought should suggest more reading, and so on, until others' thoughts and our own have become so completely amalgamated that they are our personal intellectual possessions.

But we may not read for information at all—recreation may be what we are after. Do not misunderstand me. Many persons have an idea that if one reads to amuse himself he must necessarily read novels. I think most highly of good novels. Narrative is a popular form of literary expression; it is used by those who wish to instruct as well as to amuse. One may obtain plenty of information from novels—often in a form nowhere else available. If we want exact statement, statistical or otherwise, we do not go to fiction for it; but if we wish to obtain what is often more important—accurate and lasting general impressions of history, society, or geography, the novel is often the only place where these may be had. Likewise, one may amuse himself with history, travel, science, or art—even with mathematics. The last is rarely written primarily to amuse, although we have such a title as "Mathematical recreations," but there are plenty of non-fiction books written for entertainment and one may read for entertainment any book whatever. The result depends not so much on the book or its contents as on the reader.

Recreation is now recognized as an essential part of education. And just as physical recreation consists largely in the same muscular movements that constitute work, only in different combinations and with different ends in view, so mental recreation consists of intellectual exercise with a similar variation of combinations and aims.

Somebody says that "play is work that you don't have to do". So reading for amusement may closely resemble study—the only difference is that it is purely voluntary. Here again, however, the written language is only an intermediary; we have as before, the contact of two minds—only here it is often the lighter contact of good-fellowship. And one who reads always for such recreation is thus like the man who is always bandying trivialities, story-telling, and jesting—an excellent, even a necessary, way of passing part of one's time, but a mistaken way of employing all of it.

The best kind of recreation is gently stimulating, but stimulation may rise easily to abnormality. There are fiction drunkards just as there are persons who take too much alcohol or too much coffee. In fact, if one is so much absorbed by the ideas that he is assimilating that the process interferes with the ordinary duties of life, he may be fairly sure that it is injuring him. If one loves coffee or alcohol, or even candy, so dearly that one can not give it up, it is time to stop using it altogether. If a reader is so fond of an exciting story that he can not lay it aside, so that he sits up late at night reading it, or if he can not drop it from his mind when he does lay it aside, but goes on thinking about the deadly combat between the hero and Lord William Fitz Grouchy when he ought to be studying his lessons or attending to his business, it is time to cut out fiction altogether. This advice has absolutely nothing to do with the quality of the fiction. It will not do simply to warn the habitual drunkard that he must be careful to take none but the best brands; he must drop alcohol altogether. If you are a fiction drunkard, enhanced quality will only enslave you further. This sort of use is no more recreation in the proper sense of the word than is gambling, or drinking to excess, or smoking opium.

And now we come to a use of books that is more important—lies more at the root of things—than their use for either information or recreation—their use for inspiration. One may get help and inspiration along with the other two—reading about how to make a box may inspire a boy to go out and make one himself. It is this kind of thing that should be the final outcome of every mental process. Nothing that goes on in the brain is really complete until it ends in a motor stimulus. The action, it is true, may not follow closely; it may be the result of years of mental adjustment; it may even take place in another body from the one where it originated. The man who tells us how to make a box, and tells it so fascinatingly that he sets all his readers to box-making, presumably has made boxes with his own hands, but there may be those who are fitted to inspire action in others rather than to undertake it themselves. And the larger literature of inspiration is not that which urges to specific deeds like box-making, or even to classes of deeds, like caring for the sick or improving methods of transportation; rather does it include in its scope all good thoughts and all good actions. It makes better men and women of those who read it; it is revolutionary and evolutionary at the same time, in the best sense of both words.

What will thus inspire me, do you ask? It would be easy to try to tell you; it would also be easy to fail. Many have tried and failed. This is a deeply personal matter. I can not tell what book, or what passage in a book, will touch the magic spring that shall make your life useful instead of useless, that shall start your thoughts and your deeds climbing up instead of grovelling or passively waiting. Only search will reveal it. The diamond-miner who expects to be directed to the precise spot where he will find a gem will never pick one up. Only he who seeks, finds. There are, however, places to look and places to avoid. The peculiar clay in which diamonds occur is well known to mineralogists. He who runs across it, looks for diamonds, though he may find none. But he who hunts for them on the rock-ribbed hills of New Hampshire or the sea-sands of Florida is doing a foolish thing—although even there he may conceivably pick up one that has been dropped by accident.

So you may know where it is best to go in your search for inspiration from books, for we know where seekers in the past have most often found it. He who could read the Bible or Shakespeare without finding some of it is the exception. It may be looked for in the great poets—Homer, Virgil, Dante, Chaucer, Milton, Hugo, Keats, Goethe; or the great historians—Tacitus, Herodotus, Froissart, Macaulay, Taine, Bancroft; or in the great travellers from Sir John Mandeville down, or in biographies like Boswell's life of Johnson, or in books of science—Laplace, Lagrange, Darwin, Tyndall, Helmholtz; in the lives of the great artists; in the great novels and romances—Thackeray, Balzac, Hawthorne, Dickens, George Eliot. Yet each and all of these may leave you cold and may pick up your gem in some out-of-the-way corner where neither you nor anyone else would think of looking for it.

Did you ever see a car-conductor fumbling about

in the dark with the trolley pole, trying to hit the wire? While he is pulling it down and letting it fly up again, making fruitless dabs in the air, the car is dark and motionless; in vain the motorman turns his controller, in vain do the passengers long for light. But sooner or later the pole strikes the wire; down it flows the current that was there all the time up in the air; in a jiffy the car is in motion and ablaze with light. So your search for inspiration in literature may be long and unsuccessful; you are dark and motionless. But the life-giving current from some great man's brain is flowing through some book not far away. One day you will make the connection and your life will in a trice be filled with light and instinct with action.

And before we leave this subject of inspiration, let us dwell for a moment on that to be obtained from one's literary setting in general—from the totality of one's literary associations and impressions, as distinguished from that gained from some specific passage or idea.

It has been said that it takes two to tell the truth; one to speak and one to listen. In like manner we may say that two persons are necessary to a great artistic interpretation—one to create and one to appreciate. And of no art is this more true than it is of literature. The thought that we are thus coöperating with Shakespeare and Schiller and Hugo in bringing out the full effect of their deathless conceptions is an inspiring one and its consideration may aid us in realizing the essential oneness of the human race, so far as its intellectual life is concerned .

Would you rather be a citizen of the United States than, we will say, of Nicaragua? You might be as happy, as well educated, as well off, there as here. Why do you prefer your present status? Simply and solely because of associations and relationships. If this is sentiment, as it doubtless is, it is the kind of sentiment that rules the world—it is in the same class as friendship, loyalty, love of kin, affection for home. The links that bind us to the past and the threads that stretch out into the future are more satisfactory to us here in the United States, with the complexity of its interests for us, than they would be in Nicaragua, or Guam, or Iceland.

Then of what country in the realm of literature do you desire to be a citizen? Of the one where Shakespeare is king and where your familiar and daily speech is with the great ones of this earth—those whose wise, witty, good, or inspiring words, spoken for centuries past, have been recorded in books? Or would you prefer to dwell with triviality and banality—perhaps with Laura Jean Libbey or even with Mary J. Holmes, and those a little better than these—or a little worse.

I am one of those who believe in the best associations, literary as well as social. And associations may have their effect even if they are apparently trivial or superficial.

When the open-shelf library was first introduced we were told that one of its chief advantages was that it encouraged "browsing"—the somewhat aimless rambling about and dipping here and there into a book. Obviously this can not be done in a closed-shelf library. But of late it has been suggested, in one quarter or another, that although this may be a pleasant occupation to some, or even to most, it is not a profitable one. Opponents of the open shelf of whom there are still one or two, here and there, find in this conclusion a reason for negativing the argument in its favor, while those of its advocates who accept this view see in it only a reason for basing that argument wholly on other grounds.

Now those of us who like a thing do not relish being told that it is not good for us. We feel that pleasure was intended as an outward sign of benefits received and although it may in abnormal conditions deceive us, we are right in demanding proof before distrusting its indications. When the cow absorbs physical nutriment by browsing, she does so without further reason than that she likes it. Does the absorber of mental pabulum from books argue wrongly from similar premises?

Many things are hastily and wrongly condemned because they do not achieve certain results that they were not intended to achieve. And in particular, when a thing exists in several degrees or grades, some one of those grades is often censured, although good in itself, because it is not a grade or two higher. Obviously everything depends on what is required. When a shopper wants just three yards of cloth, she would be foolish to buy four. She would, of course, be even more foolish to imagine that, if she really wished four, three would do just as well. But if a man wants to go to the eighth story of a building, he should not be condemned because he does not mount to the ninth; if he wishes a light lunch, he should not be found fault with for not ordering a seven-course dinner. And yet we continually hear persons accused of "superficiality" who purposely and knowingly acquire some slight degree of knowledge of a subject instead of a higher degree. And others are condemned, we will say, for reading for amusement when they might have read for serious information, without inquiring whether amusement, in this instance, was not precisely what they needed.

It may be, therefore, that browsing is productive

of some good result, and that it fails to effect some
other, perhaps some higher, result which its critics
have wrongly fixed upon as the one desirable thing
in this connection.

When a name embodies a figure of speech, we
may often learn something by following up the figure to see how far it holds good. What does an animal do, and what does it not do, when it "browses"?
In the first place it eats food—fresh, growing food;
but, secondly, it eats this food by cropping off the
tips of the herbage, not taking much at once, and
again, it moves about from place to place, eating
now here and now there and then making selection,
from one motive or another, but presumably following the dictates of its own taste or fancy. What does
it not do? First, it does not, from choice, eat anything bad. Secondly, it does not necessarily con-
sume all of its food in this way. If it finds a particularly choice spot, it may confine its feeding to
that spot; or, if its owner sees fit, he may remove it
to the stable, where it may stand all day and eat
what he chooses to give it. The benefits of browsing
are, first, the nourishment actually derived from the
food taken, coupled with the fact that it is taken in
small quantities, and in great variety; and secondly,
the knowledge of good spots, obtained from the testing of one spot after another, throughout the whole
broad pasture.

Now I submit that our figure of speech holds
good in all these particulars. The literary "browser"
partakes of his mental food from books and is thereby nourished and stimulated; he takes it here and
there in brief quantities, moving from section to section and from shelf to shelf, selecting choice morsels
of literature as fancy may dictate. He does not, if
he is a healthy reader, absorb voluntarily anything

that will hurt him, and this method of literary absorption does not preclude other methods of mental nourishment. He may like a book so much that he proceeds to devour it whole, or his superiors in knowledge may remove him to a place where necessary mental food is administered more or less forcibly. And having gone so far with our comparison, we shall make no mistake if we go a little further and say that the benefits of browsing to the reader are twofold, as they are to the material feeder—the absorption of actual nutriment in his own wilful, wayward manner—a little at a time and in great variety; and the knowledge of good reading obtained from such a wide testing of the field.

Are not these real benefits, and are they not desirable? I fear that our original surmise was correct and that browsing is condemned not for what it does, but because it fails to do something that it could not be expected to do. Of course, if one were to browse continuously he would be unable to feed in any other way. Attendance upon school or the continuous reading of any book whatever would be obviously impossible. To avoid misunderstanding, therefore, we will agree at this point that whatever may be said here in commendation of browsing is on condition that it be occasional and not excessive and that the normal amount of continuous reading and study proceed together with it.

Having settled, therefore, that browsing is a good thing when one does not occupy ones' whole time with it, let us examine·its advantages a little more in detail.

First: about the mental nourishment that is absorbed in browsing; the specific information, the appreciation of what is good, the intellectual stimulation—not that which comes from reading suggested

or guided by browsing, but from the actual process itself. I have heard it strenuously denied that any
such absorption occurs; the bits taken are too small,
the motion of the browser is too rapid, the whole
process is too desultory. Let us see. In the first place
a knowledge of authors and titles and of the general
character of their works is by no means to be despised. I heard the other day of a presumably educated woman who betrayed in a conversation her ignorance of Omar Khayyam—not lack of acquaintance with his works, but lack of knowledge that such
a person had ever existed. If at some period in her
life she had held in her hand a copy of "The Rubai-
yat," and had glanced at its back, without even opening it, how much embarrassment she might have
been spared! And if, in addition, she had glanced
within for just ten seconds and had discovered that
he wrote poetry in stanzas of four lines each, she
would have known as much about Omar as do many
of those who would contemptuously scoff at her ignorance. With so brief effort may we acquire literary knowledge sufficient to avoid embarrassment in
ordinary conversation. Browsing in a good library,
if the browser has a memory, will soon equip him
with a wide range of knowledge of this kind. Nor
is such knowledge to be sneered at as superficial. It
is all that we know, or need to know, about scores of
authors. One may never study higher mathematics,
but it may be good for him to know that Lagrange
was a French author who wrote on analytical mechanics, that Euclid was a Greek geometer, and that
Hamilton invented quaternions. All this and vastly
more may be impressed on the mind by an hour in
the mathematical alcove of a library of moderate
size. And it will do no harm to a boy to know that
Benvenuto Cellini wrote his autobiography, even if

the inevitable perusal of the book is delayed for several years, or that Felicia Hemans, James Thomson, and Robert Herrick wrote poetry, independently of familiarity with their works, or that "Lamia" is not something to eat or "As you like it" a popular novel. Information of this kind is almost impossible to acquire from lists or from oral statement, whereas a moment's handling of a book in the concrete may fix it in the mind for good and all. So far, we have not supposed that even a word of the contents has been read. What, now, if a sentence, a stanza, a paragraph, a page, passes into the brain through the eye? Those who measure literary effect by the thousand words or by the hour are making a great mistake. The lightning flash is over in a fraction of a second, but in that time it may reveal a scene of beauty, may give the traveller warning of the fatal precipice, or may shatter the farmer's home into kindling wood. Intellectual lightning may strike the "browser" as he stands there book in hand before the shelf. A word, a phrase, may sear into his brain —may turn the current of his whole life. And even if no such epoch-making words meet his eye, in how brief a time may he read, digest, appreciate, some of the gems of literature! Leigh Hunt's "Jennie kissed me" would probably take about thirty seconds; on a second reading he would have it by heart—the joy of a life-time. How many meaty epigrams would take as long? The whole of Gray's "Elegy" is hardly beyond the browser's limit.

In an editorial on the Harvard Classics in the "Chicago evening post", (April 22), we read, "the cultural tabloid has very little virtue; . . . to gain everything that a book has to give one must be submerged in it, saturated and absorbed". This is very much like saying, "there is very little nourishment in a sandwich; to get the full effect of a luncheon you must eat everything on the table". It is a truism to say that you can not get everything in a book without reading all of it; but it by no means follows that the virtue of less than the whole is negligible.

So much for the direct effect of what one may thus take in, bit by bit. The indirect effect is even more important. For by sampling a whole literature, as he does, he not only gets a bird's-eye view of it, but he finds out what he likes and what he dislikes; he begins to form his taste. Are you afraid that he will form it wrong? I am not. We are assuming that the library where he browses is a good one; here is no chance of evil, only a choice between different kinds of good. And even if the evil be there, it is astonishing how the healthy mind will let it slip and fasten eagerly on the good. Would you prefer a taste fixed by someone who tells the browser what he ought to like? Then that is not the reader's own taste at all, but that of his informant. We have too much of this sort of thing—too many readers without an atom of taste of their own who will say, for instance, that they adore George Meredith, because some one has told them that all intellectual persons do so. The man who frankly loves George Ade and can yet see nothing in Shakespeare may one day discover Shakespeare. The man who reads Shakespeare merely because he thinks he ought to is hopeless.

But what a triumph, to stand spell-bound by the art of a writer whose name you never heard, and then discover that he is one of the great ones of the world! Nought is comparable to it except perhaps to pick out all by yourself in the exhibition the one picture that the experts have chosen for the museum

or to be able to say you liked olives the first time
you tasted them.

Who are your favorites? Did some one guide you
to them or did you find them yourselves? I will
warrant that in many cases you discovered them and
that this is why you love them. I discovered De-
Quincey's romances, Praed's poetry, Béranger in
French, Heine in German, "The Arabian nights",
Molière, Irving's "Alhambra," hundreds of others
probably. I am sure that I love them all far more
than if some one had told me they were good books.
If I had been obliged to read them in school and pass
an examination on them, I should have hated them.
The teacher who can write an examination paper on
Gray's "Elegy", would, I firmly believe, cut up his
grandmother alive before the physiology class.

And next to the author or the book that you have
discovered yourself comes the one that the discoverer
himself—your boy or girl friend—tells you about.
He knows a good thing—*she* knows it! No school
nonsense about that; no adult misunderstanding. I
found out Poe that way, and Thackeray's "Major
Gahagan", and many others.

To go back to our old illustration and consider
for a moment not the book but the mind, the personality whose ideas it records, such association with
books represents association with one's fellowmen in
society—at a reception, in school or college, at a
club. Some we pass by with a nod, with some we
exchange a word; sometimes there is a warm hand-
grasp; sometimes a long conversation. No matter
what the mental contact may be, it has its effects—
we are continually gaining knowledge, making new
friends, receiving fresh inspiration. The complexion of this kind of daily association determines the

cast of one's mind, the thoroughness of his taste, the usefulness or uselessness of what he does. A man is known by the company he keeps, because that company forms him; he gets from it what becomes brain of his brain and soul of his soul.

And no less is he formed by his mental associations with the good and the great of all ages whom he meets in books and who talk to him there. More rather than less; for into a book the writer puts generally what is best in him, laying aside the pettiness, the triviality, the downright wickedness that may have characterized him in the flesh.

I have often heard the comment from one who had met face to face a writer whose work he loved— "Oh! he disappointed me so!" How disappointed might we be with Thackeray, with Dickens, even with Shakespeare, could we meet them in the flesh! Now they can not disappoint us, for we know only what they have left on record—the best, the most enduring part, purified from what is gross and earthly.

In and among such company as this it is your privilege to live and move, almost without money and without price. Thank God for books; let them be your friends and companions through life—for information, for recreation, but above all for inspiration.

ATOMIC THEORIES OF ENERGY *

A theory involving some sort of a discrete or discontinuous structure of energy has been put forward by Prof. Max Planck of the University of Berlin. The various aspects of this theory are discussed and elaborated by the late M. Henri Poincaré in a paper entitled "L'Hypothèse des Quanta," published in the *Revue Scientifique* (Paris, Feb. 21, 1912).

A paper in which a discontinuous or "atomic" structure of energy was suggested was prepared by the present writer fifteen years ago but remains unpublished for reasons that will appear later. Although he has no desire to put in a claim of priority and is well aware that failure to publish would put any such claim out of court, it seems to him that in connection with present radical developments in physical theory the paper, together with some correspondence relating thereto, has historical interest. Planck's theory was suggested by thermodynamical considerations. In the paper now to be quoted the matter was approached from the standpoint of a criterion for determining the identity of two portions of matter or of energy. The paper is as follows:

Some Consideration on the Identity of Definite Portions of Energy

It has been remarked recently that physicists are now divided into two opposing schools according to the way in which they view the subject of energy, some regarding it as a mere mathematical abstraction and others looking upon it as a physical entity,

* Read before the St. Louis Academy of Science.

filling space and continuously migrating by definite paths from one place to another. It may be added that there are numerous factions within these two parties; for instance, not all of those who consider energy to be something more than a mere mathematical expression would maintain that a given quantity of it retains its identity just as a given quantity of matter does. In fact a close analysis would possibly show that opinions are graded very closely and continuously from a view hardly differing from that of Lagrange, who clearly saw and freely used the mathematical considerations involving energy before the word had been invented or its physical meaning developed, up to that stated recently in its extreme form by Professor Ostwald, who would replace what he terms a mechanical theory of the universe by an "energetical" theory, and would dwell exclusively on energy as opposed to its vehicles.

Differences of opinion of this sort very frequently reduce to differences of definition, and in this case the meaning of the word "identity" or some similar word or phrase has undoubtedly much to do with the view that is taken of the matter. It may be interesting, for instance, to look for a moment at our ideas of the identity of matter and the extent to which they are influenced by the accepted theory of its constitution.

Very few persons would hesitate to admit that the matter that now constitutes the universe is identical in amount with that which constituted it one million years ago, and that any given portion of that matter is identical with an equal amount of matter that then existed, although the situations of the parts of that portion might be and probably were widely different in the two classes. To assert this is of course a very different thing from asserting that the identity of the two portions or any parts thereof could have been practically shown by following them during all their changes of location or state. That cannot be done even in the case of some simple changes that are effected in a fraction of a second. For instance, if water from the pail A be mixed with water from the pail B there is no possible way of telling which pail any given portion of the mixture came from or in what proportions, yet it is certain that such portion is identical with a portion of equal mass that recently occupied part of one or both pails.

How far our certainty as to this is influenced by our ideas regarding the ultimate constitution of the water is worthy of investigation. All who accept the molecular theory, for instance, will regard our inability to trace the elements of a mixture as due to purely physical limitations. A set of Maxwell's "demons" if bidden to watch the molecules of the water in pail A, one demon being assigned to each molecule, would be able to tell us at any time the precise proportions of any given part of the mixture. But if we should not accept the molecular theory and believe for instance, that water is a continuum, absolutely homogeneous, no matter how small portions of it be selected, then our demons would be as powerless as we ourselves now are to trace the constituents in the mixture.

We are now in a position to ask the question: Is the matter in a mixture of two continua identical with that of its constituents? The identity certainly seems of a different kind or degree from that which obtains in the first case, for there is no part, however small, that was derived from one pail alone. The mixture is something more than a mere juxtaposition of elements each of which has retained its identity; it is now of such nature that no part of it is identical with any part of A alone or of B alone, nor of A+B, where the sign + denotes simple juxtaposition. It is identical, to be sure, with a perfect mixture of certain parts of A and B, but this is simply saying that it is identical with what it is now, that is, with itself, not with something that went before.

Probably no one now believes that water or any other kind of matter is a continuum, but the bearing of what has been said may be seen when we remember that this is precisely the present stage of our belief regarding energy.

No one, so far as I know, has ventured to suggest what may be termed a molecular theory of energy, a somewhat remarkable fact when we consider the control now exercised over all thought in physics by molecular theories of matter. While we now believe, for instance, that a material body, say a crystal, can by no possibility increase continuously in mass, but must do so step by step, the minimum mass of matter that can be added being the molecule, we believe on the contrary that the energy possessed by the same body can and may increase with absolutely perfect continuity, being hampered by no such restriction.

It is not the purpose of this paper to discuss whether we have grounds for belief that there is such a thing as a minimum quantity, or atom, of energy, that does not separate into smaller parts, no matter what changes it undergoes. Suffice it to say that there appears to be no *a priori* absurdity in such an idea. At first sight both matter and energy appear non-molecular in structure. But we have been forced to look upon the gradual growth of a crystal as a step-by-step process, and we may some day, by equally cogent considerations, be forced to regard the gradual increase of energy of an accelerating body as also a step-by-step process, although the discontinuity is as invisible to the eye in the latter case as in the former.

Without following this out any farther, however, the point may be here emphasized that it is hardly possible for one who, like the majority of physicists, regards matter as molecular and energy as a continuum, to hold the same ideas regarding the identity of the two. Efforts to show that definite portions of energy, like definite portions of matter, retain their identity have hitherto been made chiefly on the lines of a demonstration that energy travels by definite and continuous paths in space just as matter does. This is very well, but it would appear to be necessary to supplement it with evidence to show that the lines representing these paths do not form at their intersections continuous blurs that not only forbid any practical attempt at identification on emergence, but make it doubtful whether we can in any true sense call the issuing path identical with the entering one. Otherwise the identity of energy can be admitted to be only that kind of identity that could be preserved by matter if its molecular structure did not exist. One who can admit that this sort of identity is the same sort that can be preserved by molecular matter may be able to hold the identity of energy in the present state of the evidence, but the present attitude of physicists would seem to show that, whether they realize the connection of the two subjects or not, they cannot take this view. In other words, modern views of the identity of matter seem closely connected with modern views of its structure, and the same connection will doubtless hold good for energy.

Regarding the probable success of an attempt to prove that energy has a "structure" analogous to the molecular structure of matter, any prediction would doubtless be rash just now. The writer has been unable, up to the present time, to disprove the proposition, but the subject is one of corresponding importance to that of the whole molecular theory of matter and should not be entered upon lightly.

* * * * *

The writer freely acknowledges at present that the illustrations in the foregoing are badly chosen and some of the statements are too strong, but it still represents essentially his ideas on the subject. No reputable scientific journal would undertake to publish it. The paper was then sent to Prof. J. Willard Gibbs of Yale, and elicited the following letter from him:

"NEW HAVEN, JUNE 2, 1897.

"MY DEAR MR. BOSTWICK:

"I regret that I have allowed your letter to lie so long unanswered. It was in fact not very easy to answer, and when one lays a letter aside to answer, the weeks slip away very fast.

"I do not think that you state the matter quite right in regard to the mixture of fluids if they were continuous. The mixing of water as I regard it would be like this, if it were continuous and not molecular. Suppose you should take strips of white and red glass and heat them until soft and twist them together. Keep on drawing them out and doubling them up and twisting them together. It would soon require a microscope to distinguish the red and white glass, which would be drawn out into thinner and thinner filaments if the matter were continuous. But it would be always only a matter of optical power to distinguish perfectly the portion of red and white glass. The stirring up of water from two pails would not really mix them but only entangle filaments from the pails.

"To come to the case of energy. All our ideas concerning energy seem to require that it is capable of gradual increase. Thus the energy due to velocity can increase continuously if velocity can. Since the energy is as the square of the velocity, if the velocity can only increase discontinuously by equal increments, the energy of the body will increase by unequal increments in such a way as to make the exchange of energy between bodies a very awkward matter to adjust.

"But apart from the question of the increase of energy by

discontinuous increments, the question of relative and absolute motion makes it very hard to give a particular position to energy, since the 'energy' we speak of in any case is not one quantity but may be interpreted in a great many ways. Take the important case of two equal elastic balls. One, moving, strikes the other at rest, we say, and gives it nearly all its energy. But we have no right to call one ball at rest and we can not say (as anything absolute) which of the balls has lost and which has gained energy. If there is such a thing as absolute energy of motion it is something entirely unknowable to us. Take the solar system, supposed isolated. We may take as our origin of coordinates the center of gravity of the system. Or we may take an origin with respect to which the center of gravity of the solar system has any (constant) velocity. The kinetic energy of the earth, for example, may have any value whatever, and the principle of the conservation of energy will hold in any case for the whole solar system. But the shifting of energy from one planet to another will take place entirely differently when we estimate the energies with reference to different origins.

"It does not seem to me that your ideas fit in with what we know about nature. If you ask my advice, I should not advise you to try to publish them.

"At best you would be entering into a discussion (perhaps not in bad company) in which words would play a greater part than precise ideas.

"This is the way I feel about it.

"I remain,

"Yours faithfully,

"J. W. Gibbs."

Professor Gibbs's criticism of the illustration of water-mixture is evidently just. Another might well have been used where the things mixed are not material—for instance, the value of money deposited in a bank. If A and B each deposits $100 to C's credit and C then draws $10, there is evidently no way of determining what part of it came from A and what from B. The structure of "value", in other words, is perfectly continuous. Professor Gibbs's objections to an "atomic" theory of the structure of energy are most interesting. The difficulties that it involves are not over-stated. In 1897 they made it unnecessary, but since that time considerations have been brought forward, and generally recognized, which may make it necessary to brave those difficulties.

Planck's theory was suggested by the apparent necessity of modifying the generally accepted theory of statistical equilibrium involving the socalled "law of equipartition," enunciated first for gases and extended to liquids and solids.

In the first place the kinetic theory fixes the number of degrees of freedom of each gaseous molecule, which would be three for argon, for instance, and five for oxygen. But what prevents either from having the six degrees to which ordinary mechanical theory entitles it? Furthermore, the oxygen spectrum has more than five lines, and the molecule must therefore vibrate in more than five modes. "Why," asks Poincaré, "do certain degrees of freedom appear to play no part here; why are they, so to speak, 'ankylosed'?" Again, suppose a system in statistical equilibrium, each part gaining on an average, in a short time, exactly as much as it loses. If the system consists of molecules and ether, as the former have a finite number of degrees of freedom and the latter an infinite number, the unmodified law of equipartition would require that the ether should finally appropriate all energy, leaving none of it to the matter. To escape this conclusion we have Rayleigh's law that the radiated energy, for a given wave length, is proportional to the absolute temperature, and for a given temperature is in inverse ratio to the fourth power of the wave-length. This is found by Planck to be experimentally unverifiable, the radiation being less for small wave-lengths and low temperatures, than the law requires.

Still again, the specific heats of solids, instead of being sensibly constant at all temperatures, are found to diminish rapidly in the low temperatures now available in liquid air or hydrogen and apparently tend to disappear at absolute zero. "All takes place," says Poincaré, "as if these molecules lost some of their degrees of freedom in cooling—as if some of their articulations froze at the limit."

Planck attempts to explain these facts by introducing the idea of what he calls "quanta" of energy. To quote from Poincaré's paper:

"How should we picture a radiating body? We know that a Hertz resonator sends into the ether Hertzian waves that are identical with luminous waves; an incandescent body must then be regarded as containing a very great number of tiny resonators. When the body is heated, these resonators acquire energy, start vibrating and consequently radiate.

"Planck's hypothesis consists in the supposition that each of these resonators can acquire or lose energy only by abrupt jumps, in such a way that the store of energy that it possesses must always be a multiple of a constant quantity, which he calls a 'quantum'—must be composed of a whole number of quanta. This indivisible unit, this quantum, is not the same for all resonators; it is in inverse ratio to the wave-length, so that resonators of short period can take in energy only in large pieces, while those of long period can absorb or give it out by small bits. What is the result? Great effort is necessary to agitate a short-period resonator, since this requires at least a quantity of energy equal to its quantum, which is great. The chances are, then, that these resonators will keep quiet, especially if the temperature is low, and it is for this reason that there is relatively little short-wave radiation in 'black radiation' . . . The diminution of specific-heats is explained similarly: When the temperature falls, a large number of vibrators fall below their quantum and cease to vibrate, so that the total energy diminishes faster than the old theories require."

Here we have the germs of an atomic theory of energy. As Poincaré now points out, the trouble is

that the quanta are not constant. In his study of
the matter he notes that the work of Prof. Wilhelm
Wien, of Würzburg, leads by theory to precisely the
conclusion announced by Planck that if we are to
hold to the accepted ideas of statistical equilibrium
the energy can vary only by quanta inversely proportional to wave-length. The mechanical property
of the resonators imagined by Planck is therefore
precisely that which Wien's theory requires. If we
are to suppose atoms of energy, therefore, they must
be variable atoms. There are other objections which
need not be touched upon here, the whole theory being in a very early stage. To quote Poincaré again:

"The new conception is seductive from a certain
standpoint: for some time the tendency has been
toward atomism. Matter appears to us as formed
of indivisible atoms; electricity is no longer continuous, not infinitely divisible. It resolves itself into
equally-charged electrons; we have also now the mag-
neton, or atom of magnetism. From this point of
view the quanta appear as *atoms* of *energy*. Unfortunately the comparison may not be pushed to the
limit; a hydrogen atom is really invariable. . . . The
electrons preserve their individuality amid the most
diverse vicissitudes, is it the same with the atoms of
energy? We have, for instance, three quanta of energy in a resonator whose wave-length is 3; this
passes to a second resonator whose wave-length is 5;
it now represents not 3 but 5 quanta, since the quantum of the new resonator is smaller and in the transformation the number of atoms and the size of each
has changed."

If, however, we replace the atom of energy by an
"atom of action," these atoms may be considered
equal and invariable. The whole study of thermo-
dynamic equilibrium has been reduced by the French

mathematical school to a question of probability. "The probability of a continuous variable is obtained by considering elementary independent domains of equal probability. . . . In the classic dynamics we use, to find these elementary domains, the theorem that two physical states of which one is the necessary effect of the other are equally probable. In a physical system if we represent by q one of the generalized coordinates and by p the corresponding momentum, according to Liouville's theorem the domain $\iint dpdq$, considered at given instant, is invariable with respect to the time if p and q vary according to Hamilton's equations. On the other hand p and q may, at a given instant take all possible values, independent of each other. Whence it follows that the elementary domain is infinitely small, of the magnitude $dpdq$. . . . The new hypothesis has for its object to restrict the variability of p and q so that these variables will only change by jumps. . . . Thus the number of elementary domains of probability is reduced and the extent of each is augmented. The hypothesis of quanta of action consists in supposing that these domains are all equal and no longer infinitely small but finite and that for each $\iint dp\,dq$ equals h, h being a constant."

Put a little less mathematically, this simply means that as energy equals action multiplied by frequency, the fact that the quantum of energy is proportional to the frequency (or inversely to the wave-length as stated above) is due simply to the fact that the quantum of action is constant—a real atom. The general effect on our physical conceptions, however, is the same: we have a purely discontinuous universe—discontinuous not only in matter but in energy and the flow of time. M. Poincaré thus puts it:

"A physical system is susceptible only of a finite number of distinct states; it leaps from one of these to the next without passing through any continuous series of intermediate states."

He notes later:

"The universe, then, leaps suddenly from one state to another; but in the interval it must remain immovable, and the divers instants during which it keeps in the same state can no longer be discriminated from one another; we thus reach a conception of the discontinuous variation of time—the atom of *time*."

I quote in conclusion, Poincaré's final remarks:

"The present state of the question is thus as follows: the old theories, which hitherto seemed to account for all the known phenomena, have met with an unexpected obstacle. Seemingly a modification becomes necessary. A hypothesis has presented itself to M. Planck's mind, but so strange a one that one is tempted to seek every means of escaping it; these means, however, have been sought vainly. The new theory, however, raises a host of difficulties, many of which are real and not simply illusions due to the indolence of our minds, unwilling to change their modes of thought. . . .

"Is discontinuity to reign through out the physical universe, and is its triumph definitive? Or rather shall we find that it is but apparent and hides a series of continuous processes? . . . To try to give an opinion just now on these questions would only be to waste ink."

It only remains to call attention again to the fact that this conception of the discontinuity of energy, the acceptance of which Poincaré says would be "the most profound revolution that natural philosophy has undergone since Newton" was suggested by

the present writer fifteen years ago. Its reception
and serious consideration by one of the first mathematical physicists of the world seems a sufficient
justification of its suggestion then as a legitimate
scientific hypothesis.

THE ADVERTISEMENT OF IDEAS

Writing is a device for the storage of ideas—the only device for this purpose prior to the invention of the phonograph, and not now likely to be generally superseded. A book consists of stored ideas; sometimes it is like a box, from which the contents must be lifted slowly and with more or less toil; sometimes like a storage battery where one only has to make the right kind of contact to get a discharge. At any rate, if we want people to use books or to use them more, or to use them better, or to use a different kind from that which they now use, we must lose sight for a moment of the material part of the book, which is only the box or the lead and acid of the storage battery, and fix our attention on the stored ideas, which are what everybody wants— everybody, that is, except those who collect books as curiosities. The subject of this lecture is thus only library advertising, about which we have heard a good deal of late, but we shall try to confine its applications to this inner or ideal substance which it is our special business as librarians to purvey. And first, in considering the matter, it may be worth while to say a word about advertising in general. Practically an advertisement is an announcement by somebody who has something to distribute. Announcements of this kind may be classified, it seems to me, as economic, uneconomic and illegitimate.

The most elementary form is that of the person who tells you where you can get something that you want—a simple statement that someone is a barber or an inn-keeper, or gives music lessons, or has shoes for sale. This may be accompanied by an effort to show that the goods offered are of specially good quality or have some feature that makes them particularly desirable, either to consumers in general or to those of a certain class. This is all surely economic, so long as nothing but the truth is told. Next we have an effort not only to supply existing wants and to direct them into some particular channel, but to create a new field, to make people realize a lack previously not felt; in other words to make people want something that they need. This may be done simply by exhibiting or describing the article or it may require long and skillful presentation of the matter. All this is still economic. But it requires only a step to carry us across the line. Next the enthusiastic advertiser strives to make someone want that which he does not need. As may be seen, the line here is difficult to determine, but this sort of advertising is surely not economic. So long as the thing not needed is not really injurious, however, the advertising cannot be called illegitimate. It is simply uneconomic. The world would be better off without it, but we may look for its abolition only to the increase of good judgment and intelligence among consumers. When an attempt however, is made to cause a man to want something that is really injurious, then the act becomes illegitimate and should be prevented. Another class of illegitimate advertising is that which would be perfectly allowable if it were truthful and becomes objectionable only because its representations are false. It may be ostensibly of any of the types noted above.

As we have already noted, the material objects distributed by the librarian are valued not for their physical characteristics but for a different reason altogether, the fact that they contain stored ideas.

Ideas which, according to some, are merely the relative positions of material particles in the brain, and which are indisputably accompanied and conditioned by such positions, here subsist in the form of peculiar and visible arrangements of particles of printer's ink upon paper, which are capable under certain conditions of generating in the human brain ideas precisely similar to those that gave them birth. And although the book cannot think for itself, but must merely preserve the idea intrusted to it, without change, it is vastly superior in stability to the brain that gave it birth, so that thousands of years after that brain has mouldered into dust it is capable of reproducing the original ideas in a second brain where they may germinate and bear fruit. How familiar all this is, and yet how perennially wonderful! The miracle of it is sufficient excuse for this digression.

Now books, beside this modern form of distribution by loan, are widely distributed commercially both by loan and by sale, and especially in the latter form advertisement is now very extensively used in connection with the distribution. In fact we have all the different types specified above—economic, uneconomic and illegitimate, both through misrepresentation and the harmful character of the subject matter. The reason for all illegitimate forms of advertising is of course not a desire to misrepresent or to do harm per se, but to make money, the profit to the distributor being proportioned to the amount of distribution done and not at all dependent on its economic value. Distribution by public officers is of course not open to this objection, nor are the distributors subject to temptation, since their compensation does not depend on the amount of distribution. If they are capable and interested, fur-

thermore, they are particularly desirous to increase
the economic value of the work that they are doing.
Since this is so and since the danger of uneconomic
or harmful forms of advertising is thus reduced to
a minimum, there would seem to be special reason
why the economic forms should be employed very
freely. But the fact is that they have been used spar-
ingly, and by some librarians shunned altogether.

Let us see what library advertising of the economic types may mean. In the first place it means
telling those who want books where they may get
them. This simple task is rarely performed completely or satisfactorily. It is astonishing how many
inhabitants of a large town do not even know where
the public library is. Everyone realizes this who
has ever tried to find a public library in a strange
place. I once asked repeatedly of passers-by in a
crowded city street a block distant from a library
(in this case not architecturally conspicuous) before
finding one who knew its whereabouts; in another
city I inquired in vain of a conductor who passed the
building every few hours in his car. In the latter
case the library was a beautiful structure calculated
to move the curiosity of a less stolid citizen. In New
York inquiry would probably cause you to reach the
nearest branch library, anything more remote than
that being beyond the local intelligence. Sometimes
I think we had better drop all our far-reaching plans
for civic betterment and devote our time for a few
years to causing citizens, lettered and unlettered
alike to memorize some such simple formula as this:
"There is a Public Library. It is on Blank street.
We may borrow books there, free."

You will notice that I have inserted in this formula one item of information that pertains to use,
not location. For of those who know of the exis-

tence and location of the Public Library there are many whose ideas of its contents and their uses, and of the conditions and value of such uses, are limited and crude. The advertising that succeeds in bettering this state of things is surely doing an economic service. All these things the self-respecting citizen should know. But beyond and above all this there is the final economic service of advertising—the causing a man to want that which he needs but does not yet desire. Every man, woman and child in every town and village needs books in some shape, degree, form or substance. And yet the proportion of those who desire them is yet outrageously small, though encouragingly on the increase. Here no memorizing of a formula, even could we compass it, could suffice. This kind of advertising means the realization of something lacking in a life. Is the awakening of such a realization too much for us? Are we to stand by and see our neighbors all about us awakening to the undoubted fact that they need telephones in their houses, and electric runabouts, and mechanical fans in hot weather, and pianolas, and new kinds of breakfast food, while we despair of awakening them to their needs of books—quite as undoubted? Are we to admit that personal gain, which was the victorious motive that spurred on the commercial advertisers in these and countless other instances, is to be counted more mighty than the desire to do a service to our fellowmen and to fulfill the duties of our positions—which should spur us on?

I am not foolish enough to suppose that by placarding the fences with the words "Books! Books!" as the patent medicine man does with "Curoline! Curoline!" we shall make any progress. The patent medicine man is right; he wants to excite curiosity

and familiarize the public with the name of his nostrum. They all know what a book is—and alas the
name is not even unknown and mysterious—would
that it were! It calls up in many minds associations
which, if we are to be successful we must combat,
overthrow, and replace by others. To many—sad it
is to say it—a book is an abhorrent thing; to more
still, it is a thing of absolute indifference. To
some a book is merely a collection of things, having no ascertainable relationships, that one is required to memorize; to others it is a collection of
statements, difficult to understand, out of which the
meaning must be extracted by hard study; to very
few indeed does the book appear to be what it really
is —a message from another mind. People will go
to a seance and listen with thrills to the silliest stuff
purporting to proceed from Plato or Daniel Webster
or Abraham Lincoln, when in the Public Library, a
few blocks away are important and authentic messages from those same persons, to which they have
never given heed. Such a message derives interest
and significance from circumstances outside itself.
Very few books create their own atmosphere unaided.
They presuppose a system of abilities, opinions, prejudices, likes and dislikes, intellectual connections
and what not, that is little less than appalling, if
we try to follow it up. Dislike of books or indifference toward them is often simply the result of a lack
of these things or of some component part of them.
We must supply what is lacking if we are to arouse
a desire for books in those who do not yet possess
it. I say that such a labor is difficult enough to interest him whose pleasure it is to essay hard tasks;
it is noble enough to attract him who loves his fellow-
man; success in it is rare enough and glorious
enough to stimulate him who likes to succeed where

others have failed. Advertising may be good or bad, noble or ignoble, right or wrong, according to what is advertised and our methods of advertising it. He who would scorn to announce the curative powers of bottled spring-water and pink aniline dye; he who regards it as a commonplace task to urge upon the spendthrift public the purchase of unnecessary gloves and neckties, may well feel a thrill of satisfaction and of anticipation in the task of advertising ideas and of persuading the unheeding citizen to appropriate what he has been accustomed to view with indifference.

To get at the root of the matter, let us inquire why it is that so many persons do not care for books. We may divide them, I think, into two classes—those who do not care, or appear not to care for ideas at all, whether stored in books or not; and those who do care for ideas but who either do not easily get them out of storage or do not realize that they can be and are stored in books. Absolute carelessness of ideas is, it seems to me, rather apparent than real. It exists only in the idiot. There are those to be sure that care about a very limited range of ideas; but about some ideas they always care.

We must, in our advertisement of ideas, bear this in mind—the necessity of offering to each that which he considers it worth his while to take. If I were asked what is the most fundamentally interesting subject to all classes, I should unhesitatingly reply "philosophy." Not, perhaps, the philosophy of the schools, but the individual philosophy that every man and woman has, and that is precisely alike in no two of us. I have heard a tiny boy, looking up suddenly from his play, ask "Why do we live?" This and its correlative "Why do we die?" Whence come we and whither do we go? What is the universe and what are our relations to it—these questions in some form have occurred to everyone who thinks at all. They are discussed around the stove at the corner grocery, in the logging camp, on the ranch, in clubs and at boarding-house tables. Sometimes they take a theological turn—free will, the origin and purpose of evil, and so on. I do not purpose to give here a catalogue of the things in which an ordinary man is interested, and I have said this only to remind you that his interest may be vivid even in connection with subjects usually considered abstruse. This interest in ideas we may call the library's raw material; anything that tends to create it, to broaden it, to extend it to new fields and to direct it into paths that are worth while is making it possible for the library to do better and wider work—is helping on its campaign of publicity. This establishes a web of connecting fibers between the library and all human activity. The man who is getting interested in his work, debaters at a labor union, students at school and college, the worker for civic reform, the poetic dreamer—all are creating a demand for ideas that makes it easier for the library to advertise them. Those who object to some of the outside work done by modern libraries should try to look at the whole matter from this standpoint. The library is taking its place as a public utility with other public utilities. Its relations with them are becoming more evident; the ties between them are growing stronger. As in all cases of such growth it is becoming increasingly difficult to identify the boundaries between them, so fast and so thoroughly do the activities of each reach over these lines and interpenetrate those of the others. And unless there is actual wasteful duplication of work, we need not bother about our respective spheres. These activities are all human;

they are mutually interesting and valuable. A library need be afraid of doing nothing that makes for the spread of interest in ideas, so long as it is not neglecting its own particular work of the collection, preservation and distribution of ideas as stored in books, and is not duplicating other's work wastefully.

When we observe those who are already interested in ideas, however, we find that not all are interested in them as they are stored up in books. Some of these cannot read; their number is small with us and growing smaller; we may safely leave the schools to deal with them. Others can read, but they do not easily apprehend ideas through print. Some of these must read aloud so that they may get the sound of the words, before these really mean anything to them. These persons need practice in reading. They get it now largely through the newspapers, but their number is still large. A person in this condition may be intellectually somewhat advanced. He may be able to discuss single-tax with some acumen, for instance. It is a mistake to suppose that because a person understands a subject or likes a thing and is able to talk well about it, he will enjoy and appreciate a book on that subject or thing. It may be as difficult for him to get at the meat of it as if it were a half-understood foreign tongue. You who know enough French to buy a pair of gloves or sufficient German to inquire the way to the station, may tackle a novel in the original and realize at once the hazy degree of such a persons' apprehension. He may stick to it and become an easy reader, but on the other hand your well-meant publicity efforts may place in his hands a book that will simply discourage and ultimately repel him, sending him to join the army of those to whom no books appeal.

Next we find those who understand how to read and to read with ease, but to whom books—at any rate certain classes of books—are not interesting. Now interest in a subject may be so great that one will wade through the driest literature about it, but such interest belongs to the few—not to the many. I have come to the conclusion that more readers have had their interest killed or lessened by books than have had it aroused or stimulated. This is a proportion that it is our business as librarians to reverse. More of this unfortunate and heart-breaking, interest-killing work than I like to think of goes on in school. Not necessarily; for the name of those is legion who have had their eyes opened to the beauties of literature by good teachers. This makes it all the more maddening when we think how many poor teachers, or good teachers with mistaken methods, or indifferent teachers, have succeeded in associating with books in the minds of their pupils simply burdensome tasks—the gloom and heaviness of life rather than its joy and lightness. Such boys and girls will no more touch a book after leaving school than you or I would touch a scorpion after one had stung us.

Perhaps it is useless to try to change this; possibly it is none of our business, though we have already seen that there are reasons to the contrary. But we can better matters, and we are daily bettering them, by our work with children. If a child has once learned to love books and to associate them powerfully with something else than a burdensome task, then the labors of the unskillful teachers will create no dislike of the book but only of the teacher and his methods; while these of the good teacher will be a thousand times more fruitful than otherwise.

So much for the ways in which interesting books

are sometimes made uninteresting. Now for the books that are uninteresting *per se*—and how many there are! When a man has something to distribute commercially for personal gain, the thing that he tries above all to do is to interest his public—to make them want what he has to sell. His success or failure in doing this, means the success or failure of his whole enterprise. He does not decide what kind of an entertainment his clients ought to attend and then try to make them go to it, or what kind of neckties they ought to wear and then try to make them wear them. Of ten promoters, if nine proceeded on this principle and one on the plan of offering something attractive and interesting, who would succeed? It is one of the marvels of all time that this never seems to have occurred to writers of books. We are almost forced to conclude that they do not care whether their volumes are read or not. In only one class of books, as a rule, do the writers endeavor to interest the reader first and foremost; you all know that I refer to fiction. What is the result? The writers of fiction are the ones read by the public. More fiction is read, as you very well know, than all the other classes of literature put together. The library that is able to show a fiction percentage of 60, points to it with pride, while there are plenty with percentages between 70 and 80. Now this is all to the credit of the fiction writers. I refuse to believe that their readers are any more fundamentally interested in the subjects of which they treat than in others. They simply follow the line of least resistance. They want something interesting to read and they know from experience where to go for it. Of course this brings on abuses. Writers use illegitimate methods to arouse interest—appeals perhaps, to unworthy instincts. We need not discuss that here, but simply focus our attention on the fact that writers of fiction always try to be interesting because they must; while writers of history, travel, biography and philosophy do not usually try, because they think it unnecessary. This is simply a survival. It used to be true that readers of these subjects read them because of their great antecedent interest in them—an interest so great that interesting methods of presentation became unnecessary. No one cared about the masses, still less about what they might or might not read. Things are changed now; we are trying to advertise stored ideas to persons unfamiliar with them and we are suddenly awakening to the fact that our stock is not all that it should be. We need history, science and travel fascinatingly presented—at least as interestingly as the fiction-writer presents his subjects. This is by no means impossible, because it has been done, in a few instances. We are by no means in the position of the Irishman who didn't know whether or not he could play the piano, because he had never tried. Some of our authors have tried—and succeeded. No one after William James can say that philosophy cannot be made interesting to the ordinary reader. Tyndall showed us long ago that physics could interest the unlearned, and there are similarly interesting writers on history and travel—more perhaps in these two classes than any other. But it remains true that the vast majority of non-fiction books do not attract, and were not written with the aim of attracting, the ordinary reader such as the libraries are now trying to reach. The result is that the fiction writers are usurping the functions of these uninteresting scribes and are putting history, science, economics, biology, medicine—all sorts of subjects, into fictional form—a sufficient answer to any who may think that the subjects themselves, as distinguished from the manner in which they are presented, are calculated to repel the ordinary reader. Fiction is thus becoming, if it has not already become, the sole form of literary expression, so far as the ordinary reader is concerned. This is interesting; it justifies the large stock of fiction in public libraries and the large circulation of that stock. It does not follow that it is commendable or desirable. For one thing it places truth and falsehood precisely on the same plane. The science or the economics in a good novel may be bad and that in a poor novel may be good. Then again, it dilutes the interesting matter with triviality. It is right that those who want to know how and when and under what circumstances Edwin and Angelina concluded to get married should have an opportunity of doing so, but it is obviously unfair that the man who likes the political discussions put into the mouth of Edwin's uncle, or the clever descriptions of country-life incident to the courtship, should be burdened with information of this sort, in which he has little interest.

To those who are interested in the increase of non-fiction percentages I would therefore say: devise some means of working upon the authors. These gentry are yet ignorant of the existence of a special library public. Some day they will wake up, and then fiction will be relieved from the burden that oppresses it at present—of carrying most of the interesting philosophy, religion, history and social science, in addition to doing its own proper work.

Meanwhile the librarian, who is interested in advertising ideas, must do what he can with his material. There is still a saving remnant of interesting non-fiction, and there is a goodly body of readers whose antecedent interest in certain subjects is great enough to attract them to almost any book on those subjects. I have purposely avoided the discussion here of the details of library publicity, which has been well done elsewhere; but I cannot refrain from expressing my opinion that the ordinary work of the library and its stock of books if properly displayed, are more effective than any other means that can be used for the purpose. From a series of articles entitled "How to Start Libraries in Small Towns" by A. M. Pendleton, I quote the following, which appears in The Library Journal for May 13, 1877:

"Plant it [the library] among the people, where its presence will be seen and felt. * * * Other things being equal, it is better to have it upon the first floor, so that passers-by will see its goodly array of books and be tempted to inspect them."

Excellent advice; we might take it if we had not built our libraries as far away from the street as possible and lifted them up on as high a pedestal as our money would buy. Who, passing by a modern library building, branch or central, can by any possibility see through the windows enough of the interior to tell whether it is a library rather than a postoffice, a bank, or an office?

Before moving into its new home the St. Louis Public Library occupied temporarily a business building having a row of six large plate-glass windows on one side, directly on the sidewalk, enabling passers-by to see clearly all that went on in the adult lending-delivery room. The effect on the circulation was noteworthy. During the last months of our occupancy we went further and utilized each of the windows for a book display. This was in charge of a special committee of the staff, and its results were beyond expectation. In one window we had a shelfful of current books, open to attractive pictures, with a sign reminding wayfarers that they might be taken out by cardholders and that cards were free. In another we had standard works, without pictures, but open at attractive pages. In another we had children's books; in another, open reference or art books in a dust-proof case—and so on. Each of these windows was seldom without its contingent of gazers, and the direct effect on library circulation was noticed by all. At the end of the year we moved into our great million-and-a-half-dollar building; and beautiful as it is—satisfactory as are its arrangements—we have had—alas—to give up our show windows. We can, it is true, have show cases in the great entrance hall, but we want to attract outsiders, not insiders. Some of our enthusiastic staff want to build permanent show cases on the sidewalk. What we may possibly do is to rent real show windows opposite. What we do not desire, is to abandon our publicity plan altogether. But when, oh when, shall we have libraries (branches at any rate, if our main buildings must be monumental) that will throw themselves open to the public eye, luring in the wayfarer to the joys of reading, as the commercial window does to the delights of gumdrops or neckties?

One of the greatest steps ever taken toward the advertisement of ideas was the adoption, on a large scale, of the open shelf. This throws the books of a library, or many of them, open to public inspection and handling; it encourages "browsing"—the somewhat aimless rambling about and dipping here and there into a volume.

If we are to present ideas to our would-be readers in great variety, hoping that among them there may be toothsome bait, surely there could be no better way than this. The only trouble is that it appeals only to those who are already sufficiently interested in stored ideas to enter the library.

We must remember, however, that by our method

of sending out books for home use we are making a great open-shelf of the whole city. While the number of volumes in any one place may be small, the books are constantly changing so that the non-reader has a good chance of seeing in his friend's house something that may attract him. That this may affect the use of the library it is essential that he who sees a library book on the table or in the hands of a fellow passenger on a car must be able to recognize its source at once, so that, if attracted, he may be led thither by the suggestion. Nothing is better for this purpose than the library seal, placed on the book where all may see it; and that all may recognize it, it should also be used wherever possible, in connection with the library—on letter heads, posters, lists, pockets and cards, so that the public association between its display and the work of the library shall become strong.

This making the whole outstanding supply of circulating books an agency in our publicity scheme for ideas is evidently more effective as the books better fit and satisfy their users; for in that case we have an unpaid agent with each book. The adaptation of book to user helps our advertisement of ideas, and that in turn aids us in adapting book to user. When a dynamo starts, the newly arisen current makes the field stronger and that in turn increases the current. Only here we must have just a little residual magnetism in the field magnet to start the whole process. In the library's work the residual magnetism is represented by the latent interest in ideas that is present in every community. And I can do no better, in closing, than to emphasize the fact that everything that advertises ideas, even if totally unconnected with their recorded form in books, helps the library and pushes forward its work.

Itself a product of the great extension of intellectual activity to classes in which it was formerly bounded by narrow limits, the library is bound to widen those limits wherever they can be stretched, and every movement of them reacts to help it. Surely advertisement on its part is an evangel—a bearing of good intellectual tidings into the darkness. We are spiritualistic mediums in the best sense—the bearers of authentic messages from all the good and great of past or present time; only with us, no turning on of the light, no publicity however glaring, will break the spell or do otherwise than aid, for whether we succeed or fail, whether we live or die, those messages, recorded as they are in books, will stand while humanity remains.

THE PUBLIC LIBRARY, THE PUBLIC SCHOOL, AND THE SOCIAL CENTER MOVEMENT *

The center of a geometrical figure is important, not for its size and content, but for its position—not for what it is in itself, but for its relations to the other elements of the figure. And words used with derived meanings are used best when their original significations are kept in mind. The business center of a city does not contain all of that city's commercial activity; when we speak of the church as a religious center, we do not mean that there is to be no religious activity in the home or in other walks of life; as for the center of population of a large and populous country, it may be out in the prairie where neither man nor his dwellings are to be seen. All these centers are what they are because of certain relationships. It is so with a social center. But social relationships cover a wide field. The relationships of business, of religion, even of mere co-existence, are all social. May we have a center for so wide a range of activities? Even the narrower relations of business or of religion tend to form subsidiary groups and to multiply subsidiary centers. In a large city we may have not only a general business center but centers of the real estate business, of the hardware or textile trades, and so on. Our religious affiliations condense into denominational centers.

In the district of a large city where newly arrived foreign immigrants gather, you will be shown the group of blocks where the Poles or the Hungarians

* Read before the National Education Association.

have segregated themselves from the rest, and even within these, the houses where dwell families from a particular province or even from one definite city or village. Man is social, but he is socially clannish, and the broadest is not so much he who refuses to recognize these clan or caste relationships as he who enters into the largest number of them—he who keeps in touch with his childhood home, has a wide acquaintance among those of his own religious faith and of his chosen business or profession, keeps up his old college friendships, is interested in collecting coins or paintings and knows all the other collectors, is active in civic and charitable societies, takes an interest in education and educators, and so on. The social democracy that should succeed in abolishing all these groups or leveling them—that should recognize no relationships but the broader ones that underly all human effort and feeling—the touches of nature that make the whole world kin—would be barren indeed.

We cannot spare these fundamentals; we could not get rid of them if we would; but civilization advances by building upon them, and to do away with these additions would be like destroying a city to get at its foundation, in the vain hope of securing some wide-reaching result in economics or aesthetics. Occupying a foremost place among these groupings is the large division embracing our educational activities. And these are social not only in the broad sense, but also in the narrower. The intercourse of student with student in the school and even of reader with reader in the library, especially in such departments as the children's room, is so obviously that of society that we need dwell on it no further.

This intercourse, while a necessary incident of education in the mass, is only an incident. It is sufficiently obtrusive, however, to make it evident that any use of school or library building for social purposes is fit and proper. There is absolutely nothing new nor strange about such use. In places that cannot afford separate buildings for these purposes, the same edifice has often served for church, schoolhouse, public library, and as assembly room for political meetings, amateur theatricals, and juvenile debating societies. The propriety of all this has never been questioned and it is difficult to see why it should not be as proper in a town of 500,000 inhabitants as in one of 500. The incidence of the cost is a matter of detail. Why should such purely social use of these educational buildings—always common in small towns—have been allowed to fall into abeyance in the larger ones? It is hard to say; but with the recent great improvements in construction, the building of schools and libraries that are models of beauty, comfort, and convenience, there has arisen a not unnatural feeling in the public that all this public property should be put to fuller use. Why should children be forced to dance on the street or in some place of sordid association when comfortable and convenient halls in library or school are closed and unoccupied? Why should the local debating club, the mothers' meeting—nay, why should the political ward meeting be barred out? Side by side with this trend of public opinion there has been an awakening realization on the part of many connected with these institutions that they themselves might benefit by such extended use.

Probably this realization has come earlier and more fully to the library, because its educational function is directed so much more upon adults. The library is coming to be our great continuation school —an institution of learning with an infinity of purely optional courses. It may open its doors to any form of adult social activity.

There are forms of activity proper to a social center that require special apparatus or equipment. These may be furnished in a building erected for the purpose, as are the Chicago fieldhouses. Here we have swimming-pools, gymnasiums for men and for women, and all the rest of it. A branch library is included and some would house the school also under the same roof. We may have to wait long for the general adoption of such a composite social center. Our immediate problem is to supply an immediate need by using means directly at our disposal. And it is remarkable how many kinds of neighborhood activity may take place in a room unprovided with any special equipment. A brief glance over our own records for only a few months past enables me to classify them roughly as athletic or outdoor, purely social, educational, debating, political, labor, musical, religious, charitable or civic, and expository, besides many that defy or elude classification

The athletic or outdoor organizations include the various turning or gymnastic clubs and the Boy and Girl Scouts; the social organizations embrace dancing-classes, "welfare" associations, alumni and graduate clubs of schools and colleges, and dramatic clubs; the educational, which are very numerous, reading circles, literary clubs galore, free classes in chemistry, French, psychology, philosophy, etc., and all such organizations as the Jewish Culture Club, the Young People's Ethical Society, the Longan Parliamentary Class, and the Industrial and Business Women's Educational leagues. Religious bodies are parish meetings, committees of mission boards, and such organizations as the Theosophical Society; charitable or civic activities include the National Conference of Day Nurseries, the Central Council of Civic Agencies, the W.C.T.U., playground rehearsals for the Child Welfare Exhibit, and the Business Men's Association; and the Advertising Men's League; musical organizations embrace St. Paul's Musical Assembly, the Tuesday Choral Club, etc. Among exhibitions are local affairs such as wild flower shows, an exhibit of birdhouses, collections from the Educational Museum, the Civil League's Municipal Exhibit, selected screens from the Child Welfare Exhibit, and the prize-winners from the St. Louis Art Exhibit held in the art room of our central library. Then we have the Queen Hedwig Branch, the Clay School Picnic Association, the Aero Club, the Lithuanian Club, the Philotechne Club, the Fathers' Club, and the United Spanish War Veterans.

I trust you will not call upon me to explain the objects of some of these, as such a demand might cause me embarrassment—not because their aims are unworthy, but because these are skilfully obscured by their names. If anyone believes that there is a limit to the capacity of the human race for forming groups and subgroups on a moment's notice, for any reason or for no reason at all, I would refer him to our assembly room and clubroom records; and he would find, I think, that these are typical of every large library offering the use of such rooms somewhat freely.

It will be noted that the library takes no part in organizing or operating any of these activities; it does not have to do so.

The successful leader is he who repairs to a hill and raises his standard, knowing that at sight of it followers will flock around him. When you drop a tiny crystal into a solution, the atoms all rush to it naturally: there is no effort or compulsion except that of the aptitudes that their Creator has implanted in them. So it is with all centers, business or religious or social. No one instituted a campaign to locate the business center of a city at precisely such a square or corner. Things aggregate, and the point to which they tend is their center; they make it, it does not make them. The leader on a hill is a leader because he has followers; without them he would be but a lone warrior. The school or the library that says proudly to itself, "Go to; I will be a social center," may find itself in the same lonely position. It can offer an opportunity: that is all. It can offer houseroom to clubs, organizations, and groups of all kinds, whether permanent or temporary, large or small, but its usefulness as a social center depends largely on the existence of these and on their desire for a meeting place. We have in St. Louis six branch libraries with assembly rooms and clubrooms—in all a dozen or so. I have before me the calendar for a single week and I find 55 engagements, running from 24 at one branch down thru 13, 8, 6, and 3 to one. If I had before me only the largest number I should conclude that branch libraries as social centers were a howling success; if only the smallest, I should say that they were dismal failures. Why the difference? For the same reason that the leader who displays his standard may or may not be surrounded with eager "flocking" followers. There may be no one within earshot, or they may have no stomach for the war, or they may not be interested in the cause that he represents. Or again, he may not shout loud or persuasively enough, or his standard may not be attractive enough in form or color, or mounted on a sufficiently high staff.

I have said that all we can offer is opportunity: to

change our figure, we can furnish the drinking-fountain—thirst must bring the horse to it. But we must not forget that we offer our opportunity in vain unless we are sure that everyone who might grasp it realizes our offer and what it means.

Here is the chance for personal endeavor. If the young people in a neighborhood continue to hold their social meetings over a saloon when the branch library or the school is perfectly willing to offer its assembly room, it is pretty certain that they do not understand that offer, or that they mistrust its sincerity, or that there is something wrong that might be remedied by personal effort. In the one of our branches that is most used by organizations there is this personal touch. But I should hesitate to say that the others do not have it too. There are plenty of organizations near this busiest library and there are no other good places for them to meet. In the neighborhood of some other branches there are other meeting-places, and elsewhere, perhaps, the social instinct is not so strong, or at any rate the effort to organize is lacking. Should the librarian step out and attempt to stimulate this social instinct and to guide this organizing effort? There is room for difference of opinion here.

Personally I think that he should not do it directly and officially as a librarian. He may do it quietly and unobtrusively like any other private citizen, but he needs all his efforts, all his influence, to bring the book and the reader together in his community. Sometimes by doing this he can be doing the other too, and he can always do it vicariously. He should bear in mind that the successful man is not he who does everything himself, but he who can induce others to do things—to do them in his way and to direct them toward his ends. Even in the most sluggish, the most indifferent community there are these potential workers with enthusiasms that need only to be awakened to be let loose for good. The magic key is often in the librarian's girdle, and his free offer of house room and sympathy, with good literature thrown in, will always be of powerful assistance in this kind of effort. He will seldom need to do more than to make clear the existence and the nature of the opportunity that he offers. I know that there are some librarians and many more teachers who hesitate to open their doors in any such way as this; who are afraid that the opportunities offered will be misused or that the activities so sheltered will be misjudged by the public. It has shocked some persons that a young people's dancing-class has been held, under irreproachable auspices, in one of our branch libraries; others have been grieved to see that political ward meetings have taken place in them, and that some rather radical political theories have been debated there. These persons forget that a library never takes sides. It places on its shelves books on the Civil War from the standpoint of both North and South, histories of the great religious controversies by both Catholics and Protestants, ideas and theories in science and philosophy from all sides and at all angles. It may give room at one time to a young people's dancing-class and at another to a meeting of persons who condemn dancing. Its walls may echo one day to the praises of our tariff system and on another to fierce denunciations of it.

These things are all legitimate and it is better that they should take place in a library or a school building than in a saloon or even in a grocery store. The influence of environment is gently pervasive. I may be wrong, but I cannot help thinking that it is easier to be a gentleman in a library, whether in social meeting or in political debate, than it is in some other places. In one of our branches there meets a club of men who would be termed anarchists by some people. The branch librarian assures me that the brand of anarchism that they profess has grown perceptibly milder since they have met in the library. It is getting to be literary, academic, philosophic. Nourished in a saloon, with a little injudicious repression, it might perhaps have borne fruit of bombs and dynamite.

In this catholicity I cannot help thinking that the library as an educational institution is a step ahead of the school. Most teachers would resent the imputation of partisanship on the part of the school, and yet it is surely partisan—in some ways rightly and inevitably so. One cannot well explain both sides of any question to a child of six and leave its decision to his judgment. This is obvious; and yet I cannot help thinking that there is one-sided teaching of children who are at least old enough to know that there is another side, and that the one-sided teaching of two-sided subjects might be postponed in some cases until two-sided information would be possible and proper. Where a child is taught one side and finds out later that there is another, his resentment is apt to be bitter; it spoils the educational effect of much that he was taught and injures the influence of the institution that taught him. My resentment is still strong against the teaching that hid from me the southern viewpoint concerning slavery and secession, the Catholic viewpoint of what we Protestants call the Reformation—dozens of things omitted from textbooks on dozens of subjects because they did not happen to meet the approval of the textbook compiler. I am no less

an opponent of slavery—I am no less a Protestant—
because I know the other side, but I think I am a better man for knowing it, and I think it a thousand
pities that there are thousands of our fellow citizens,
on all sides of all possible lines, from whom our educative processes have hid even the fact that there is
another side. This question, as I have said, does not
affect the library, and fortunately need not affect it.
And as we are necessarily two-sided in our book material so we can open our doors to free social or neighborhood use without bothering our heads about whether the users are Catholics, Protestants, or Jews;
Democrats, Republicans, or Socialists; Christian Scientists or suffragists. The library hands our suffrage
and anti-suffrage literature to its users with the same
smile, and if it hands the anti-suffrage books to the
suffragist, and vice versa, both sides are certainly the
better for it.

I have tried to make it clear in what I have said
that in this matter of social activity, public institutions should go as far as they can in furnishing facilities without taking upon themselves the burden of
administration. I believe fully in municipal ownership of all kinds of utilities, but rarely in municipal
operation. Municipal ownership safeguards the city,
and private or corporate operation avoids the numerous objections to close municipal control of detail.
So the library authorities may retain sufficient control of these social activities by the power that they
have of admitting them to the parts of the buildings
provided for them, or of excluding them at any time.
These activities themselves are better managed by voluntary bodies, and, as I have said, there is no indica-
tion that the formation of such bodies is on the wane.
The establishment and operation of a musical or ath-

letic club, a debating society, or a Boy Scouts company, are surely quite as educational as the activities themselves in which their members engage. Do not let us arrogate to ourselves such opportunities as these. I should be inclined to take this attitude also with regard to the public playgrounds, were they not somewhat without the province of this paper; and I take it very strongly with regard to the public school. Throw open the school buildings as soon as you can, and as freely as you can to every legitimate form of social activity, but let your relationship to this activity be like that of the center to the circle—in it and of it, but embracing no part of its areal content. So, I am convinced, will it be best for all of us—for ourselves, the administrators of public property, and for the public, the owning body which is now demanding that it should not be barred out by its servants from that property's freest and fullest use.

THE SYSTEMATIZATION OF VIOLENCE

The peace propaganda has suffered much from the popular impression that many of those engaged in it are impractical enthusiasts who are assuming the possibility of doing away with passions and prejudices incident to our very humanity, and of bringing about an ideal reign of love and good will. Whether this impression is or is not justified we need not now inquire. It is the impression itself that is injuring the cause of peace, and will continue to injure it until it is removed.

It may at least be lessened by allowing the mind to dwell for a time on another aspect of the subject in which the regime of peace that would follow the discontinuance of all settlement of disputes by violence will appear to consist not so much in the total disappearance of violence from the earth as in the use of it for a different purpose, namely, the preservation of the peaceful status quo, by a systematic and lawful use of force, or at any rate, the readiness to employ it.

A state of peace, whether between individuals or nations, whether without or within a regime of law, always partakes of the nature of an armed truce: under one regime, however, the arms are borne by the possible contestants themselves; under the other, by the community whose members they are. If there is a resort to arms, violence ensues under both regimes; in both cases it tends ultimately to restore peace, but the action is more certain and more systematic when the violence is exerted by the community.

These laws may apply indifferently to a community of individuals or to one of nations. The most cogent and the most valid argument at the disposal of the peace advocate is the fact that we no longer allow the individual to take the law into his own hand, and that logically we should equally prohibit the nation from doing so. This is unanswerable, but its force has been greatly weakened by the assumption, which it requires no great astuteness to find unwarranted, that the settlement of individual quarrels by individual force has resulted from—or at least resulted in—the discontinuance of violence altogether, or in the dawn of a general era of good-will, man to man. On the contrary, it is very doubtful whether there is less violence to-day than there would be if the operation of law were suspended altogether; the difference, is that the violence has shifted its incidence and altered its aim—it is civic and social and no longer individual.

If we are to introduce the regime of law among nations as among individuals, our first step must be similarly to shift the incidence of violence. In so doing we may not decrease it, we may, indeed, increase it—but we shall none the less be taking that step in the only possible direction to achieve our purpose.

Among individuals, custom, crystallizing into law, generally precedes the enforcement of that law by the community. Hence, a somewhat elaborate code may exist side by side with the settlement of disputes, under that code, by personal combat. We have among nations such a code, and we yet admit the settlement of disputes by war, because the incidence of violence has not yet completely shifted. We have established a tribunal to act, in certain cases, on behalf of the community of nations, but we have not yet given that tribunal complete jurisdiction and we have given it no power whatever to enforce its decrees. It is on this latter point that I desire to dwell. In a community of individuals, there are two ways of using violence to enforce law—by the professional police force and by the posse of citizens. The former is more effective, but the latter is often readier and more certain in particular instances, especially in primitive communities. To give it force we must have readiness on the part of every citizen to respond to a call from the proper officer, and ability to do effective service, especially by the possession of arms and skill in their use. These requisites are not generally found in more advanced communities.

In like manner, the decrees of an international tribunal might be enforced either by the creation of an international army or by calling upon as many of the nations as necessary to aid in coercing the non-law-abiding member of the international community. Each nation is already armed and ready.

Whatever may be thought of the ultimate possibility of an international army, it must be evident that the principle of the posse must serve us at the outset. An international army would always consist in part of members of the nation to be coerced, whereas, in selecting a posse those furthest in race and in sympathy from the offender might always be chosen, just as members of a hostile clan would make up the best posse to arrest a Highlander for sheep-stealing.

Moreover, the posse has been used internationally more than once, as when decrees have been pronounced by a general European Congress and some particular nation or nations have been charged with their execution.

When a frontier community that has been a law unto itself gets its first sheriff, the earliest visible result is not impossibly a sudden increase, instead of a decrease, of violence. There is a war of the community, represented by the sheriff and the good citizens, against all the bad ones. Even so it may be expected that among the first results of an effective agreement to enforce the decrees of an international tribunal, would be an exceptionally great and violent war. Sooner or later some nation would be sure to take issue with an unpopular decree and refuse to obey it. This would probably be one of the larger and more powerful nations, for a weaker power would not proceed to such lengths in protest.

Not improbably other nations might join the protesting power. The result would be a war; it might even be the world war that we have been fearing for a generation. It might conceivably be the greatest and the bloodiest war that the world has yet seen. Yet it would be far the most glorious war of history, for it would be a struggle on behalf of law and order in the community of nations—a fight to uphold that authority by whose exercise alone may peace be assured to the world. The man who shudders at the prospect of such a war, who wants peace, but is unwilling to fight for it, should cease his efforts on behalf of a universal agreement among nations, for there is no general agreement without power to quell dissension.

This is not the place to discuss the details of an international agreement to enforce the decrees of an international tribunal. It may merely be said that if the most powerful and intelligent communities of men that have ever existed cannot devise machinery to do what puny individuals have long been successfully accomplishing, they had better disband and coalesce in universal anarchy.

My object here is neither to propose plans nor to

discuss details, but merely to point out that not the abandonment, but the systematization of violence is the goal of a rational peace propaganda, and that when this is once acknowledged and universally realized, an important step will have been taken toward winning over a class of persons who now oppose a world-peace as impractical and impossible.

These persons disapprove of disarmament: and from the point of view here advocated, a general disarmament would be the last thing to be desired. The possible member of a posse must bear arms to be effective. Armaments may have to be limited and controlled by international decree, but to disarm a nation would be as criminal and foolish as it would be to take away all weapons from the law-abiding citizens of a mining town as a preliminary to calling upon them to assist in the arrest of a notorious band of outlaws.

Again: a common objection to the peace propaganda is that without war we shall have none of the heroic virtues that war calls into being. This objection fails utterly when we consider that what we shall get under a proper international agreement is not the abolition of war, but simply an assurance that when there is a war it will be one in which every good citizen can take at once the part of international law and order—a contest between the law and the lawbreaker, and not one in which both contestants are equally lawless. Thus the profession of arms will still be an honorable one—it will, in fact, be much more honorable than it is to-day, when it may at any moment be prostituted to the service of greed or commercialism.

THE ART OF RE-READING

"I have nothing to read," said a man to me once. "But your house seems to be filled with books." "O, yes; but I've read them already." What should we think of a man who should complain that he had no friends, when his house was thronged daily with guests, simply because he had seen and talked with them all once before? Such a man has either chosen badly, or he is himself at fault. "Hold fast that which is good" says the Scripture. Do not taste it once and throw it away. To get at the root of this matter we must go farther back than literature and inquire what it has in common with all other forms of art to compel our love and admiration. Now, a work of art differs from any other result of human endeavor in this—that its effect depends chiefly on the way in which it is made and only secondarily upon what it is or what it represents. Were this not true, all statues of Apollo or Venus would have the same art-value; and you or I, if we could find a tree and a hill that Corot had painted, would be able to produce a picture as charming to the beholder as his.

The way in which a thing is done is, of course, always important, but its importance outside of the sphere of art differs from that within. The way in which a machine is constructed makes it good or bad, but the thing that is aimed at here is the useful working of the machine, toward which all the skill of the maker is directed. What the artist aims at is not so much to produce a likeness of a god or a picture of a tree, as to produce certain effects in the person who looks at his complete work; and this he does by the way in which he performs it. The fact that a painting represents certain trees and hills is here only secondary; the primary fact is what the artist has succeeded in making the on-looker feel.

While Sorolla is painting a group of children on the beach, I may take a kodak picture of the same group. My photograph may be a better likeness than Sorolla's picture, but it has no art-value. Why? Because it was made mechanically, whereas Sorolla put into his picture something of himself, making it a unique thing, incapable of imitation or of reproduction.

The man who has a message, one of those pervasive, compelling messages that are worth while, naturally turns to art. He chooses his subject not as an end, but as a vehicle, and he makes it speak his message by his method of treatment, conveying it to his public more or less successfully in the measure of his skill.

We have been speaking of the representative arts of painting and sculpture, but the same is true of art in any form. In music, not a representative art, in spite of the somewhat grotesque claims of so-called program music, the method of the composer is everything, or at least his subject is so vague and immaterial that no one would think of exalting it as an end in itself. There is, however, an art in which the subject stands forth so prominently that even those who love the art itself are continually in danger of forgetting the subject's secondary character. I mean the art of literature. Among the works of written speech the boundaries of art are much more ill-defined than they are elsewhere. There is, to be sure, as much difference between Shelley's "Ode to a Skylark" and Todhunter's "Trigonometry" as there is between the Venus de Milo and a battleship; and I conceive that the difference is also of precisely the same kind, being that by which, as we have seen above, we may always discriminate between a work of art and one of utility. But where art-value and utility are closely combined, as they are most frequently in literature, it is, I believe, more difficult to divide them mentally and to dwell on their separate characteristics, than where the work is a concrete object. This is why we hear so many disputes about whether a given work does or does not belong to the realm of "pure literature," and it is also the reason why, as I have said, some, even among those who love literature, are not always ready to recognize its nature as an art, or mistakenly believe that in so far as its art-value is concerned, the subject portrayed is of primary importance—is an aim in itself instead of being a mere vehicle for the conveyance of an impression.

Take, if you please, works which were intended by their authors as works of utility, but have survived as works of art in spite of themselves, such as Walton's "Compleat Angler" and White's "Natural History of Selborne." Will anyone maintain that the subject-matter of those books has much to do with their preservation, or with the estimation in which they are now held? Nay; we may even be so bold as to enter the field of fiction and to assert that those fictional works that have purely literary value are loved not for the story they tell, but for the way in which the author tells it and for the effect that he thereby produces on the reader.

I conceive that pure literature is an art, subject to the rules that govern all art, and that its value depends primarily on the effect produced on the reader —the message conveyed—by the way in which the writer has done his work, the subject chosen being only his vehicle. Where a man who has something to

say looks about for means to say it worthily, he may
select a tale, a philosophical disquisition, a familiar
essay, a drama or a lyric poem. He may choose badly
or well, but in any case it is his message that matters.

My excuse for dwelling on this matter must be
that unless I have carried you with me thus far what
I am about to say will have no meaning, and I had
best fold my papers, make my bow, and conclude an
unprofitable business. For my subject is re-reading,
the repetition of a message; and the message that we
would willingly hear repeated is not that of utility
but of emotion. It is the word that thrills the heart,
nerves the arm, and puts new life into the veins, not
that which simply conveys information. The former
will produce its effect again and again, custom can
not stale it. The latter, once delivered, has done its
work. I see two messengers approaching; one, whom
I have sent to a library to ascertain the birth-date of
Oliver Cromwell, tells me what it is and receives my
thanks. The other tells me that one dear to my heart,
long lying at death's door, is recovering. My blood
courses through my veins; my nerves tingle; joy suf-
fuses me where gloom reigned before. I cry out; I
beg the bearer of good tidings to tell them again and
again; I keep him by me, so that I may ask him a
thousand questions, bringing out his message in a
thousand variant forms. But do I turn to the other
and say, "O, that blessed date! was Cromwell truly
born thereon? Let me, I pray, hear you recite it
again and again!" I trow, not.

The message that we desire to hear again is the
one that produces its effect again and again; and that
is the message of feeling, the message of art—not that
of mere utility. This is so true that I conceive we
may use it as a test of art-value. The great works of
literature do not lose their effect on a single reading.

One makes response to them the hundredth time as he did the first. Their appeal is so compelling that there is no denying it—no resisting it. There are snatches of poetry—and of prose, too—that we have by heart; that we murmur to ourselves again and again, sure that the response which never failed will come again, thrilling the whole organism with its pathos, uplifting us with the nobility of its appeal, warming us with its humor. There is a little sequence of homely verse that never fails to bring the tears to my eyes. I have tested myself with it under the most unfavorable circumstances. In the midst of business, amid social jollity, in the mental dullness of fatigue, I have stopped and repeated to myself those three verses. So quickly acts the magic of the author's skill that the earlier verses grip the fibers of my mind and twist them in such fashion that I feel the pathos of the last lines just as I felt them for the first time, years ago. You might all tell similar stories. I believe that this is a characteristic of good literature, and that all of it will bear reading, and re-reading, and reading again.

But I hear someone say, "Do you mean to tell me that those three little verses that bring the tears to your eyes, will bring them also to mine and my neighbor's? I might listen to them appreciatively but dry-eyed; my neighbor might not care for them enough to re-read them once. All about us we see this personal equation in the appreciation of literature. Unless you are prepared, then, to maintain that literature may be good for one and bad for another, your contention will scarcely hold water."

Even so, brother. The messenger who told me of the safety of my dear one did not thrill your heart as he did mine. She was dear to me, not to you, and the infinitely delicate yet powerful chain of conditions and relations that operated between the messenger's voice and my emotional nature did not connect him with yours. Assuredly, the message that reaches one man may not reach another. It may even reach a man in his youth and fall short in manhood, or vice versa. It may be good for him and inoperative on all the rest of the world. We estimate literature, it is true, by the universality of its appeal or by the character of the persons whom alone that appeal reaches. The message of literature as art may thus be to the crowd or to a select few. I could even imagine intellect and feeling of such exquisite fineness, such acknowledged superiority, that appeal to it alone might be enough to fix the status of a work of art, though it might leave all others cold. Still, in general I believe, that the greatest literature appeals to the greatest number and to the largest number of types. I believe that there are very few persons to whom Shakespeare, properly presented, will not appeal. In him, nevertheless, the learned and those of taste also delight. There are authors like Walter Pater who are a joy to the few but do not please the many. There are others galore, whom perhaps it would be invidious to name, who inspire joy in the multitude but only distaste in the more discriminating. We place Pater above these, just as we should always put quality above quantity; but I place Shakespeare vastly higher, because his appeal is to the few and the many at once.

But we must, I think, acknowledge that an author whose value may not appeal to others may be great to one reader; that his influence on that reader may be as strong for good as if it were universal instead of unique. We may not place such a writer in the Walhalla, but I beseech you, do not let us tear him rudely from the one or two to whom he is good and great.

Do not lop off the clinging arms at the elbow, but rather skilfully present some other object of adoration to the intent that they may voluntarily untwine and enfold this new object more worthily.

The man who desires to own books but who can afford only a small and select library can not do better than to make his selection on this basis—to get together a collection of well-loved books any one of which would give him pleasure in re-reading. Why should a man harbor in his house a book that he has read once and never cares to read again? Why should he own one that he will never care to read at all? We are not considering the books of the great collectors, coveted for their rarity or their early dates, for their previous ownership or the beauty of their binding—for any reason except the one that makes them books rather than curiosities. These collections are not libraries in the intellectual or the literary sense. Three well thumbed volumes in the attic of one who loves them are a better library for him than those on which Pierpont Morgan spent his millions.

This advice, it will be noted, implies that the man has an opportunity to read the book before he decides whether to buy it or not. Here is where the Public Library comes in. Some regard the Public Library as an institution to obviate all necessity of owning books. It should rather be regarded from our present standpoint as an institution to enable readers to own the books that they need—to survey the field and make therefrom a proper and well-considered selection. That it has acted so in the past, none may doubt; it is the business of librarians to see that this function is emphasized in the future. The bookseller and the librarian are not rivals, but co-workers. Librarians complain of the point of view of those publishers and dealers who regard every library user as a lost customer. He is rather, they say, in many cases a customer won—a non-reader added to the reading class—a possible purchaser of books. But have not librarians shared somewhat this mistaken and intolerant attitude? How often do we urge our readers to become book-owners? How often do we give them information and aid directed toward this end? The success of the Christmas book exhibitions held in many libraries should be a lesson to us. The lists issued in connection with these almost always include prices, publishers' names, and other information intended especially for the would-be purchaser. But why should we limit our efforts to the holiday season? True, every librarian does occasionally respond to requests for advice in book-selection and book-purchase, but the library is not yet recognized as the great testing field of the would-be book owner; the librarian is not yet hailed as the community's expert adviser in the selection and purchase of books, as well as its book guardian and book distributor. That this may be and should be, I believe. It will be if the librarian wills it.

Are we straying from our subject? No; for from our present standpoint a book bought is a book re-read. My ideal private library is a room, be it large or small, lined with books, every one of which is the owner's familiar friend, some almost known by heart, others re-read many times, others still waiting to be re-read.

But how about the man whose first selection for this intimate personal group would be a complete set of the works of George Ade? Well, if that is his taste, let his library reflect it. Let a man be himself. That there is virtue in merely surrounding oneself with the great masters of literature all unread and unloved, I can not see. Better acknowledge your poor taste than be a hypocrite.

The librarian can not force the classics down the unwilling throats of those who do not care for them and are perhaps unfitted to appreciate them. There has been entirely too much of this already and it has resulted disastrously. Surely, a sane via media is possible, and we may agree that a man will never like Eschylus, without assuring him that Eschylus is an out-of-date old fogy, while on the other hand we may acknowledge the greatness of Homer and Milton without trying to force them upon unwilling and incompetent readers. After all it is not so much a question of Milton versus George Ade, as it is of sanity and wholesomeness against vulgarity and morbidity. And if I were to walk through one city and behold collections of this latter sort predominating and then through another, where my eyes were gladdened with evidences of good taste, of love for humor that is wholesome, sentiment that is sane, verse that is tuneful and noble, I should at once call on the public librarian and I should say to him, "Thou art the man!" The literary taste of your community is a reflection of your own as shown forth in your own institution— its collection of books, the assistants with which you have surrounded yourself, your attitude and theirs through you toward literature and toward the public.

But, someone asks, suppose that I am so fortunate and so happy as to sit in the midst of such a group of friendly authors; how and how often shall I re-read? Shall I traverse the group every year? He who speaks thus is playing a part; he is not the real thing. Does the young lover ask how and how often he shall go to see his sweetheart? Try to see whether you can keep him away! The book-lover reopens his favorite volume whenever he feels like it. Among the works on his shelves are books for every mood, every shade of varying temper and humor. He chooses for the moment the friend that best corresponds to it, or it may be, the one that may best woo him away from it. It may be that he will select none of them, but occupy himself with a pile of newcomers, some of whom may be candidates for admission to the inner group. The whole thing—the composition of his library, his attitude toward it, the books that he re-reads oftenest, the favorite passages that he loves, that he scans fondly with his eye while yet he can repeat them by heart, his standards of admission to his inner circle—all is peculiarly and personally his own. There is no other precisely like it, just as there is no other human being precisely like its owner. There is as much difference between this kind of a library and some that we have seen as there is between a live, breathing creature with a mind and emotions and aspirations, and a wax figure in the Eden Musee.

Thus every book lover re-reads his favorites in a way of his own, just as every individual human being loves or hates or mourns or rejoices in a way of his own.

One can no more describe these idiosyncrasies than he can write a history of all the individuals in the world, but perhaps, in the manner of the ethnological or zoological classifier, it may interest us to glance at the types of a few genera or species.

And first, please note that re-reading is the exact repetition of a dual mental experience, so far at least as one of the minds is concerned. It is a replica of mind-contact, under conditions obtainable nowhere else in this world and of such nature that some of them seem almost to partake of other-worldliness. My yesterday's interview with Smith or Jones, trivial as it is, I can not repeat. Smith can not remember what he said, and even if he could, he could not say it to me in the same way and to the same purpose. But my interview with Plato—with Shakespeare, with Emerson; my talk with Julius Caesar, with Goethe, with Lincoln! I can duplicate it once, twice, a hundred times. My own mind—one party to the contact—may change, but Plato's or Lincoln's is ever the same; they speak no "various language" like Byrant's nature, but are like that great Author of Nature who has taken them to Himself, in that in them "is no variableness, neither shadow of turning." To realize that these men may speak to me today, across the abyss of time, and that I can count on the same message tomorrow, next year and on my death bed, in the same authentic words, producing the same effect, assures me that somewhere, somehow, a miracle has been wrought.

I have said that one of the minds that come thus into contact changes not, while the other, the reader's, is alterable. This gives him a sort of standard by which he can measure or at least estimate, the changes that go on within him, the temporary ones due to fluctuations in health, strength or temper, the progressive ones due to natural growth or to outside influences.

In his "Introduction to Don Quixote," Heine tells us how that book, the first that he ever read, was his mental companion through life. In that first perusal knowing not "how much irony God had interwoven into the world," he looked upon the luckless knight as a real hero of romance and wept bitterly when his chivalry and generosity met with ingratitude and violence. A little later, when the satire dawned upon his comprehension, he could not bear the book. Still later he read it with contemptuous laughter at the poor knight. But when in later life, he lay racked on a bed of pain his attitude of sympathy returned. "Dulcinea del Toboso," he says "is still the most beautiful woman in the world; although I lie stretched upon the earth, helpless and miserable, I will never take back that assertion. I can not do otherwise. On with your lances, ye Knights of the Silver Moon; ye disguised barbers!"

So every reader's viewpoint shifts with the years.

Our friend who welcomes George Ade to his inner sanctuary may find as the years go on that his reaction to that contact has altered. I should not recommend that the author be then be cast into outer darkness. Once a favorite, always a favorite, for old sake's sake even if not for present power and influence. Our private libraries will hold shelf after shelf of these old-time favorites—milestones on the intellectual track over which we have wearily or joyously traveled.

There will always be a warm spot in my heart and a nook on my private shelf for Oliver Optic and Horatio Alger. Though I bar them from my library (I mean my Library with a big L) I have no right to exclude them from my private collection of favorites, for once I loved them. I scarcely know why or how. If there had been in those far-off days of my boyhood, children's libraries and children's librarians, I might not have known them; as it is, they are incidents in my literary past that can not be blinked, shameful though they may be. The re-reading of such books as these is interesting because it shows us how far we have traveled since we counted them among our favorites.

Then there is the book that, despite its acknowledged excellence, the reader would not perhaps admit to his inner circle if he read it now for the first time.

It holds its place largely on account of the glamour with which his youth invested it. It thrills him now as it thrilled him then, but he half suspects that the thrill is largely reminiscent. I sometimes fancy that as I re-read Ivanhoe and my heart leaps to my mouth when the knights clash at Ashby, the propulsive power of that leap had its origin in the emotions of 1870 rather than those of 1914. And when some of Dickens' pathos—that death-bed of Paul Dombey for instance—brings the tears again unbidden to my eyes, I suspect, though I scarcely dare to put my suspicion into words, that the salt in those tears is of the vintage of 1875. I am reading Arnold Bennett now and loving him very dearly when he is at his best; but how I shall feel about him in 1930 or how I might feel if I could live until 2014, is another question.

Then there is the book that, scarce comprehended or appreciated when it was first read, but loved for some magic of expression or turn of thought, shows new beauties at each re-reading, unfolding like an opening rose and bringing to view petals of beauty, wit, wisdom and power that were before unsuspected. This is the kind of book that one loves most to re-read, for the growth that one sees in it is after all in oneself—not in the book. The gems that you did not see when you read it first were there then as they are now. You saw them not then and you see them now, for your mental sight is stronger—you are more of a man now than you were then.

Not that all the changes of the years are necessarily for the better. They may be neither for better nor for worse. As the moving train hurries us onward we may enjoy successively the beauties of canyon, prairie and lake, admiring each as we come to it without prejudice to what has gone before. In youth we love only bright colors and their contrasts —brilliant sunsets and autumn foliage; in later life we come to appreciate also the more delicate tints and their gradations—a prospect of swamp-land and distant lake or sea on a gray day; a smoky town in the fog; the tender dove colors of early dawns. So in youth we eagerly read of blood and glory and wild adventure; Trollope is insufferably dull. Jane Austen is for old maids; even such a gem as Cranford we do not rate at its true value. But in after life how their quiet shades and tints come out! There is no glory in them, no carnage, no combat; but there is charm and fascination in the very slowness of their movement, the shortness of their range, their lack of intensity, the absence of the shrill, high notes and the tremendous bases.

Then there is the re-reading that accuses the reader of another kind of change—a twist to the right or the left, a cast in the mental eye, or perhaps the correction of such a cast. The doctrines in some book seemed strange to you once—almost abhorrent; you are ready to accept them now. Is it because you then saw through a glass darkly and now more clearly? Or is your vision darker now than it was? Your re-reading apprizes you that there has been a change of some sort. Perhaps you must await corroborative testimony before you decide what its nature has been. Possibly you read today without a blush what your mind of twenty years ago would have been shocked to meet. Are you broader-minded or just hardened? These questions are disquieting, but the disturbance that they cause is wholesome, and I know of no way in which they can be raised in more uncompromising form than by re-reading an old favorite, by bringing the alterable fabric of your living, growing and changing mind into contact with the stiff, unyielding yardstick of an unchangeable mental record—the cast of one phase of a master mind that once was but has passed on.

Here I can not help saying a word of a kind of re-reading that is not the perusal of literature at all with most of us—the re-reading of our own words, written down in previous years—old letters, old lectures, articles—books, perhaps, if we chance to be authors. Of little value, perhaps, to others, these are of the greatest interest to ourselves because instead of measuring our minds by an outside standard they enable us to set side by side two phases of our own life—the ego of 1892, perhaps, and that of 1914. How boyish that other ego was; how it jumped to conclusions; how ignorant it was and how self-confident! And yet, how fresh it was; how quickly responsive to new impressions; how unspoiled; how aspiring! If you want to know the changes that have transformed the mind that was into the very different one that now is, read your own old letters.

I have tried to show you that pure literature is an art and like other arts depends primarily upon manner and only secondarily upon matter. That the artist, who in this case is the author, uses his power to influence the reader usually through his emotions or feelings and that its effects to a notable extent, are not marred by repetition. That on this account all good literature may be re-read over and over, and that the pleasure derived from such re-reading is a sign that a book is peculiarly adapted in some way to the reader. Finally, that one's private library, especially if its size be limited, may well consist of personal favorites, often re-read.

When the astronomer Kepler had reduced to simple laws the complicated motions of the planets he cried out in ecstacy: "O God! now think I Thy thoughts after Thee!" Thus when a great writer of old time has been vouchsafed a spark of the divine fire we may think his divine thoughts after him by re-reading. And Shakespeare tells us in that deathless speech of Portia's, that since mercy is God's attribute we may by exercising it become like God. Thus, by the mere act of tuning our brains to think the thoughts that the Almighty has put into the minds of the good and the great, may it not be that our own thoughts may at the last come to be shaped in the same mould?

"Old wine, old friends, old books," says the old adage; and of the three the last are surely the most satisfying. The old wine may turn to vinegar; old friends may forget or forsake us; but the old book is ever the same. What would the old man do without it? And to you who are young I would say— that you may re-read, you first must read. Choose worthy books to love. As for those who know no book long enough either to love or despise it—who skim through good and bad alike and forget page ninety-nine while reading page 100, we may simply say to them, in the words of the witty Frenchman, "What a sad old age you are preparing for yourself!"

HISTORY AND HEREDITY*

In one of his earlier books, Prof. Hugo Munster-berg cites the growing love for tracing pedigrees as evidence of a dangerous American tendency toward aristocracy. There are only two little things the matter with this—the fact and the inference from it. In the first place, we Americans have always been proud of our ancestry and fond of tracing it; and in the second place, this fondness is akin, not to aristocracy but to democracy. It is not the purpose of this paper to prove this thesis in detail, so I will merely bid you note that aristocratic pedigree-tracers confine themselves to one line, or to a few lines. Burke will tell you that one of the great-great-grandfathers of the present Lord Foozlem was the First Baron; he is silent about his great-grandfather, the tinker, and his great-grandfather, the pettifogging country lawyer. Americans are far more apt to push their genealogical investigations in all directions, because they are prompted by a legitimate curiosity rather than by desire to prove a point. American genealogical research is biological, while that of Europe is commercial.

An obvious advantage of interest in our ancestors is that it ought to make history a more vital thing to us; for to them, history was merely current events in which they took part, or which, at least, they watched. This linking up of our personal ancestral lines with past events is done too seldom. Societies like the New England Society are doing it, and it is

* Read before the New England Society of St. Louis.

for this reason that I have chosen to bring the subject briefly before you.

It has been noted that our historical notions of the Civil War are now, and are going to be in the future, more just and less partisan than those of the Revolution. This is not because we are nearer the Civil War; for nearness often tends to confuse historical ideas rather than to clear them up. It is because the descendants of those who fought on both sides are here with us, citizens of our common country, intermarrying and coming into contact in a thousand ways. We are not likely to ignore the Southern standpoint regarding the rights of secession and the events of the struggle so long as the sons and daughters of Confederate soldiers live among us. Nor shall we ever forget the Northern point of view while the descendants of those who fought with Grant and Sherman are our friends and neighbors.

It is otherwise with the Revolution. We are the descendants only of those who fought on one side. Of the others, part went back to their homes in England, the rest, our old neighbors and friends, we despoiled of their lands and drove across our northern border with execrations, to make new homes in a new land and view us with a hatred that has not yet passed away. If you doubt it, discuss the American Revolution for fifteen minutes with one of the United Empire Loyalists of Toronto. It will surprise you to know that your patriot ancestors were thieves, blacklegs and scoundrels. I do not believe that they were; but possibly they were not the impossible archangels of the school histories.

Of one thing I am sure; that if the descendants of those who fought against us in '76 had been left to mingle with our own people, the historical recollections of the struggle would have been surer and truer on both sides than they are to-day. Here is a case where ancestry has perverted history, but simply because there has been an unnatural segregation of descendants. Let me note another where we have absolutely forgotten our ancestral predilections and have gone over to the other side, simply because the other side made the records. When we read a Roman account of encounters between the legions and the northern tribes, where do we place ourselves in imagination, as readers? Always with the Roman legions. But our place is not there; it is with our hardy and brave forefathers, fighting to defend their country and their firesides against the southern intruders. How many teachers of history try to utilize race-consciousness in their pupils to make them attain a clearer knowledge of what it all meant? Should we not be proud that we are of the blood of men who withstood the self-styled rulers of the world and won their freedom and their right to shape their own personal and civic development?

I should like to see a book tracing the history and development of an imaginary Anglo-Saxon American line of ancestry, taking it from the forests of Northern Germany across to Britain, through the Norman conquest and down the stream of subsequent English history across seas to America—through savage wars and Revolution, perhaps across the Alleghenies, to settle finally in the great West. I would try to make the reader realize that here was no fairy tale— no tale of countries and races with which we have naught to do, but the story of our own fathers, whose features and whose characteristics, physical and mental, have been transmitted by heredity to us, their sons and daughters of the year 1913.

It is unfortunate perhaps, for our perceptions of racial continuity, that we are rovers by disposition.

Who runs across the sea, says the Latin poet, changes his sky but not his mind. True enough, but it is difficult for some of us to realize it. It is hard for some of us to realize that our emigrant ancestors were the same men and women when they set foot on these shores as when they left the other side some weeks before. Our trans-Atlantic cousins labor under the same difficulties, for they assure us continually that we are a "new" country. We have, they say, the faults and the advantages of "youth." It would be interesting to know at just what point in the passage the education and the habits and the prejudices of the incoming Englishman dropped off. Change of environment works wonders with habits and even with character; we must of course recognize that; but it certainly does not make of the mind a *tabula rasa* on which the fresh surroundings may absolutely work their will.

I must say that our migrations within the limits of our own continent have not been productive of so much forgetfulness. I have been struck, for instance, since I came to St. Louis, with what I may call the source-consciousness of our western population. Everyone, whether he is particularly interested in genealogy or not, knows that his people came from Vermont or Virginia or Pennsylvania. He may not be able to trace his ancestry, or even to name his great-grandfather; but with the source of that ancestry he is always acquainted. I believe this to be the case throughout the Middle West. From this point of view the population is not so well mixed as it is in the East. No one in Massachusetts or Connecticut can point out to you, offhand, the families that came from particular counties in England. And yet in England, a migration from one county to another is always recognized and remembered. A cousin of mine, visiting on an English estate, was casually informed by his host, "Our family are newcomers in this county. We moved in only about 300 years ago." From this point of view we are all newcomers in America. It is to be hoped that as the years go on, the elements of our western population will not so thoroughly lose sight of their sources as have the Easterners. It is not likely that they will, for those sources are more accessible. We have Virginia families who still keep up friendly intercourse with the old stock; Vermont families who spend each summer on the old homestead; and so on. The New Englander did not and could not keep up similar relations with Old England. Even the Southerner, who did it for a time, had to drop it. Our inter-communication with Europe has grown enormously in volume, but little of it, if any, is due to continuous ancestral interest, although a revived general interest has sprung up and is to be commended.

I fear, however, that the greater part of this interest in sources, where it exists, is very far from an intelligent connection with the body of historical fact. When a man is proud of the fact that an ancestor took part in the famous Boston Tea Party, has he taken any pains to ascertain what actually took place on that occasion? If he claims descent from Pocahontas, can he tell us just how much of what we currently believe of her is fact and how much is myth? If he knows that his family came from Cheshire, England, and was established and well-known there for centuries, what does he know of the history of Cheshire and of the connection of his ancestors with it? Our interest, when it exists, is concentrated too much on trivial happenings. We know and boast that an ancestor came over in the Mayflower without knowing of the family doings before and after that event. Of course, connection with some one picturesque event serves to stimulate the imagination and focus the interest, but these events should serve as starting points for investigation rather than resting points where interest begins and ends. Historical students are beginning to realize that it is not enough to know about the battle of Hastings without understanding the causes and forces that led to it and proceeded from it, and the daily lives and thoughts of those who took part in it, from captain to spearman.

This failure to link up family history with general history is responsible for many sad losses of historical material. Many persons do not understand the value of old letters and diaries; many who do, keep them closely in the family archives where they are unknown and unappreciated. Old letters containing material that bears in any way on the events, customs or life of the time, should be turned over to the local historical society. If they contain private matter, seal up the packet and require that it shall remain sealed for a century, if you wish; but do not burn it. The feeling that destroys such documents is simply evidence that we are historically valuing the individual and the family above the community, just as we still are in so many other fields of thought. I cannot tolerate the idea that we shall ultimately think only in terms of the common good; the smaller units, the man, the family must not lose their influence, but the connection between them and the general welfare must be better understood and more generally recognized; and this must be done, in the first place, in all that relates to their historical records and to our historical consciousness.

Ancestral feeling should, in this way, always be

historical, not individual. A man is right to be personally proud of his own achievements, but it is difficult to see how he can properly take the same kind of pride in that of others, whether related to him by blood or not. But there are other kinds of legitimate pride—family pride, racial pride, group pride of all sorts, where the feeling is not personal. If any member of a family, a profession or any association, has so conducted himself that credit is gained for the whole body, it is proper that this kind of group pride should be felt by each member of the body, and in the case of a family, where the bond is one of blood, the group feeling should be stronger and the group pride, if it is proper to feel it at all, may be of peculiar strength, provided it be carefully distinguished from the pride due to personal achievement. And when the member of the family in whom one takes pride is an ancestor, this means, as I have said, that feeling should be historical, not individual. And anything that tends to lift our interest from the individual to the historical plane—to make us cease from congratulating ourselves personally on some connection with the good and great and substitute a feeling of group pride shared in common by some body to which we all belong, is acting toward this desirable end. The body may be a family; it may be the community or the state; it may be as broad as humanity itself, for we may all be proud of the world's greatest. Or it may be a body like our own, formed to cherish the memories of forebears in some particular line of endeavor, in some particular place or at some particular era. Our ancestry is part of our history; so long as our regard for it is properly interwoven with our historical sense, no one can properly charge us with laying the foundation for aristocracy. We are rather making true democracy possible, for such is the case only when the elements of a community are closely united by ties of blood, interest and knowledge—by pride in those who have gone before and by determination that the standard set by these men and women of old shall be worthily upheld.

WHAT THE FLAG STANDS FOR*

The most important things in the world are ideas. We are so familiar with the things that are the material embodiment of ideas—buildings, roads, vehicles and machines—that we are prone to forget that without the ideas that gave them birth all these would be impossible. A house is a mass of wood, stone and metal, but all these substances, collected in a pile, do not suffice to make a house.

A locomotive is made of steel and brass, but although the ancient Romans had both the metal and the alloy, they had no locomotives.

The vital thing about the house—the thing that differentiates it from other masses of the same materials—is the idea—the plan—that was in the architect's mind while wood and stone and iron were still in forest, quarry and mine. The vital thing about the locomotive is the builder's idea or plan, which he derived, in turn, from the inventor.

The reason why there were no locomotives in ancient Rome is that in those days the locomotive had not yet been invented, and when we say this we refer not to the materials, which the Romans had in abundance, but to the idea or plan of the locomotive. So it is with the whole material world about us. The things that result, not from man's activities, but from the operations of nature, are no exceptions; for, if we are Christians, we believe that the idea or plan of a man, or a horse, or a tree, was in the mind of the great architect, the great machinist, before the world

* An address on Flag Day made in St. Peter's Church, St. Louis.

began, and that this idea is the important thing about each.

A man, a house, an engine—these are ideas that lead to things that we can feel, and see and hear. But there are other ideas that have nothing of the kind to correspond to them—I mean such ideas as charity, manliness, religion and patriotism—what sometimes are called abstract qualities. These are real things and their ideas are even more important than the others, but we cannot see nor feel them.

Now, man likes to use his senses, and it is for this reason that he is fond of using for these abstract ideas, symbols that he can see and feel. We of St. Louis should appreciate this to the full just now, for we have just set before the world the greatest assemblage of symbolic images and acts, portraying our pride in the past and our hope and confidence for the future, that any city on this earth ever has been privileged to present or to witness. *   Whether we were actors or spectators; whether we camped with the Indians, marched with De Soto or La Salle and felled the forests of early St. Louis with Laclede and Chouteau, or whether we were part of that great host on the hillside, we can say no longer that we do not understand the importance of the idea, or the value and cogency of the visible symbols that fix it in the memory and grip it to the heart.

The Church of Christ always has understood and used this property of the visible and tangible symbol to enforce the claims of the abstract idea.

We revere the cross, not because there is anything in its shape or substance to make us venerate it, but because it is the symbol of the Christian religion— of all that it has done for the world in the past and all that it may do in the future.   That is why we

* The Pageant and Masque of St. Louis, 1915.

love and honor the flag—not because it is a piece of cloth bearing certain figures and colors, but because it is to us, the symbol of all that our country has meant to our fathers; all it means to us and all that it may mean to our children, generation after generation.

A nation's flag did not always mean all this to those who gazed upon it. In very old times the flag was for the soldier alone and had no more meaning for the ordinary citizen than a helmet or a spear. When the soldier saw it uplifted in the thick of the battle he rallied to it. Then the flag became the personal emblem of a king or a prince, whether in battle or not; then it was used to mark what belonged to the government of a country. It is still so used in many parts of Europe, where the display of a flag on a building marks it as government property, as our flag does when it is used on a post office or a custom-house. Nowhere but in our own country is the flag used as the general symbol of patriotic feeling and displayed alike by soldier and citizen, by Government office and private dwelling. So it comes about that the stars and stripes means to us all that his eagles did to the Roman soldier; all that the great Oriflamme did to the medieval Frenchman; all that the Union Jack now means to the Briton or the tricolor to the Frenchman—and more, very much more, beside.

What ideas, then, does the flag stand for? First, it stands for union. It was conceived in union, it was dipped in blood to preserve union, and for union it still stands. Its thirteen stripes remind us of that gallant little strip of united colonies along the Atlantic shore that threw down the gage of battle to Britain a century and a half ago. Its stars are symbols of the wider union that now is. Both may be held to signify the great truth that in singleness of purpose among many there is effective strength that no one by himself can hope to achieve. Our union of States was formed in fear of foreign aggression; we have need of it still though our foes be of our own household. If we are ever to govern our cities properly, hold the balance evenly betwixt capital and labor, develop our great natural resources without undue generosity on the one hand or parsimony on the other—solve the thousand and one problems that rise to confront us on every hand—we shall never accomplish these things by struggling singly—one man at a time or even one State at a time, but by concerted, united effort, the perfect union of which our flag is a symbol, and which we need to-day even more than we did in 1776 or 1861.

We stand on the threshold of an effort to alter our city government. Whether that effort should or should not succeed, every citizen must decide for himself, with the aid of such intelligence and judgment as it has pleased God to give him. But if he should decide in its favor, be certain that his individual vote at the polls will go a very little way toward bringing his desires to pass. We are governed by majorities, and a majority is a union of many. He who would win must not only vote, but work. Our flag, with its assemblages of stripes and stars, is a perpetual reminder that by the union of the many, and not merely by the rectitude of the individual, are policies altered and charters changed.

Again, our flag stands for love. It is a beautiful flag and it stands for a beautiful land. We all love what is our own, if we are normal men and women— our families, our city, our country. They are all beautiful to us, and it is right that they should be

I confess that the movement that has for its

motto "See America First" has my hearty sympathy. Not that the Rockies or the Sierras are necessarily more beautiful than the Alps or the Missouri fairer than the Danube; we should have no more to do here with comparisons than the man who loves his children. He does not, before deciding that he will love them, compare them critically with his neighbors'. If we do not love the Grand Canyon and the Northern Rockies, the wild Sierras and the more peaceful beauties of the Alleghenies or the Adirondacks, simply because leaving these all unseen we prefer the lakes and mountains of foreign lands, we are like a man who should desert his own children, whom he had never seen, to pass his time at a moving-picture show, because he believed that he saw there faces and forms more fair than those of his own little ones. When we sing in our hymn of "America"

> I love thy rocks and rills
> Thy woods and templed hills,

we should be able to do it from the heart.

It is indeed fitting that we should love our country, and thrill when we gaze at the old flag that symbolizes that love. Does this mean that when our country makes an error we are to shut our eyes to it? Does it require us to call wrong right and black white?

There is a sentiment with which you are all familiar, "My country, may she ever be right; but, right or wrong, my country!"

Understood aright, these are the noblest and truest of words, but they are commonly misinterpreted, and they have done much harm. To love and stand by a friend who has done wrong is a fine thing; but it would be very different to abet him in his wrong-doing and assure him that he had done right. We may dearly love a son or a brother who is the worst of sinners, without joining him in sin or persuading him that he is righteous.

So we may say, "Our country, right or wrong" without forfeiting the due exercise of our judgment in deciding whether she is right or wrong, or the privilege of exerting our utmost power to make her do right.

If she is fighting for an unrighteous cause, we should not go over to the enemy, but we should do our best to make her cease and to make amends for the wrong she has done.

Another thing for which the flag stands is freedom or liberty. We all are familiar with the word. It means different things to different persons. When hampering conditions press hard upon a man, all that he thinks of for the moment is to be rid of them. Without them he deems that he will be free. The freedom of which our fathers thought, for which they fought and which they won, was freedom from government by what had become to them a foreign power. The freedom that the black man longed for in the sixties was freedom from slavery.

To-day men and women living in intolerable industrial conditions are panting for freedom—the freedom that seems to them just now more desirable than aught else in the world. All this the flag stands for, but it stands for much more. Under its folds we are entitled to live our own lives in the fullest way compatible with the exercise of the same privilege by others. This includes political freedom, industrial freedom, social freedom and all the rest. Despite much grumbling and some denials, I believe that it is all summed up under political freedom, and that we have it all, though we may not always take advantage of it. The people who groan under an industrial yoke do so because they do not choose to exert the power given them by law, under the flag, to throw it off. The boss-ridden city is boss-ridden only because it is satisfied to be so. The generation that is throttled by trusts and monopolies may at any time effect a peaceful revolution. The flag gives us freedom, but even a man's eternal salvation cannot be forced upon him against his will.

Another thing for which the flag stands is justice—the "square deal," as it is called by one of our Presidents. To every man shall come sooner or later, under its folds, that which he deserves. This means largely "hands off," and is but one of the aspects of freedom, or liberty, since if we do not interfere with a man, what happens to him is a consequence of what he is and what he does. If we oppress him, or interfere with him, he gets less than he merits; and if, on the contrary we coddle him and give him privileges, he may get more than his due.

Give a man opportunity and a free path and he will achieve what is before him in the measure of his strength. That the American Flag stands for all this, thousands will testify who have left their native shores to live under its folds and who have contributed here to the world's progress what the restraints and injustice of the old world forbade then to give.

This sense of the removal of bonds, of sudden release and the entry into free space, is well put by a poet of our own, Henry Van Dyke, when he sings,

So it's home again, and home again, America for me!
My heart is turning home again, and there I long to be,
In the land of youth and freedom beyond the ocean bars,
Where the air is full of sunlight and the flag is full of stars.

I know that Europe's wonderful, yet something seems to lack:
The Past is too much with her, and the people looking back,
But the glory of the Present is to make the Future free—
We love our land for what she is and what she is to be.

Oh, it's hom、again, and home again, America for me!
I want a ship that's westward bound to plough the rolling sea,
To the blessed Land of Room Enough beyond the ocean bars,
Where the air is full of sunlight and the flag is full of stars.

Finally, the flag stands for the use of physical force where it becomes necessary.

This simple statement of facts will grieve many good people, but to omit it would be false to the truth and dishonorable to the flag that we honor to-day.

Its origin, as we have seen, was in its service as a rallying point in battle. We are still battling, and we still need it. And at times our contests still inevitably take the physical form. One may earnestly pray for peace; one may even pay his dues to the Peace Society and still realize that to preserve peace we may have to use the sword.

Northward, across the Canadian border, good men* are striving even now to keep us in peace and to assure peace to a neighbor severely torn by internal conflict. Can any of us doubt that our good friend and fellow-citizen—nay, can anyone doubt that our neighbors of the Southern Continent—are doing their best to save human lives, to preserve our young men and the young men of Mexico to build and operate machines, to raise crops and to rebuild and beautify cities, instead of sending them to fill soldiers' graves, as our bravest and best did in the "sixties?" And yet, should they succeed, as God grant they may, who can doubt that what will give strength and effect to their decisions will be the possibility of force, exerted in a righteous cause, symbolized by the flag? Who can be sorry that back of the flag there are earnest men; nay, that there are ships there, and guns? One need not be a Jingo; one can hate war

* United States and "A-B-C" Commissions on the State of Mexico.

and love peace with all one's heart and yet rejoice that the flag symbolizes authority—the ability to back up a decision without which the mind itself cannot decide in calmness and impartiality.

Surely, to say that the flag stands for the exertion of force, is only to say that it stands for peace; for it is by force only, or by the possibility of it, that peace is assured and maintained.

These are a few of the many things for which our flag of the Stars and Stripes stands. We are right to doff our hats when it passes; we are right to love it and to reverence it, for in so doing we are reverencing union, patriotism, liberty and justice. That it shall never become an empty symbol; that it shall never wave over a land disunited, animated by hate, shackled by indifference and feebleness, permeated by injustice, unable to exert that salutary strength which alone can preserve peace without and within—this is for us to see and for our children and grandchildren. We must not only exercise that "eternal vigilance" of which the fathers spoke, but we must be eternally ready, eternally active. The Star-Spangled Banner! Long may it wave over a land whose sons and daughters are both free and brave—free because they are brave, and brave because they are free, and both because they are true children of that eternal father without whom both freedom and bravery are but empty names.

THE PEOPLE'S SHARE IN THE PUBLIC LIBRARY *

The change that has come over the library in the last half century may be described, briefly but comprehensively, by saying that it has become predominently a social institution; that is, that its primary concern is now with the service that it may render to society—to the people. Books, of course, were always intended to be read, and a library would have no meaning were it never to be used; yet in the old libraries the collection and preservation of the books was primary and their use secondary, whereas the modern institution exists primarily for public service, the collection of the books, their preservation, and whatever is done to them being directed to this end. To a social institution—a family, a school, a club, a church or a municipality—the persons constituting it, maintaining it, or served by it are all-important. A family without parents and children, a school without pupils, a club without members, a church with no congregation, a city without citizens—all are unthinkable. We may better realize the change in our conception of the public library by noting that it has taken its place among bodies of this type. A modern library with no readers is unthinkable; it is no library, as we now understand the word; though it be teeming with books, housed in a palace, well cataloged and properly manned.

It is no longer possible to question this view of the library as a social institution— a means of rendering general service to the widest public. We have

* Read before the Chicago Woman's Club, January 6, 1915.

to deal not with theories of what the library ought
to be, but with facts indicating what it actually is;
and we have only to look about us to realize that the
facts give the fullest measure of support to what I
have just said. The library is a great distributing
agency, the commodities in which it deals being ideas
and its customers the citizens at large, who pay,
through the agency of taxation, for what they receive.
This democratic and civic view of the public library's
functions, however, does not commend itself to those
who are not in sympathy with democratic ideals. In
a recent address, a representative librarian refers to
it as "the commercial-traveler theory" of the library.
The implication, of course, is that it is an ignoble
or unworthy theory. I have no objection to accepting the phrase, for in my mind it has no such con-
notation. The commercial traveler has done the
world service which the library should emulate
rather than despise. He is the advance guard of
civilization. To speak but of our own country and
of its recent years, he is responsible for much of our
improvement in transit facilities and hotel accommo-
dations. Personally, he is becoming more and more
acceptable. The best of our educated young men
are going into commerce, and in commerce to-day
no one can reach the top of the ladder who has not
proved his efficiency "on the road." Would that we
could place men of his type at the head of all our
libraries!

We need not think, however, that there is anything new in the method of distribution by personal
travel. Homer employed it when he wished his
heroic verse to reach the great body of his countrymen. By personal travel he took it to the cross-roads
—just as the distributor of food and clothing and
labor-saving appliances does to-day; just as we li-

brarians must do if we are to democratize all literature as Homer democratized a small part of it. Homer, if you choose to say so, adopted the "commercial-traveler theory" of literary distribution; but I prefer to say that the modern public library, in laying stress on the necessity of distributing its treasures and in adopting the measures that have proved effective in other fields, is working on the Homeric method.

Now, without the people to whom he distributed his wares, Homer would have been dead long ago. He lives because he took his wares to his audience. And without its public, as we have already said, the public library, too, would soon pass into oblivion. It must look to the public for the breath of life, for the very blood in its veins, for its bone and sinew. What, then, is the part that the community may play in increasing the efficiency of a public institution like the public library? Such an institution is, first of all, a medium through which the community does something for itself. The community employs and supports it, and at the same time is served by it. To use another homely illustration, which I am sure will not please those who object to comparing great things with small, this type of relationship is precisely what we find in domestic service. A cook or a housemaid has a dual relation to the mistress of the house, who is at the same time her employer and the person that she directly serves. This sort of relation does not obtain, for instance, in the case of a railroad employe, who is responsible to one set of persons and serves another. The public library is established and maintained by a given community in order that it may perform certain service for that same community directly. It seems to me that this dual relationship ought to make for efficiency. If it does not, it is because its existence and significance are not always realized. The cook knows that if she does not cook to suit her mistress she will lose her job— the thing works almost automatically. If the railroad employe does not serve the public satisfactorily there is no such immediate reaction, although I do not deny that the public displeasure may ultimately reach the railroad authorities and through them the employe. In most public institutions the reaction is necessarily somewhat indirect. The post office is a public institution, but public opinion must act on it generally through the channels of Congressional legislation, which takes time. Owing to this fact, very few postmen, for instance, realize that the persons to whom they deliver letters are also their employers. In all libraries the machinery of reaction is not the same. In St. Louis, for instance, the library receives the proceeds of a tax voted directly by the people; in New York City it receives an appropriation voted by the Board of Apportionment, whose members are elected by the people. The St. Louis Public Library is therefore one step nearer the control of the people than the New York Public Library. If we could imagine the management of either library to become so objectionable as to make its abolition desirable, a petition for a special election could remove public support in St. Louis very soon. In New York the matter might have to become an issue in a general election, at which members of a Board of Apportionment should be elected under pledge to vote against the library's appropriation. Nevertheless, in both cases there is ultimate popular control. Owing to this dual relation, the public can promote the efficiency of the library in two ways— by controlling it properly and by its attitude toward the service that is rendered. Every member of the public, in fact, is related to the library somewhat as a railway stockholder, riding on a train, is related to the company. He is at once boss and beneficiary.

Let us see first what the public can do for its library through its relation of control. Besides the purse-strings, which we have seen are sometimes held directly by the public and sometimes by its elected representatives, we must consider the governing board of the institution—its trustees or directors. These may be elected by the people or appointed by an elected officer, such as the mayor, or chosen by an elected body, such as the city council or the board of education.

Let us take the purse-strings first. Does your public library get enough public money to enable it to do the work that it ought to do? What is the general impression about this in the community? What does the library board think? What does the librarian think? What do the members of his staff say? What has the library's annual report to say about it? It is not at all a difficult matter for the citizen to get information on this subject and to form his own opinion regarding it. Yet it is an unusual thing to find a citizen who has either the information or a well-considered opinion. The general impression always seems to be that the library has plenty of money—rather more, in fact, than it can legitimately use. It is probably well for the library, under these circumstances, that the public control of its purse-strings is indirect. If the citizens of an average American city had to go to the polls annually and vote their public library an appropriation, I am sure that most libraries would have to face a very material reduction of their income.

The trouble about this impression is that it is gained without knowledge of the facts. If a majority of the citizens, understanding how much work a modern public library is expected to do and how their own library does it, should deliberately conclude that its management was extravagant, and that its expenditure should be cut down, the minority would have nothing to do, as good citizens, but submit. The citizens have nothing to say as directly as this, but the idea, so generally held, that libraries are well off, does operate in the long run to limit library appropriations and to prevent the library from doing much useful work that it might do and ought to do.

It is then, every citizen's business, as I conceive it, to inform himself or herself of the work that the public library is doing, of that which it is leaving undone, and of the possibilities of increased appropriations. If the result is a realization that the library appropriation is inadequate, that realization should take the form of a statement that will sooner or later reach the ears, and tend to stimulate the action, of those directly responsible. And it should, above all, aid in the formation of a sound public opinion. Ours is, we are told, a government of public opinion. Such government will necessarily be good or bad as public opinion is based on matured judgment or only on fleeting impressions.

Inadequacy of support is responsible for more library delinquency than the average citizen imagines. Many a librarian is deservedly condemned for the unsatisfactory condition of his institution when his fault is not, as his detractors think, failure to see what should be done, or lack of ability to do it, so much as inability to raise funds to do it with. This is doubtless a fault, and its possessor should suffer, but how about the equally guilty accessories? How about the city authorities who have failed to vote the library adequate support? How about the board of trustees who have accepted such a situation without protest? And what is more to our purpose here, how about the citizens who have limited their efforts to pointing out the cracks in the edifice, with not a bit of constructive work in propping it up and making possible its restoration to strength and soundness?

In conversation with a friend, not long ago, I referred to the financial limitations of our library's work, and said that we could add to it greatly and render more acceptable service if our income were larger. He expressed great surprise, and said: "Why, I thought you had all the money you want; your income must be all of $100,000 a year." Now, our income actually is about $250,000, but how could I tell him that? I judiciously changed the subject.

Let us look next, if you please, at the library board and examine some of its functions. There appears to be much public misapprehension of the duties of this body, and such misapprehension assumes various and opposing forms. Some appear to think that the librarian is responsible for all that is done in the library and that his board is a perfunctory body. Others seem to believe that the board is the direct administrative head of the library, in all of its working details and that the librarian is its executive in the limited sense of doing only those things that he is told to do. Unfortunately there are libraries that are operated in each of these ways, but neither one relationship nor the other, nor any modification of either, is the ideal one between a librarian and his board. The board is supreme, of course, but it is a body of non-experts who have employed an expert to bring about certain results. They ought to know what they want, and what they have a right to expect, and if their expert does not give them this, the relation between him and them should terminate; but if they are men of sense they will not attempt to dictate methods or supervise details. They are the delegated representatives of the great public, which owns the library and operates it for a definite purpose. It is this function of the board as the representative of the public that should be emphasized here. Has the public a definite idea of what it wants from the public library, and of what is reasonable for it to ask? If so, is it satisfied that it is represented by a board that is of the same mind? The citizens may be assured that the composition of the library board rests ultimately upon its will. If the board is elective, this is obvious; if appointive, the appointing officer or body would hardly dare to go counter to the expressed desire of the citizens.

What has been said above may be put into a very few words. The public library is public property, owned and controlled by the citizens. Every citizen, therefore, should be interested in setting standards for it and playing his part toward making it conform to them—in seeing that its governing body represents him in also recognizing those standards and trying to maintain them—in laboring for such a due apportionment of the public funds as shall not make an attempt to live up to such standards a mere farce.

So much for the things that the citizen can and should do in his capacity of library boss. His possibilities as a beneficiary are still more interesting and valuable.

Perhaps you remember the story of the man who attempted to board the warship and, on being asked his business, replied, "I'm one of the owners." One version of the tale then goes on to relate how the sailor thus addressed picked up a splinter from the deck, and, handing it to the visitor, remarked: "Well, I guess that's about your share. Take it and get out!"

I have always sympathized with the sailor rather than with his visitor. Most of us librarians have had experiences with these bumptious "owners" of public property. The fact has already been noted that in a case like this the citizen is both an owner and a beneficiary. He has duties and privileges in both capacities, but he sometimes acts the owner in the wrong place. The man on the warship was doubtless an owner, but at that particular moment he was only a visitor, subject to whatever rules might govern visitors; and he should have acted as such. Every citizen is a part owner of the public library; he should never forget that fact. We have seen how he may effectively assert his ownership and control. But when he enters the library to use it his role is that of beneficiary, and he should act as such. He may so act and at the same time be of the greatest service to the institution which he, as a member of the public, has created and is maintaining.

I know of no way in which a man may show his good citizenship or the reverse—may either demonstrate his ability and willingness to live and work in community harness, or show that he is fit for nothing but individual wild life in the woods—better than in his use of such a public institution as a library. The man who cannot see that what he gets from such an institution must necessarily be obtained at the price of sacrifice—that others in the community are also entitled to their share, and that sharing always means yielding—that man has not yet learned the first lesson in the elements of civic virtue. And when one sees a thousand citizens, each of whom would surely raise his voice in protest if the library were to waste public money by buying a thousand copies of the latest novel, yet find fault with the library because each cannot borrow it before all the others, one is tempted to wonder whether we really have here a thousand bad citizens or whether their early education in elementary arithmetic has been neglected.

Before the present era there were regulations in all institutions that seemed to be framed merely to exasperate—to put the public in its place and chasten its spirit. There are now no such rules in good libraries. He who thinks there are may find that there is a difference of opinion between him and those whom he has set in charge of the library regarding what is arbitrary and what is necessary; but at any rate he will discover that the animating spirit of modern library authority is to give all an equal share in what it has to offer, and to restrain one man no more than is necessary to insure to his brother the measure of privilege to which all are equally entitled.

Another way in which the citizen, in his capacity of the library's beneficiary, can aid it and improve its service is his treatment of its administrators. Librarians are very human: they react quickly and surely to praise or blame, deserved or undeserved. Blame is what they chiefly get. Sometimes they deserve it and sometimes not. But the occasions on which some citizen steps in and says, "Well done, good and faithful servant," are rare indeed. The public servant has to interpret silence as praise; so sure is he that the least slip will be caught and condemned by a vigilant public. No one can object to discriminating criticism; it is a potent aid to good administration. Mere petulant fault-finding, however, especially if based on ignorance or misapprehension, does positive harm. And a little discriminating praise, now and then, is a wonderful stimulant. No service is possible without the men and women who render it; and the quality of service depends, more than we often realize, on the spirit and temper of a staff—something that is powerfully affected, either for good or for evil, by public action and public response.

Years ago, at a branch library in a distant city, a reader stood at the counter and complained loudly because the library would not send her a postal reserve notice unless she defrayed the cost, which was one cent. The assistant to whom she was talking had no option in the matter and was merely enforcing a rule common, so far as I know, to all American public libraries; but she had to bear the brunt of the reader's displeasure, which she did meekly, as it was all in the day's work. The time occupied in this useless business spelled delay to half a dozen other readers, who were waiting their turn. Finally, one of them, a quiet little old lady in black, spoke up as follows: "Some of us hereabouts think that we owe a great debt of gratitude to this library. Its assistants have rendered service to us that we can never repay. I am glad to have an opportunity to do something in return, and it therefore gives me pleasure to pay the cent about which you are taking up this young lady's time, and ours." So saying, she laid the coin on the desk and the line moved on. I have always remembered these two points of view as typical of two kinds of library users. Their respective effects on the temper and work of a library staff need, I am sure, no explanation.

In what I have said, which is such a small fraction of what might be said, that I am almost ashamed to offer it to you, I have in truth only been playing the variations on one tune, which is—Draw closer to the library, as it is trying to draw closer to you. There is no such thing, physicists tell us, as a one-sided force. Every force is but one aspect of a stress, which includes also an equal and opposing force. Any two interacting things in this world are either approaching each other or receding from each other. So it should be with library and public. A forward movement on the one hand should necessarily involve one to meet it.

The peculiarity of our modern temper is our hunger for facts—our confidence that when the facts are known we shall find a way to deal with them, and that until the facts are known we shall not be able to act—not even to think. Our ancestors thought and acted sometimes on premises that seem to us frightfully flimsy—they tried, as Dean Swift painted them in his immortal satire, to get sunbeams from cucumbers. There are some sunbeam-chasers among us to-day, but even they recognize the need of real cucumbers to start with; the imaginary kind will not do. I recently heard a great teacher of medicine say that the task of the modern physician is merely to ascertain the facts on which the intelligent public is to act. How different that sounds from the dicta of the medicine of a past generation! It is the same everywhere: we are demanding an accurate survey—an ascertainment of the facts in any field in which action, based on inference and judgment, is seen to be necessary. Now the library is nothing more nor less than a storehouse of recorded facts. It is becoming so more truly and more fully every day, thereby adjusting itself to the modern temper of which I have already spoken. The library and its users are coming more closely together, in sympathy, in aims and in action, than ever before—partly a result and partly a justification for that

Homeric method of popularizing it which has been characterized and condemned as commercial. The day when the librarian, or the professor, or the clergyman could retire into his tower and hold aloof from the vulgar herd is past. The logical result of such an attitude is now being worked out on the continent of Europe. Not civilizations, as some pessimists are lamenting, but the forces antagonistic to civilization are there destroying one another, and there is hope that a purified democracy will arise from the wreckage. May our American civilization never have to run the gantlet of such a terrible trial!

Meanwhile, there can be no doubt that the hope for the future efficiency of all our public institutions, including the library, lies in the success of democracy, and that depends on the existence and improvement of the conditions in whose absence democracy necessarily fails. Foremost among these is the homogeneity of the population. The people among whom democracy succeeds must have similar standards, ideas, aims and abilities. Democracy may exist in a pack of wolves, but not in a group that is half wolves and half men. Either the wolves will kill the men or the men the wolves. This is an extreme case, but it is true in general that in a community made up of irreconcilable elements there can be no true democracy. And the same oneness of vision and purpose that conduces to the success of democracy will also bring to perfection such great democratic institutions as the library, which have already borne such noteworthy fruit among us just because we are homogeneous beyond all other nations on the earth. And here progress is by action and reaction, as we see it so often in the world. The unity of aims and abilities that makes democracy and democratic institutions possible is itself facilitated and increased by the work of those institutions. The more work the library does, the more its ramifications multiply, and the further they extend, the more those conditions are favored that make the continuance of the library possible. In working for others, it is working for itself, and every additional bit of strength and sanity that it takes on does but enable it to work for others the more. And if the democracy whose servant it is will but realize that it has grown up as a part of that American system to which we are all committed—to which we owe all that we are and in which we must place all our hopes for the future—then neither democracy nor library will have aught to fear. Democracy will have its "true and laudable" service from the library, and the library in its turn will have adequate sympathy, aid and support from the people.

It is no accident that I make this appeal for sympathy and aid to a club composed of women. The bonds between the modern public library and the modern woman's club have been particularly strong in this country. The two institutions have grown up together, making their way against suspicion, contempt and hostility, aided by the same public demand, and now, when both are recognized as elements in the intellectual strength of our nation, they are rendering mutual service. The club turns to the library daily. Hitherto the library has turned to the club only in some emergency—a bill to be passed, an appropriation to be made, an administration to be purified. I have tried to show you how, apart from these great services, which no one would think of minimizing, the women of this country, as citizens, can uphold the hands of the library daily. Ours is a government of public opinion, and in the formation of that opinion there is no more powerful element than the sentiment of our women, especially when organized in such bodies as yours.

"To be aristocratic in taste and democratic in service," says Bliss Perry, "is the privilege and glory of the public library." In appealing thus to both your aristocracy and your democracy, I feel, then, that I have not gone astray.

SOME TENDENCIES OF AMERICAN
THOUGHT*

The modern American mind, like modern America, itself, is a melting pot. We are taking men and women of all races and fusing them into Americans. In the same way we are taking points of view, ideas, standards and modes of action from whatever source we find them, combining them and fusing them into what will one day become American thoughts and standards. We are thus combining the most varied and opposing things—things that it would seem impossible to put together. Take our modern American tendency in government, for instance. Could there be two things more radically different than despotism and democracy?—the rule of the one and the rule of the many? And yet I believe that we are taking steps toward a very successful combination of the two. Such a combination is essentially ancient. No despotism can hold its own without the consent of the governed. That consent may be unwilling and sooner or later it is then withheld, with the result that a revolution takes place and the despot loses his throne —the oldest form of the recall. Every despotism is thus tempered by revolution, and Anglo-Saxon communities have been ready to exercise such a privilege on the slightest sign that a despotic tendency was creeping into their government.

It is not remarkable, then, that our own Federal government, which is essentially a copy of the British government of its day, should have incorporated this

* Read before the New York Library Association at Squirrel Inn, Haines Falls, September 28, 1915.

feature of the recall, which in England had just
passed from its revolutionary to its legal stage. It
was beginning to be recognized then that a vote of the
people's representatives could recall a monarch, and
the English monarchy is now essentially elective. But
to make assurance doubly sure, the British government, in its later evolution, has been practically separated from the monarch's person, and any government may be simply overthrown or "recalled" by a
vote of lack of confidence in the House of Commons,
followed, if need be, by a defeat in a general election.
We have not yet adopted this feature. Our President is still the head of our government, and he and
all other elected Federal officers serve their terms
out, no matter whether the people have confidence in
them or not. But the makers of our Constitution improved on the British government as they found it.
They made the term of the executive four years instead of life and systematized the "recall" by providing for impeachment proceedings—a plan already
recognized in Britain in the case of certain administrative and judicial officers.

As it stands at present we have a temporary elective monarch with more power, even nominally, than
most European constitutional monarchs and more
actually than many so-called absolute monarchs such
as the Czar or the Sultan. In case he should abuse
the power that we have given him, he may be removed
from office after due trial, by our elected representatives.

In following out these ideas in later years, we are
gradually evolving a form of government that is both
more despotic and more democratic. We are combining the legislative and executive power in the hands
of a few persons, hampering them very little in their
exercise of it, and making it possible to recall them

by direct vote of the body of citizens that elected them. I think we may describe the tendency of public thought in governmental matters as a tendency toward a despotism under legalized democratic control. It may be claimed, I think, that the best features of despotism and democracy may thus be utilized, with a minimum of the evils of each.

It was believed by the ancients, and we frequently see it stated today, that the ideal government would be government by a perfectly good despot. This takes the citizens into account only as persons who are governed, and not as persons who govern or help to govern. It is pleasant, perhaps, to have plenty of servants to wait upon one, but surely health, physical, mental and moral, waits on him who does most things for himself. I once heard Lincoln Steffens say: "What we want is not 'Good Government'; it is *Self-Government.*" But is it not possible to get the advantage of government by a few, with its possibilities of continuous policy and its freedom from "crowd-psychology," with its skillful utilization of expert knowledge, while admitting the public to full knowledge of what is going on, and full ultimate control of it? We evidently think so, and our present tendencies are evidence that we are attempting something of the kind. Our belief seems to be that if we elect our despot and are able to recall him we shall have to keep tab on him pretty closely, and that the knowledge of statecraft that will thus be necessary to us will be no less than if we personally took part in legislation and administration—probably far more than if we simply went through the form of delegating our responsibilities and then took no further thought, as most of us have been accustomed to do.

Whether this is the right view or not—whether it is workable—the future will show; I am here discussing tendencies, not their ultimate outcome. But it would be too much to expect that this or any other eclectic policy should be pleasing to all.

"The real problem of collectivism," says Walter Lippmann, "is the difficulty of combining popular control with administrative power. . . . The conflict between democracy and centralized authority . . . is the line upon which the problems of collectivism will be fought out."

In selecting elements from both despotism and democracy we are displeasing the adherents of both. There is too much despotism in the plan for one side and too much democracy for the other. We constantly hear the complaint that concentrated responsibility with popular control is too despotic, and at the same time the criticism that it is too democratic. To put your city in the hands of a small commission, perhaps of a city manager, seems to some to be a return to monarchy; and so perhaps it is. To give Tom, Dick and Harry the power to unseat these monarchs at will is said to be dangerously socialistic; and possibly it is. Only it is possible that by combining these two poisons—this acid and this alkali—in the same pill, we are neutralizing their harmful qualities. At any rate this would seem to be the idea on which we are now proceeding.

We may now examine the effects of this tendency toward eclecticism in quite a different field—that of morals. Among the settlers of our country were both Puritans and Cavaliers—representatives in England of two moral standards that have contended there for centuries and still exist there side by side. We in America are attempting to mix them with some measure of success. This was detected by the German lady of whom Mr. Bryce tells in his "American Commonwealth," who said that American women were

"furchtbar frei und furchtbar fromm"—frightfully
free and frightfully pious! In other words they are
trying to mix the Cavalier and Puritan standards.
Of course those who do not understand what is going
on think that we are either too free or too pious. We
are neither; we are trying to give and accept freedom
in cases where freedom works for moral efficiency and
restraint where restraint is indicated. We have not
arrived at a final standard. We may not do so. This
effort at mixture, like all our others, may fail; but
there appears to be no doubt that we are making it.
To take an obvious instance, I believe that we are trying, with some success, to combine ease of divorce
with a greater real regard for the sanctity of marriage. We have found that if marriage is made absolutely indissoluble, there will be greater excuse for
disregarding the marriage vow than if there are legal
ways of dissolving it.

Americans are shocked at Europeans when they
allude in ordinary conversation to infractions of the
moral code that they treat as trivial. They on the
other hand are shocked when we talk of divorce for
what they consider insufficient causes. In the former
case we seem to them "frightfully pious"; in the latter, "frightfully free." They are right; we are both;
it is only another instance of our tendency towards
eclecticism, this time in moral standards.

In some directions we find that this tendency to
eclecticism is working toward a combination not of
two opposite things, but of a hundred different ones.
Take our art for instance, especially as manifested in
our architecture. A purely native town in Italy, Arabia, or Africa, or Mexico, has its own atmosphere; no
one could mistake one for the other any more than he
could mistake a beaver dam for an ant hill or a bird's
nest for a woodchuck hole.

But in an American city, especially where we have enough money to let our architects do their utmost, we find streets where France, England, Italy, Spain, Holland, Arabia and India all stand elbow to elbow, and the European visitor knows not whether to laugh or to make a hasty visit to his nerve-specialist. It seems all right to us, and it *is* all right from the standpoint of a nation that is yet in the throes of eclecticism. And our other art—painting, sculpture, music—it is all similarly mixed. Good of its kind, often; but we have not yet settled down to the kind that we like best—the kind in which we are best fitted to do something that will live through the ages.

We used to think for instance that in music the ordinary diatonic major scale, with its variant minor, was a fact of nature. We knew vaguely that the ancient Greeks had other scales, and we knew also that the Chinese and the Arabs had scales so different that their music was generally displeasing to us. But we explained this by saying that our scale was natural and right and that the others were antiquated, barbaric and wrong. Now we are opening our arms to the exotic scales and devising a few of our own. We have the tonal and the semi-tonal scales and we are trying to make use of the Chinese, Arabic and Hindu modes. We are producing results that sound very odd to ears that are attuned to the old-fashioned music, but our eclecticism here as elsewhere is cracking the shell of prejudice and will doubtless lead to some good end, though perhaps we can not see it yet.

How about education? In the first place there are, as I read the history of education, two main methods of training youth—the individual method and the class method. No two boys or girls are alike; no two have like reactions to the same stimulus.

Each ought to have a separate teacher, for the methods to be employed must be adapted especially to the material on which we have to work. This means a separate tutor for every child.

On the other hand, the training that we give must be social—must prepare for life with and among one's fellow beings, otherwise it is worthless. This means training in class, with and among other students, where each mind responds not to the teacher's alone but to those of its fellow-pupils.

Here are two irreconcilable requirements. In our modern systems of education we are trying to respond to them as best we may, teaching in class and at the same time giving each pupil as much personal attention as we can. The tutorial system, now employed in Princeton University, is an interesting example of our efforts as applied to the higher education.

At the same time, eclecticism in our choice of subjects is very manifest, and at times our success here seems as doubtful as our mixture of architectural styles. In the old college days, not so very long ago, Latin, Greek, and mathematics made up the curriculum. Now our boys choose from a thousand subjects grouped in a hundred courses. In our common schools we have introduced so many new subjects as to crowd the curriculum. Signs of a reaction are evident. I am alluding to the matter here only as another example of our modern passion for wide selection and for the combination of things that apparently defy amalgamation.

What of religion? Prof. George E. Woodberry, in his interesting book on North Africa, says in substance that there are only two kinds of religion, the simple and the complex. Mohammedanism he considers a simple religion, like New England Puritanism, with which he thinks it has points in common.

Both are very different from Buddhism, for instance. Accepting for the moment his classification I believe that the facts show an effort to combine the two types in the United States. Many of the Christian denominations that Woodberry would class as "simple"—those that began with a total absence of ritual, are becoming ritualized. Creeds once simple are becoming complicated with interpretation and comment. On the other hand we may see in the Roman Catholic Church and among the so-called "High Church" Episcopalians a disposition to adopt some of the methods that have hitherto distinguished other religious bodies. Consider, for example, some of the religious meetings held by the Paulist Fathers in New York, characterized by popular addresses and the singing of simple hymns. As another example of the eclectic spirit of churches in America we may point to the various efforts at combination or unity, with such results as the Federation of the Churches of Christ in America—an ambitious name, not yet justified by the facts—the proposed amalgamation of several of the most powerful Protestant bodies in Canada, and the accomplished fact of the University of Toronto—an institution whose constituent colleges are controlled by different religious denominations, including the Roman Catholic Church. I may also mention the present organization of the New York Public Library, many of whose branch libraries were contributions from religious denominations, including the Jews, the Catholics and the Episcopalians. All these now work together harmoniously. I know of nothing of this kind on any other continent, and I think we shall be justified in crediting it to the present American tendency to eclecticism.

Turn for a moment to philosophy. What is the philosophical system most widely known at present

as American? Doubtless the pragmatism of William
James. No one ever agreed with anyone else in a
statement regarding philosophy, and I do not expect
you to agree with me in this; but pragmatism seems
to me essentially an eclectic system. It is based on
the character of results. Is something true or false?
I will tell you when I find out whether it works practically or not. Is something right or wrong? I rely
on the same test. Now it seems to me that this is the
scheme of the peasant in later Rome, who was perfectly willing to appeal to Roman Juno or Egyptian
Isis or Phoenician Moloch, so long as he got what he
wanted. If a little bit of Schopenhauer works, and
some of Fichte; a piece of Christianity and a part of
Vedantism, it is all grist to the mill of pragmatism.
Any of it that works must of necessity be right and
true. I am not criticizing this, or trying to contro-
vert it; I am merely asserting that it leads to eclecticism; and this, I believe, explains its vogue in the
United States.

It would be impossible to give, in the compass of
a brief address, a list of all the domains in which this
eclecticism—this tendency to select, combine and
blend—has cropped out among us Americans of to-
day. I have reserved for the last that in which we are
particularly interested—the Public Library, in which
we may see it exemplified in an eminent degree. The
public library in America has blossomed out into a
different thing, a wider thing, a combination of more
different kinds of things, than in any other part of the
world. Foreign librarians and foreign library users
look at us askance. They wonder at the things we are
trying to combine under the activities of one public
institution; they shudder at our extravagance. They
wonder that our tax-payers do not rebel when they are
compelled to foot the bills for what we do. But the

taxpayers do not seem to mind. They frequently complain, but not about what we are doing. What bothers them is that we do not try to do more. When we began timidly to add branch libraries to our system they asked us why we did not build and equip them faster; when we placed a few books on open shelves they demanded that we treat our whole stock in the same way; when we set aside a corner for the children they forced us to fit up a whole room and to place such a room in every building, large or small. We have responded to every such demand. Each response has cost money and the public has paid the bill. Apparently librarians and public are equally satisfied. We should not be astonished, for this merely shows that the library is subject to the same laws and tendencies as all other things American.

Hence it comes about that whereas in a large library a century ago there were simply stored books with no appliances to do anything but keep them safe, we now find in library buildings all sorts of devices to facilitate the quick and efficient use of the books both in the building and in the readers' homes, together with other devices to stimulate a desire to use books among those who have not yet felt it; to train children to use and love books; to interest the public in things that will lead to the use of books. This means that many of the things in a modern library seem to an old-fashioned librarian and an old-fashioned reader like unwarranted extensions or even usurpations. In our own Central building you will find collections of postal cards and specimens of textile fabrics, an index to current lectures, exhibitions and concerts, a public writing-room, with free note-paper and envelopes, a class of young women studying to be librarians, meeting places for all sorts of clubs and groups, civic, educational, social, political and religious; a bindery in full operation, a photographic copying-machine; lunch-rooms and rest-rooms for the staff; a garage, with an automobile in it, a telephone switchboard, a paintshop, a carpenter-shop, and a power-plant of considerable capacity. Not one of these things I believe, would you have found in a large library fifty years ago. And yet the citizens of St. Louis seem to be cheerful and are not worrying over the future. We are eclectic, but we are choosing the elements of our blend with some discretion and we have been able, so far, to relate them all to books, to the mental activities that are stimulated by books and that produce more books, to the training that instils into the rising generation a love for books. The book is still at the foundation of the library, even if its walls have received some architectural embellishment of a different type.

When anyone objects to the introduction into the library of what the colleges call "extra-curriculum activities," I prefer to explain and justify it in this larger way, rather than to take up each activity by itself and discuss its reasonableness—though this also may be undertaken with the hope of success. In developing as it has done, the Library in the United States of America has not been simply obeying some law of its own being; it has been following the whole stream of American development. You can call it a drift if you like; but the Library has not been simply drifting. The swimmer in a rapid stream may give up all effort and submit to be borne along by the current, or he may try to get somewhere. In so doing, he may battle with the current and achieve nothing but fatigue, or he may use the force of the stream, as far as he may, to reach his own goal. I like to think that this is what many American institutions are doing, our libraries among them. They are using the present tendency to eclecticism in an effort toward wider public service. When, in a community, there seems to be a need for doing some particular thing, the library, if it has the equipment and the means, is doing that thing without inquiring too closely whether there is logical justification for linking it with the library's activities rather than with some others. Note, now, how this desirable result is aided by our prevailing American tendency toward eclecticism. Suppose precisely the same conditions to obtain in England, or France, or Italy, the admitted need for some activity, the ability of the library and the inability of any other institution, to undertake it. I submit that the library would be extremely unlikely to move in the matter, simply from the lack of the tendency that we are discussing. That tendency gives a flexibility, almost a fluidity, which under a pressure of this kind, yields and ensures an outlet for desirable energy along a line of least resistance.

The Englishman and the American, when they are arguing a case of this kind, assume each the condition of affairs that obtains in his own land—the rigidity on the one hand, the fluidity on the other. They assume it without stating it or even thoroughly understanding it, and the result is that neither can understand the conclusions of the other. The fact is that they are both right. I seriously question whether it would be right or proper for a library in a British community to do many of the things that libraries are doing in American communities. I may go further and say that the rigidity of British social life would make it impossible for the library to achieve these things. But it is also true that the fluidity of American social life makes it equally impossible for the library to withstand the pressure that is brought to

bear on it here. To yield is in its case right and
proper and a failure of response would be wrong and
improper.

It is usually assumed by the British critic of
American libraries that their peculiarities are due to
the temperament of the American librarian. We
make a similar assumption when we discuss British
libraries. I do not deny that the librarians on both
sides have had something to do with it, but the determining factor has been the social and tempera-
mental differences between the two peoples. Americans are fluid, experimental, eclectic, and this finds
expression in the character of their institutions and
in the way these are administered and used.

Take if you please the reaction of the library on
the two sides of the water to the inevitable result of
opening it to home-circulation—the necessity of
knowing whether a given book is or is not on the
shelves. The American response was to open the
shelves, the British, to create an additional piece of
machinery—the indicator. These two results might
have been predicted in advance by one familiar with
the temper of the two peoples. It has shown itself in
scores of instances, in the front yards of residences,
for instance—walled off in England and open to the
street in the United States.

I shall be reminded, I suppose, that there are
plenty of open shelves in English libraries and that
the open shelf is gaining in favor. True; England is
becoming "Americanized" in more respects than this
one. But I am speaking of the immediate reaction to
the stimulus of popular demand, and this was as I
have stated it. In each case the reaction, temporarily
at least, satisfied the demand; showing that the difference was not of administrative habit alone, but of
community feeling.

This rapid review of modern American tendencies, however confusing the impression that it may give, will at any rate convince us, I think, of one thing—the absurdity of objecting to anything whatever on the ground that it is un-American. We are the most receptive people in the world. We "take our good things where we find them," and what we take becomes "American" as soon as it gets into our hands. And yet, if anything new does not happen to suit any of us, the favorite method of attack is to denounce it as "un-American." Pretty nearly every element of our present social fabric has been thus denounced, at one time or another, and as it goes on changing, every change is similarly attacked.

The makers of our Constitution were good conservative Americans—much too conservative, some of our modern radicals say—yet they provided for altering that Constitution, and set absolutely no limits on the alterations that might be made, provided that they were made in the manner specified in the instrument. We can make over our government into a monarchy tomorrow, if we want, or decree that no one in Chicago shall wear a silk hat on New Year's Day. It was recently the fashion to complain that the amendment of the Constitution has become so difficult as to be now practically a dead letter. And yet we have done so radical a thing as to change absolutely the method of electing senators of the United States; and we did it as easily and quietly as buying a hat—vastly more easily than changing a cook. The only obstacle to changing our Constitution, no matter how radically and fundamentally, is the opposition of the people themselves. As soon as they want the change, it comes quickly and simply. Changes like these are not un-American if the American people like them well enough to make them. They, and they alone, are the judges of what peculiarities they shall adopt as their own customs and characteristics. So that when we hear that this or that is un-American, we may agree only in so far as it is not yet an American characteristic. That we do not care for it today is no sign that we may not take up with it tomorrow, and it is no legitimate argument against our doing so, if we think proper.

And now what does this all mean? The pessimist will tell us, doubtless, that it is a sign of decadence. It does remind us a little of the later days of the Roman empire when the peoples of the remotest parts of the known world, with their arts, customs and manners, were all to be found in the imperial city—when the gods of Greece, Syria and Egypt were worshipped side by side with those of old Rome, where all sorts of exotic art, philosophy, literature and politics took root and flourished. That is usually regarded as a period of decadence, and it was certainly a precursor of the empire's fall. When we consider that it was contemporaneous with great material prosperity and with the spread of luxury and a certain loosening of the moral fiber, such as we are experiencing in America today, we can not help feeling a little perturbed. Yet there is another way of looking at it. A period of this sort is often only a period of readjustment. The Roman empire as a political entity went out of existence long ago, but Rome's influence on our art, law, literature and government is still powerful. Her so-called "fall" was really not a fall but a changing into something else. In fact, if we take Bergson's viewpoint—which it seems to me is undoubtedly the true one, the thing we call Rome was never anything else but a process of change. At the time of which we speak the visible part of the change was accelerated—that is all. In like manner each one of you as an individual is not a fixed entity. You are changing every instant and the reality about you is the change, not what you see with the eye or photograph with the camera—that is merely a stage through which you pass and in which you do not stay—not for the thousand millionth part of the smallest recognizable instant. So our current American life and thought is not something that stands still long enough for us to describe it. Even as we write the description it has changed to another phase. And the phenomena of transition just now are particularly noticeable—that is all. We may call them decadent or we may look upon them as the beginnings of a new and more glorious national life.

"The size and intricacy which we have to deal with," says Walter Lippmann, "have done more than anything else, I imagine, to wreck the simple generalizations of our ancestors."

This is quite true, and so, in place of simplicity we are introducing complexity, very largely by selection and combination of simple elements evolved in former times to fit earlier conditions. Whether organic relations can be established among these elements, so that there shall one day issue from the welter something well-rounded, something American, fitting American conditions and leading American aspirations forward and upward, is yet on the knees of the gods. We, the men and women of America, and may I not say, we, the Librarians of America, can do much to direct the issue.

DRUGS AND THE MAN*

The graduation of a class of technically trained persons is an event of special moment. When we send forth graduates from our schools and colleges devoted to general education, while the thought of failure may be disquieting or embarrassing, we know that no special danger can result, except to the man who has failed. The college graduate who has neglected his opportunities has thrown away a chance, but he is no menace to his fellows. Affairs take on a different complexion in the technical or professional school. The poorly trained engineer, physician or lawyer, is an injury to the community. Failure to train an engineer may involve the future failure of a structure, with the loss of many lives. Failure to train a doctor means that we turn loose on the public one who will kill oftener than he will cure. Failure to train a lawyer means wills that can be broken, contracts that will not hold, needless litigation.

Congressman Kent, of California, has coined a satisfactory word for this sort of thing—he calls it "mal-employment." Unemployment is a bad thing. We have seen plenty of it here during the past winter. But Kent says, and he is right, that malemployment is a worse thing. All these poor engineers and doctors and lawyers are busily engaged, and every thing on the surface seems to be going on well. But as a matter of fact, the world would be better off if each one of them should stop working and never do another stroke. It would pay the community to support them in idleness.

* A Commencement address to the graduating class of the School of Pharmacy, St. Louis, May 19, 1915.

I have always considered pharmacy to be one of the occupations in which malemployment is particularly objectionable. If you read Homer badly it affects no one but yourself. If you think Vera Cruz is in Italy and that the Amazon River runs into the Arctic Ocean, your neighbor is as well off as before; but if you are under the impression that strychnine is aspirin, you have failed in a way that is more than personal.

I am dwelling on these unpleasant possibilities partly for the reason that the Egyptians displayed a skeleton at their banquets—because warnings are a tonic to the soul—but also because, if we are to credit much that we see in general literature, including especially the daily paper and the popular magazine, *all* druggists are malemployed. And if it would really be better for the community that you should not enter upon the profession for which you have been trained, now, of course, is the time for you to know it.

There seems to be a widespread impression—an assumption—that the day of the drug is over—that the therapeutics of the future are to be concerned alone with hygiene and sanitation, with physical exercise, diet, and mechanical operations. The very word "drug" has come to have an objectionable connection that did not belong to it fifty years ago. Even some of the druggists themselves, it seems to me, are a little ashamed of the drug part of their occupation. Their places of business appear to be news-agencies, refreshment parlors, stationery stores—the drugs are "on the side," or rather in the rear. Sometimes, I am told, the proprietors of these places know nothing at all about pharmacy, but employ a prescription clerk who is a capable pharmacist. Here the druggist has stepped down from his former position as the manager of a business and has become a servant. All of which looks to me as if the pharmacist himself might be beginning to accept the valuation that some people are putting upon his services to the community.

Now these things affect me, not as a physician nor as a pharmacist, for I am neither, but they do touch me as a student of physics and chemistry and as one whose business and pleasure it has been for many years to watch the development of these and other sciences. The fact that I am addressing you this evening may be taken, I suppose, as evidence that you may be interested in this point of view. The action of most substances on the human organism is a func tion of their chemical constitution. Has that chemical constitution changed? It is one of the most astonishing discoveries of our age that many, perhaps all, substances undergo spontaneous disintegration, giving rise to the phenomena now well known as "radio-activity." No substances ordinarily known and used in pharmacy, however, possess this quality in measurable degree, and we have no reason to suppose that the alkaloids, for instance, or the salts of potash or iron, differ today in any respect from those of a century ago. How about the other factor in the reaction—the human organism and its properties? That our bodily properties have changed in the past admits of no doubt. We have developed up to the point where we are at present. Here, however, evolution seems to have left us, and it is now devoting its attention exclusively to our mental and moral progress. Judging from what is now going on upon the continent of Europe, much remains to be accomplished. But there is no reason to believe that if Cæsar or Hannibal had taken a dose of opium, or ipecac, or aspirin, the effect would have been different from that experienced today by one of you. This is what a physicist or a chemist would expect. If the action of a drug on the organism is chemical, and if neither the drug nor the organism has changed, the action must be the same. If we still desire to bring about the action and if there is no better way to do it, we must use the drug, and there is still need for the druggist. As a matter of fact, the number of drugs at your disposal today is vastly greater than ever before, largely owing to the labor, and the ingenuity, of the analytical chemist. And there are still great classes of compounds of whose existence the chemist is assured, but which he has not even had time to form, much less to investigate. Among these may lurk remedies more valuable than any at our disposal today. It does not look, at any rate, as if the druggist were going to be driven out of business from lack of stock, whether we regard quantity or variety. To what, then, must we attribute the growth of the feeling that the treatment of disease by the administration of drugs is on the decline? From the standpoint of a layman it seems to be due to two facts, or at least to have been strongly affected by them: (1) The discovery and rapid development of other therapeutic measures, such as those dependent on surgical methods, or on the use of immunizing serums, or on manipulations such as massage, or on diet, or even on mental suggestion; and (2) the very increase in the number and variety of available drugs alluded to above, which has introduced to the public many new and only partially tried substances, the results of whose use has often been unexpectedly injurious, including a considerable number of new habit-forming drugs whose ravages are becoming known to the public.

The development of therapeutic measures that are independent of drugs has been coincident with popular emancipation from the mere superstition of drug-administration. The older lists of approved remedies were loaded with items that had no curative properties at all, except by suggestion. They were purely magical—the thumb-nails of executed criminals, the hair of black cats, the ashes of burned toads and so on. Even at this moment your pharmacopœia contains scores of remedies that are without effect or that do not produce the effects credited to them. I am relying on high therapeutical authority for this statement. Now when the sick man is told by his own physician to discard angleworm poultices, and herbs plucked in the dark of the moon, on which he had formerly relied, it is any wonder that he has ended by being suspicious also of calomel and ipecac, with which they were formerly classed? And when the man who believed that he received benefit from some of these magical remedies is told that the result was due to auto-suggestion, is it remarkable that he should fall an easy prey next day to the Christian Scientist who tells him that the effects of calomel and ipecac are due to nothing else than this same suggestion? The increased use and undoubted value of special diets, serums, aseptic surgery, baths, massage, electrical treatment, radio-therapeutics, and so on, makes it easy for him to discard drugs altogether, and further, it creates, even among those who continue to use drugs, an atmosphere favorable to the belief that they are back numbers, on the road to disuse. Just here comes in the second factor to persuade the layman, from what has come under his own observation, that drugs are injurious, dangerous, even fatal. Newly discovered chemical compounds with valuable properties, have been adopted and used in medicine before the necessary time had elapsed to disclose the fact that they possessed also other properties, more elusive than the first, but at potent for harm as these were for good. Many were narcotics or valuable anesthetics, local or otherwise, which have proved to be the creators of habits more terrible than the age-long enemies of mankind, alcohol and opium. When the man whose wife takes a coal-tar derivative for headache finds that it stills her heart forever, the incident affects his whole opinion of drugs. When the patient for whom one of the new drugs has been prescribed by a practitioner without knowledge of his idiosyncrasies reacts to it fatally, it is slight consolation to his survivors that his case is described in print under the heading, "A Curious Case of Umptiol Poisoning." When a mother sees her son go to the bad by taking cocaine, or heroin, or some other drug of whose existence she was ignorant a dozen years ago, she may be pardoned for believing that all drugs, or at least all newly discovered drugs, are tools of the devil.

And this feeling is intensified by one of our national faults—the tendency to jump at conclusions, to overdo things, to run from one evil to its opposite, without stopping at the harmless mean. We think we are brighter and quicker than the Englishman or the German. They think we are more superficial. Whatever name you give the quality it causes us to "catch on" sooner, to work a good thing to death more thoroughly and to drop it more quickly for something else, than any other known people, ancient or modern. Somebody devises a new form of skate roller that makes roller-skating a good sport. We find it out before anyone else and in a few months the land is plastered from Maine to California with huge skating halls or sheds. Everybody is skating at once and the roar of the rollers resounds across the oceans. We skate ourselves out in a year or two, and then the roar ceases, the sheds decay and roller-skating is once more a normal amusement. Then someone invents the safety bicycle, and in a trice all America, man, woman and child, is awheel. And we run this good horse to death, and throw his body aside in our haste to discover something new. Shortly afterward someone invents a new dance, or imports it from Spanish America, and there is hardly time to snap one's finger before we are all dancing, grandparents and children, the cook in the kitchen and the street-cleaner on the boulevard.

We display as little moderation in our therapeutics. We can not get over the idea that a remedy of proved value in a particular case may be good for all others. Our proprietary medicines will cure everything from tuberculosis to cancer. If massage has relieved rheumatism, why should it not be good also for typhoid? The Tumtum Springs did my uncle's gout so much good; why doesn't your cousin try them for her headaches? And even so, drugs must be all good or bad. Many of us remember the old household remedies, tonics or laxatives or what not, with which the children were all dosed at intervals, whether they were ill or not. That was in the days when all drugs were good: when one "took something" internally for everything that happened to him. Now the pendulum has swung to the other side —that is all. If we can ever settle down to the rational way of regarding these things, we shall discover, what sensible medical men have always known, and what druggists as well as mere laymen can not afford to neglect, that there is no such thing as a panacea, and that all rational therapeutics is based on common sense study of the disease—finding out what is the cause and endeavoring to abate that cause. The cause may be such that surgery is indicated, or serum, or regulation of diet, or change of scene. It may obviously indicate the administration of a drug. I once heard a clever lawyer in a poisoning case, in an endeavor to discredit a physician, whom we shall call Dr. Jones, tell the following anecdote: (Dr. Jones, who had been called in when the victim was about to expire, had recommended the application of ice). Said the lawyer:

"A workman was tamping a charge of blasting-powder with a crowbar, when the charge went off prematurely and the bar was driven through the unfortunate man's body, so that part of it protruded on either side. A local physician was summoned, and after some study he pronounced as follows: 'Now, if I let that bar stay there, you'll die. If I pull it out, you'll die. But I'll give you a pill that may melt it where it is!' In this emergency," the lawyer went on to say, "Dr. Jones doubtless would have prescribed *ice.*"

Now the pill to melt the crowbar may stand for our former excessive and absurd regard for drugs. The application of ice in the same emergency may likewise represent a universal resort to hydrotherapy. Neither of them is logical. There is place for each, but there are emergencies that can not be met with either. Still, to abandon one method of treatment simply because additional methods have proved to be valuable, would be as absurd as to give up talking upon the invention of writing or to prohibit the raising of corn on land that will produce wheat.

No: we shall doubtless continue to use drugs and we shall continue to need the druggist. What can he do to make his business more valued and respected, more useful to the public and more profitable to himself? For there can be no doubt that he will finally succeed in attaining all these desirable results together, or fail in all. Here and there we may find a man who is making a fortune out of public credulity and ignorance, or, on the other hand, one who is giving the public more service than it pays for and ruining himself in the process; but in general and on the average personal and public interest run pretty well hand in hand. Henry Ford makes his millions because he is producing something that the people want. St. Jacob's Oil, once the most widely advertised nostrum on the continent, cost its promoters a fortune because there was nothing in it that one might not find in some other oil or grease.

What then, I repeat, must the pharmacist do to succeed, personally and professionally? I welcome this opportunity to tell you what I think. My advice comes from the outside—often the most valuable source. I have so little to do with pharmacy, either as a profession or as a business that I stand far enough away to get a bird's-eye view. And if you think that any advice, based on this view, is worthless, it will be a consolation to all of us to realize that no force on earth can compel you to take it.

It is doubtless too late to lament or try to resist the course of business that has gone far to turn the pharmacy into a department store. But let me urge you not to let this tendency run wild. There are sidelines that belong properly to pharmacy, such as all those pertaining to hygiene or sanitation; to the toilet, to bodily refreshment. I do not see why one should not expect to find at his pharmacist's, soap, or tooth-brushes, or sponges. I do not see why the thirsty man should not go there for mineral water as well as the dyspeptic for pills. But I fail to see the connection between pharmacy and magazines, or stationery or candy. By selling these the druggist puts himself at once into competition with the department stores. There can be no doubt about who will win out in any such competition as that. But I believe there is still a place in the community for any special line of business if its proprietor sticks to his specialty and makes himself a recognized expert in it. The department store spreads itself too thin—there is no room for intensive development at any point of its vast expanse. Its general success is due to this very fact. I am not now speaking of the rural community where there is room only for one general store selling everything that the community needs. But my statement holds good for the city and the large town.

Let me illustrate by an instance in which we librarians are professionally interested—the book store. Once every town had its book-store. Now they are rare. We have few such stores even in a city of the size of St. Louis. Every department store has its book-section. They are rarely satisfactory. Everybody is lamenting the disappearance of the old bookstore, with its old scholarly proprietor who knew books and the book-market; who loved books and the book-business. Quarts of ink have been wasted in trying to account for his disappearance. The Public Library, for one thing, has been blamed for it. I have no time now to disprove this, though it is very clear to me that libraries help the book trade instead of hindering it. I shall simply give you my version of the trouble. The book-dealer disappeared, as soon as he entered into competition with the department store. He put in side lines of toys, and art supplies, and cameras and candy. He began to spread himself thin and had no time for expert concentration on his one specialty. Thus he lost his one advantage over the department store—his strength in the region where it was weak; and of course he succumbed. If you will think for a moment of the special businesses that have survived the competition of the department store, you will see that they are precisely the ones that have resisted this temptation to spread themselves and have been content to remain experts. Look at the men's furnishing stores. Would they have survived if they had begun to sell cigars and lawn-mowers? Look at the retail shoe stores, the opticians, the cigar stores, the bakers, the meat markets, the confectioners, the restaurants of all grades! They have all to compete with the department stores, but their customers realize that they have something to offer that can be offered by no department store—expert service in one line, due to some one's life-long training, experience and devotion to the public.

I do not want the pharmacist to go the way of the book dealers. Already some of the department stores include drug departments. I do not see how these can be as good as independent pharmacies. But I do not see the essential difference between a drug department in a store that sells also cigars and stationery and confectionery, and a so-called independent pharmacy that also distributes these very things.

I am assuming that the druggist is an expert. That is the object of our colleges of pharmacy, as I understand the matter. As a librarian I want to deal with a book man who knows more of the book business than I do. I want to ask his advice and be able to rely on it. When I have printing to be done, I like to give it to a man who knows more about the printed page than I do. When I buy bread, or shoes, or a house, or a farm I like to deal with recognized experts in these articles. How much more when I am purchasing substances where expert knowledge will turn the balance between life and death. I have gossiped with pharmacists enough to know that all physicians do not avoid incompatibles in their prescriptions, and that occasionally a combination falls into

the prescription clerk's hands, which, if made up as
he reads it would produce a poisonous compound, or
perhaps even an explosive mixture. Two heads are
better than one, and if my physician ever makes a
mistake of this kind I look to my pharmacist to see
that it shall not reach the practical stage.

I recognize the great value and service of the department store, but I do not go there for my law or
medicine; neither do I care to resort thither for my
pharmacy. I want our separate drug stores to per-
sist, and I want them to remain in charge of experts.

And when the store deals in other things than
purely therapeutic preparations—which I have already said I think probably unavoidable,—I want it to
present the aspect of a pharmacy that deals also in
toilet preparations and mineral water, not of an establishment for dispensing soda-water and soap,
where one may have a prescription filled on the side,
in an emergency. And when the emergency does
arise, I should have the pharmacy respond to it. It
is the place where we naturally look in an emergency
—the spot to which the victim of an accident is carried directly—the one where the lady bends her steps
when she feels that she is going to faint. In hundreds
of cases the drug store is our only standby, and it
should be the druggist's business to see that it never
fails us. There are pharmacies where a telephone
message brings an unfailing response; there are
others to which one would as soon think of sending
an inquiry regarding a Biblical quotation. To which
type, do you think, will the public prefer to resort?

Then there are those little courtesies that no retail business is obliged to offer, but that the public
has been accustomed to expect from the druggist—
the cashing of checks, the changing of bills, the
furnishing of postage stamps, the consultation of the

city directory. There can be no reason for resorting to a drug store for all these favors except that the pharmacist has an enviable reputation as the man who is most likely to grant them. And yet I begin to hear druggists complaining of the results of this reputation, of which they ought to be proud; I see them pointing out that there is no profit on postage stamps and no commission for changing a bill. They intimate, further, that although it may be proper for them to put themselves out for regular customers, it is absurd for strangers to ask for these courtesies. I marvel when I hear these sentiments. If this popular impression regarding the courtesy of the druggist did not exist, it would be worth the expenditure of vast sums and the labor of a lifetime to create it. To deliberately undo it would be as foolish as to lock the door in the face of customers.

I do not believe that in St. Louis the pharmaceutical profession is generally averse to a reputation for generous public service, and I base my belief on some degree of personal knowledge. The St. Louis Public Library operates about sixty delivery stations in various parts of the city. These stations are all in drug stores. The work connected with them, though light, is by no means inconsiderable, and yet not one of the druggists who undertake it charges the library a cent for his space or his services. Doubtless they expect a return from the increased attractiveness of their places to the public. I hope that they get it and I believe that they do. At any rate we have evidence here of the pharmacist's belief that the bread of public service, cast upon the waters, will sooner or later return.

You will notice that I am saying nothing about advertising. One would think from the pharmaceutical papers, with which I am not unfamiliar, that the druggist's chief end was to have a sensational show window of some kind. These things are not unimportant, but I do not dwell on them because I believe that if a druggist realizes the importance of his profession; if he makes himself a recognized expert in it; if he sticks to it and magnifies it; if he makes his place indispensable to the community around him, the first point to which the citizens resort for help in an emergency, an unfailing center of courtesy and favor—he may fill his window with toilet soap, or monkeys, or with nothing at all—there will still be a trodden path up to his door.

Gentlemen, you have chosen as your life work a profession that I believe to be indispensable to human welfare—one of enviable tradition and honor and with standing and reputation in the community that set it apart, in some degree from all others. And while I would not have you neglect the material success that it may bring you, I would urge you to expect this as a result rather than strive for it as an immediate end. I would have you labor to maintain and develop the special knowledge that you have gained in this institution, to hold up the standard of courtesy and helpfulness under which you can best do public service, confident that if you do these things, business standing and financial success will also be added unto you.

HOW THE COMMUNITY EDUCATES ITSELF*

In endeavoring to distinguish between self-education and education by others, one meets with considerable difficulty. If a boy reads Mill's "Political Economy" he is surely educating himself; but if after reading each chapter he visits a class and answers certain questions propounded for the purpose of ascertaining whether he has read it at all, or has read it understandingly, then we are accustomed to transfer the credit for the educative process to the questioner, and say that the boy has been educated at school or college. As a matter of fact, I think most of us are self-educated. Not only is most of what an adult knows and can do, acquired outside of school, but in most of what he learned even there he was self-taught. His so-called teachers assigned tasks to him and saw that he performed them. If he did not, they subjected him to discipline. Once or twice in a lifetime most of us have run up against a real teacher—a man or a woman that really played a major part in shaping our minds as they now are—our stock of knowledge, our ways of thought, our methods of doing things. These men have stood and are still standing (though they may have joined the great majority long ago) athwart the stream of sensation as it passes through us, and are determining what part shall be stored up, and where; what kind of action shall ultimately result from it. The influence of a good teacher spreads farther and lasts longer than that of any other man. If his words have been recorded in books it may reach across the seas and down the ages.

* Read before the American Library Association, Asbury Park, N. J., June 27, 1916.

There is another reason why the distinction between school education and self-education breaks down. If the boy with whom we began had any teacher at all it was John Stuart Mill, and this man was his teacher whether or not his reading of the book was prescribed and tested in a class-room. I would not have you think that I would abolish schools and colleges. I wish we had more of the right kind, but the chief factor in educative acquirement will still be the pupil.

So when the community educates itself, as it doubtless does and as it must do, it simply continues a process with which it has always been familiar, but without control, or under its own control. Of all the things that we learn, control is the most vital. What we are is the sum of those things that we do not repress. We begin without self-repression and have to be controlled by others. When we learn to exercise control ourselves, it is right that even our education should revert wholly to what it has long been in greater part—a voluntary process.

This does not mean that at this time the pupil abandons guidance. It means that he is free to choose his own guides and the place and method of using them. Some rely wholly on experience; others are wise enough to see that life is too short and too narrow to acquire all that we need, and they set about to make use also of that acquired by others. Some of these wiser ones use only their companions and acquaintances; others read books. The wisest are opportunists; they make use of all these methods as they have occasion. Their reading does not make them avoid the exchange of ideas by conversation, nor does the acquirement of ideas in either way preclude learning daily by experience, or make reflection useless or unnecessary.

He who lives a full life acquires ideas as he may, causes them to combine, change and generate in his own mind, and then translates them into action of some kind. He who omits any of these things cannot be said to have really lived. He cannot, it is true, fail to acquire ideas unless he is an idiot; but he may fail to acquire them broadly, and may even make the mistake of thinking that he can create them in his own mind.

He may, however, acquire fully and then merely store without change or combination; that is, he may turn his brain into a warehouse instead of using it as a factory.

And the man who has acquired broadly and worked over his raw material into a product of his own, may still stop there and never do anything. Our whole organism is subsidiary to action and he who stops short of it has surely failed to live.

Our educative processes, so far, have dwelt heavily on acquirement, somewhat lightly on mental assimilation and digestion, and have left action almost un touched. In these two latter respects, especially, is the community self-educated.

The fact that I am saying this here, and to you, is a sufficient guaranty that I am to lay some emphasis on the part played by books in these self-educative processes. A book is at once a carrier and a tool; it transports the idea and plants it. It is a carrier both in time and in space—the idea that it implants may be a foreign idea, or an ancient idea, or both. Either of its functions may for the moment be paramount; a book may bring to you ideas whose implantation your brain resists, or it may be used to implant ideas that are already present, as when an instructor uses his own text book. Neither of these two cases represents education in the fullest sense.

You will notice that I have not yet defined education. I do not intend to try, for my time is limited. But in the course of my own educative processes, which I trust are still proceeding, the tendency grows stronger and stronger to insist on an intimate connection with reality in all education—to making it a realization that we are to do something and a yearning to be able to do it. The man who has never run up against things as they are, who has lived in a world of moonshine, who sees crooked and attempts what is impossible and what is useless—is he educated? I used to wonder what a realist was. Now that I am becoming one myself I begin dimly to understand. He certainly is not a man devoid of ideals, but they are real ideals, if you will pardon the bull.

I believe that I am in goodly company. The library as I see it has also set its face toward the real. What else is meant by our business branches, our technology rooms, our legislative and municipal reference departments? They mean that slow as we may be to respond to community thought and to do our part in carrying on community education, we are vastly more sensitive than the school, which still turns up its nose at efforts like the Gary system; than the stage, which still teaches its actors to be stagy instead of natural; even than the producers of the very literature that we help to circulate, who rarely know how even to represent the conversation of two human beings as it really is. And when a great new vehicle of popular artistic expression arises, like the moving picture, those who purvey it spend their millions to build mock cities instead of to reproduce the reality that it is their special privilege to be able to show. And they hire stage actors to show off their staginess on the screen—staginess that is a thousand times more stagy because its background is of waving foliage and glimmering water, instead of the painted canvas in front of which it belongs. The heart of the community is right. Its heroine is Mary Pickford. It rises to realism as one man. The little dog who cannot pose, and who pants and wags his tail on the screen as he would anywhere else, elicits thunderous applause. The baby who puckers up its face and cries, oblivious of its environment, is always a favorite. But the trend of all this, these institutions cannot see. We librarians are seeing it a little more clearly. We may see it—we shall see it, more clearly still.

The self-education of a community often depends very closely on bonds of connection already established between the minds of that community's individual members. Sometimes it depends on a sudden connection made through the agency of a single event of overwhelming importance and interest. Let me illustrate what I mean by connection of this kind. For many years it was my duty to cross the Hudson river twice daily on a crowded ferry-boat, and it used to interest me to watch the behavior of the crowds under the influence of simple impulses affecting them all alike. I am happy to say that I never had an opportunity of observing the effect of complex impulses such as those of panic terror. I used particularly to watch, from the vantage point of a stairway whence I could look over their heads, the behavior of the crowd standing in the cabin just before the boat made its landing. Each person in the crowd stood still quietly, and the tendency was toward a loose formation to ensure comfort and some freedom of movement. At the same time each was ready and anxious to move forward as soon as the landing should be made. Only those in front could see the bow of the ferryboat; the others could see nothing but the persons directly in front of them. When those in the front rank saw that the landing was very near they began to move forward; those just behind followed suit and so on to the rear. The result was that I saw a wave of compression, of the same sort as a sound-wave in air, move through the throng. The individual motions were forward but the wave moved backward. No better example of a wave of this kind could be devised. Now the actions and reactions between the air-particles in a sound wave are purely mechanical. Not so here. There was neither pushing nor pulling of the ordinary kind. Each person moved forward because his mind was fixed on moving forward at the earliest opportunity, and because the forward movement of those just in front showed him that now was the time and the opportunity. The physical link, if there was one, properly speaking, between one movement and another was something like this: A wave of light, reflected from the body of the man in front, entered the eye of the man just behind, where it was transformed into a nerve impulse that reached the brain through the optic nerve. Here it underwent complicated transformations and reactions whose nature we can but surmise, until it left the brain as a motor impulse and caused the leg muscles to contract, moving their owner forward. All this may or may not have taken place within the sphere of consciousness; in the most cases it had happened so often that it had been relegated to that of unconscious cerebration.

I have entered into so much detail because I want to make it clear that a connection may be established between members of a group, even so casual a group as that of persons who happen to cross on the same ferry boat, that is so real and compelling, that its results simulate those of physical forces. In this case the results were dependent on the existence in the crowd of one common bond of interest. They all wanted to leave the ferry boat as soon as possible, and by its bow. If some of them had wanted to stay on the boat and go back with it, or if it had been a river steamboat where landings were made from several gangways in different parts of the boat the simple wave of compression that I saw would not have been set up. In like manner the ordinary influences that act on men's minds tend in all sorts of directions and their results are not easily traced. Occasionally, however, there occurs some event so great that it turns us all in the same direction and establishes a common network of psychical connections. Such an event fosters community education.

We have lately witnessed such a phenomenon in the sudden outbreak of the great European War. Probably no person in the community as we librarians know it remained unaffected by this event. In most it aroused some kind of a desire to know what was going on. It was necessary that most of us should know a little more than we did of the differences in racial temperament and aim among the inhabitants of the warring nations, of such movements as Pan-Slavism and Pan-Germanism, of the recent political history of Europe, of modern military tactics and strategy, of international law, of geography, of the pronunciation of foreign place-names, of the chemistry of explosives—of a thousand things regarding which we had hitherto lacked the impulse to inform ourselves. This sort of thing is going on in a community every day, but here was a catastrophe setting in motion a mighty brain-wave that had twisted us all in one direction. Notice now what a conspicuous rôle our public libraries play in phenomena of this kind. In the first place, the newspaper and periodical press reflects at once the interest that has been aroused. Where man's unaided curiosity would suggest one question it adds a hundred others. Problems that would otherwise seem simple enough now appear complex—the whole mental interest is intensified. At the same time there is an attempt to satisfy the questions thus raised. The man who did not know about the Belgian treaty, or the possible use of submarines as commerce-destroyers, has all the issues put before him with at least an attempt to settle them. This service of the press to community education would be attempted, but it would not be successfully rendered, without the aid of the public library, for it has come to pass that the library is now almost the only non-partisan institution that we possess; and community education, to be effective, must be non-partisan. The press is almost necessarily biassed. The man who is prejudiced prefers the paper or the magazine that will cater to his prejudices, inflame them, cause him to think that they are reasoned results instead of prejudices. If he keeps away from the public library he may succeed in blinding himself; if he uses it he can hardly do so. He will find there not only his own side but all the others; if he has the ordinary curiosity that is our mortal heritage he cannot help glancing at the opinions of others occasionally. No man is really educated who does not at least know that another side exists to the question on which he has already made up his mind—or had it made up for him.

Further, no one is content to stop with the ordinary periodical literature. The flood of books inspired by this war is one of the most astonishing things about it. Most libraries are struggling to keep up with it in some degree. Very few of these books would be within the reach of most of us were it not for the library.

I beg you to notice the difference in the reaction of the library to this war and that of the public school as indicative of the difference between formal educative processes, as we carry them on, and the self-education of the community. I have emphasized the freedom of the library from bias. The school is necessarily biassed—perhaps properly so. You remember the story of the candidate for a district school who, when asked by an examining committeeman whether the earth was round or flat, replied, "Well, some says one and some t'other. I teach either round or flat, as the parents wish."

Now, there are books that maintain the flatness of the earth, and they properly find a place on the shelves of large public libraries. Those who wish to compare the arguments pro and con are at liberty to do so. Even in such a *res adjudicata* as this the library takes no sides. But in spite of the obliging school candidate, the school cannot proceed in this way. The teaching of the child must be definite. And there are other subjects, historical ones for instance, in which the school's attitude may be determined by its location, its environment, its management. When it is a public school and its controlling authority is really trying to give impartial instruction there are some subjects that must simply be skipped, leaving them to be covered by post-scholastic community education. This is the school's limitation. Only the policy of caution is very apt to be carried too far. Thus we find that in the school the immense educational drive of the European War has not been utilized as it has in the community at large. In some places the school authorities have erected a barrier against it. So far as they are concerned

the war has been non-existent. This difference be-
between the library and the school appears in such
reports as the following from a branch librarian:

"Throughout the autumn and 'most of the winter
we found it absolutely impossible to supply the demand for books about the war. Everything we had
on the subject or akin to it—books, magazines,
pamphlets—were in constant use. Books of travel
and history about the warring countries became
popular—things that for years had been used but
rarely became suddenly vitally interesting.

"I have been greatly interested by the fact that
the high school boys and girls never ask for anything
about the war. Not once during the winter have I
seen in one of them a spark of interest in the subject. It seems so strange that it should be necessary to keep them officially ignorant of this great
war because the grandfather of one spoke French
and of another German."

Another librarian says:

"The war again has naturally stimulated an interest in maps. With every turn in military affairs,
new ones are issued and added to our collection.
These maps, as received, have been exhibited for
short periods upon screens and they have never
lacked an appreciative line of spectators, representing all nationalities."

One noticeable effect of the war in libraries has
been to stimulate the marking of books, periodicals
and newspapers by readers, especially in periodical
rooms. Readers with strong feelings cannot resist
annotating articles or chapters that express opinions
in which they cannot concur. Pictures of generals
or royalties are especially liable to defacement with
opprobrious epithets. This feeling extends even to
bulletins. Libraries receive strenuous protests

against the display of portraits and other material relating to one of the contesting parties without similar material on the other side to offset it.

"Efforts to be strictly neutral have not always met with success, some readers apparently regarding neutrality as synonymous with suppression of everything favorable to the opposite side. One library reports that the display of an English military portrait called forth an energetic protest because it was not balanced by a German one."

Such manifestations as these are merely symptoms. The impulse of the war toward community education is a tremendous one and it is not strange that it should find an outlet in all sorts of odd ways. The German sympathizer who would not ordinarily think of objecting to the display of an English portrait, and in fact would probably not think of examining it closely enough to know whether it was English or Austrian, has now become alert. His alertness makes him open to educative influences, but it may also show itself in such ways as that just noted.

Keeping the war out of the schools is of course a purely local phenomenon, to be deprecated where it occurs. The library can do its part here also.

"G. Stanley Hall believes that the problem of teaching the war is how to utilize in the very best way the wonderful opportunity to open, see and feel the innumerable and vital lessons involved." Commenting on this a children's librarian says: "The unparalleled opportunity offered to our country, and the new complex problems presented by these new conditions should make the children's librarian pause and take heed.

"Can we do our part toward using the boy's loyalty to his gang or his nine, his love of his country, his respect for our flag, his devotion to our heroes, in developing a sense of human brotherhood which alone can prevent or delay in the next generation another such catastrophe as the one we face to-day?"

Exclusion of the war from the schools is partly the outcome of the general attitude of most of our schoolmen, who object to the teaching of a subject as an incidental. Arithmetic must be studied for itself alone. To absorb it as a by-product of shop-work, as is done in Gary, is inadmissible. But it is also a result of the fear that teaching the war at all would necessarily mean a partisan teaching of it—a conclusion which perhaps we cannot condemn when we remember the partisan instruction in various other subjects for which our schools are responsible.

Again, this exclusion is doubtless aided by the efforts of some pacifists, who believe that, ostrich-like, we should hide our heads in the sand, to avoid acknowledging the existence of something we do not like. "Why war?" asks a recent pamphlet. Why, indeed? But we may ask in turn "Why fire?" "Why flood?" I cannot answer these questions, but it would be foolish to act as if the scourges did not exist. Nay, I hasten to insure myself against them, though the possibility that they will injure me is remote. This ultra-pacifist attitude has gone further than school education and is trying to put the lid on community education also. Objection, for instance, has been made to an exhibit of books, prints and posters about the war, which was displayed in the St. Louis Public Library for nearly two months. We intended to let it stand for about a week, but the public would not allow this. The community insists on self-education even against the will of its natural allies. The contention that we are cultivating the innate bloodthirstiness of our public, I regard as absurd.

What can we do toward generating or taking advantage of other great driving impulses toward community education? Must we wait for the horrors of a great war to teach us geography, industrial chemistry and international law? Is it necessary to burn down a house every time we want to roast a pig? Certainly not. But just as one would not think of bringing on any kind of a catastrophe in order to utilize its shock for educational purposes, so also I doubt very much whether we need concern ourselves about the initiation of any impulse toward popular education. These impulses exist everywhere in great number and variety and we need only to select the right one and reinforce it. Attempts to generate others are rarely effective. When we hear the rich mellow tone of a great organ pipe, it is difficult to realize that all the pipe does is to reinforce a selected tone among thousands of indistinguishable noises made by the air rushing through a slit and striking against an edge. Yet this is the fact. These incipient impulses permeate the community all about us; all we have to do is to select one, feed it and give it play and we shall have an "educational movement." This fact is strongly impressed upon anyone working with clubs. If it is desired to foster some movement by means of an organization, it is rarely necessary to form one for the purpose. Every community teems with clubs, associations and circles. All that is needed is to capture the right one and back it up. Politicians well understand this art of capture and use it often for evil purposes. In the librarian's hands it becomes an instrument for good. Better than to offer a course of twenty lectures under the auspices of the library is it to capture a club, give it house-room, and help it with its program. I am proud of the fact that in fifteen public rooms in our library, about four thousand meetings are held in the course of the year; but I am inclined to be still prouder of the fact that not one of these is held formally under the auspices of the library or is visibly patronized by it. To go back to our thesis, all education is self-education; we can only select, guide and strengthen, but when we have done these things adequately, we have done a very great work indeed.

What is true of assemblies and clubs is also true of the selection and use of books. A book purchased in response to a demand is worth a dozen bought because the librarian thinks the library ought to have them. The possibilities of free suggestion by the community are, it seems to me, far from realized, yet even as it is, I believe that librarians have an unexampled opportunity of feeling out promising tendencies in this great flutter of educational impulses all about us, and so of selecting the right ones and helping them on.

Almost while I have been writing this I have been visited by a delegate from the foundrymen's club— an organization that wants more books on foundry practice and wants them placed together in a convenient spot. Such a visit is of course a heaven-sent opportunity and I suppose I betrayed something of my pleasure in my manner. My visitor said, "I am so glad you feel this way about it; we have been meaning for some time to call on you, but we were in doubt about how we should be received." Such moments are humiliating to the librarian. Great heavens! Have we advertised, discussed, talked and plastered our towns with publicity, only to learn at last that the spokesman of a body of respectable men, asking legitimate service, rather expects to be kicked downstairs than otherwise when he approaches us? Is our publicity failing in quantity or in quality?

Whatever may be the matter, it is in response to demands like this that the library must play its part in community education. Here as elsewhere it is the foundrymen who are the important factors—their attitude, their desires, their capabilities. Our function is that of the organ pipe—to pick out the impulse, respond to it and give it volume and carrying power. The community will educate itself whether we help or not. It is permeated by lines of intelligence as the magnetic field is by lines of force. Thrust in a bit of soft iron and the forcelines will change their direction in order to pass through the iron. Thrust a book into the community field, and its lines of intelligence will change direction in order to take in the contents of the book. If we could map out the field we should see great masses of lines sweeping through our public libraries.

All about us we see men who tell us that they despair of democracy; that at any rate, whatever its advantages, democracy can never be "efficient." Efficient for what? Efficiency is a relative quality, not absolute. A big German howitzer would be about as inefficient a tool as could be imagined, for serving an apple-pie. Beside, democracy is a goal; we have not reached it yet; we shall never reach it if we decide that it is undesirable. The path toward it is the path of Nature, which leads through conflicts, survivals, and modifications. Part of it is the path of community education, which I believe to be efficient in that it is leading on toward a definite goal. Part of Nature is man, with his desires, hopes and abilities. Some men, and many women, are librarians, in whom these desires and hopes have definite aims and in whom the corresponding abilities are more or less developed. We are all thus cogs in Nature's great scheme for community education; let us be intelligent cogs, and help the movement on instead of hindering it.

CLUBWOMEN'S READING

I—*The Malady*

A WELL-DRESSED woman entered the Art Department of a large public library. "Have you any material on the Medici?" she asked the custodian. "Yes; just what kind of material do you want?" "Stop a minute," cried the woman, extending a detaining hand; "before you get me anything, just tell me what they are!" Librarians are trained not to laugh. No one could have detected the ghost of a smile on this one's face as she lifted the "M" volume of a cyclopedia from a shelf and placed it on the table before the seeker after knowledge. "There; that will tell you," she said, and returned to her work.

Not long afterward she was summoned by a beckoning finger. "I can't tell from this book," said the perplexed student, "whether the Medici were a family or a race of people." The Art Librarian tried to untie this knot, but it was not long before another presented itself." "This book doesn't explain," said the troubled investigator, "whether the Medici were Florentines or Italians." Still without a quiver, the art assistant emitted the required drop of information. "Shan't I get you something more now?" she asked. "Oh, no; this will be quite sufficient," and taking out pencil and paper the inquirer began to write rapidly with the cyclopedia propped before her. Presently, when the Art Librarian looked up, her guest had disappeared. But she was on hand the next morning. "May I see that book again?" she asked sweetly. "There are some words here in my copy that I can't quite make out."

On another occasion a reader, of the same sex, wandered into the reading-room and began to gaze about her with that peculiar sort of perplexed aimlessness that librarians have come to recognise instinctively as an index to the wearer's state of mind. "Have you anything on American travels?" she asked.

"Do you mean travels in America, or travels by Americans in foreign countries?"

"Well; I don't know—exactly."

"Do you want books like Dickens's *American Notes,* that give a foreigner's impression of this country?"

"Ye-es—possibly."

"Or books like Hawthorne's *Note Book,* telling how a foreign country appears to an American?"

"We-ell; perhaps."

"Are you following a programme of reading?"

"Yes."

"May I see it? That may give me a clue."

"I haven't a copy here."

"Can you give me the name of the person or committee who made it?"

"Oh, I *made* it *myself.*"

This was a "facer"; the librarian seemed to have brought up against a stone wall, but she waited, knowing that a situation, unlike a knot, will sometimes untie itself.

The seeker after knowledge also waited for a time. Then she broke out animatedly:

"Why, I just wanted American travels, don't you know? Funny little stories and things about the sort of Americans that go abroad with a bird-cage!"

Just what books were given to her I do not know;

but in due time her interesting paper before the Olla
Podrida Club was properly noticed in the local
papers.

In another case a perplexed club-woman came to
a library for aid in making a programme of reading.
" Have you some ideas about the subject you want to
take up?" asked the reference assistant.

"Well, we had thought of England, or perhaps
Scotland; and some of us would like the Elizabethan
Period."

The assistant, after some faithful work, produced
a list of books and articles on each of these somewhat comprehensive subjects and sent them to the
reader for selection. "Which did you finally take?"
she asked when the inquirer next visited the library.

"Oh, they were so good, we decided to use all of
them this year!"

The writer is no pessimist. These stories which
are as true, word for word, as any tales not taken
down by a stenographer (and far more so than some
that are) seemed to throw the persons who told them
into a sort of dumb despair, but I hastened to reas-
sure them. I pointed out that the inquirers after
knowledge had, beyond all doubt, obtained some
modicum of what they wanted. If the lady in the
first tale, for instance, had mistakenly supposed that
the Medici were a new kind of dance or something to
eat, she surely has been disabused. And her cyclopedia
article was probably as well written as most of its
kind, so that a literal transcript of it could have done
no harm either to the copyist or to her clubmates.
And the paper on "American Travels," and the combined lists on England, Scotland and the Elizabethan
Period; did not those who laboured on them, or with
them, acquire information in the process? Most assuredly!

Still, I must confess that, in advancing these arguments, I feel somewhat like an *advocatus diaboli*. It is all very well to treat the puzzled clubwoman as a joke. When a man slips on a banana-peel and goes down, we may laugh at his plight; but suppose the whole crowd of passers-by began to pitch and slide and tumble! Should we not think that some horrible epidemic had laid its hand on us? The ladies with their Medici and their Travels are not isolated instances. Ask the librarians; they know, but in countless instances they do not tell, for fear of casting ridicule upon the hundreds of intelligent clubwomen whom they are proud to help. In many libraries there is a standing rule against repeating or discussing the errors and slips of the public, especially to the everhungry reporter. I break this rule here with equanimity, and even with a certain degree of hope, for my object is to awaken my readers to the knowledge that part of the reading public is suffering from a malady of some kind. Later I may try my hand at diagnosis and even at therapeutics. And I am taking as an illustration chiefly the reading done by women's clubs, not because men do not do reading of the same kind, or because it is not done by individuals as well as by groups; but because, just at the present time, women in general, and clubwomen in particular, seem especially likely to be attacked by the disease. It must be remembered also that I am writing from the standpoint of the public library, and I here make humble acknowledgement of the fact that many things in the educational field, both good and bad, go on quite outside of that institution and beyond its ken.

The intellectual bonds between the library and the woman's club have always been close. Many libraries are the children of such clubs; many clubs have been formed in and by libraries. If any mistakes are being made in the general policies and programmes of club reading, the librarian would naturally be the first to know it, and he ought to speak out. He does know it, and his knowledge should become public property at once. But, I repeat, although the trouble is conspicuous in connection with the reading of women's clubs, it is far more general and deeply rooted than this.

The malady's chief symptom, which is well known to all librarians, is a lack of correspondence between certain readers and the books that they choose. Reading, like conversation, is the meeting of two minds. If there is no contact, the process fails. If the cogs on the gearwheels do not interact, the machine can not work. If the reader of a book on algebra does not understand arithmetic; if he tackles a philosophical essay on the representative function without knowing what the phrase means; if he tries to read a French book without knowing the language, his mind is not fitted for contact with that of the writer, and the mental machinery will not move.

In the early days of the Open Shelf, before librarians had realised the necessity of copious assignments to "floor duty," and before there were children's librarians, I saw in a branch library a small child staggering under the weight of a volume of Schaff's *History of the Christian Church,* which he had taken from the shelves and was presenting at the desk to be charged. "You are not going to read that, are you?" said the desk assistant.

"It isn't for me; it's for me big brudder."

"What did your big brother ask you to get?"

"Oh, a Physiology!"

Nowadays, our well-organised children's rooms make such an occurrence doubtful with the little ones, but apparently there is much of it with adults.

Too much of our reading—I should rather say our attempts at reading—is of this character. Such attempts are the result of a tendency to regard the printed page as a fetich—to think that if one knows his alphabet and can call the printed words one after another as his eye runs along the line, some unexplained good will result, or at least that he has performed a praiseworthy act, has "accumulated merit" somehow or somewhere, like a Thibetan with his prayer-wheel.

It is probably a fact that if a man should meet you in the street and say, "In beatific repentance lies jejune responsibility," you would stare at him and pass him by, or perhaps flee from him as from a lunatic; whereas if you saw these words printed in a book you might gravely study them to ascertain their meaning, or still worse, might succeed in reading your own meaning into them. The words I have strung together happen to have no meaning, but the result would be the same if they meant something that was hidden from the reader by his inability to understand them, no matter what the cause of that inability might be.

This malady is doubtless spontaneous in some degree, and dependent on failings of the human mind that we need not discuss here, but there are signs that it is being fostered, spread, and made more acute by special influences. Probably our educational methods are not altogether blameless. The boy who trustfully approached a Reference Librarian and said, "I have to write a composition on what I saw between home and school; have you got a book about that?" had doubtless been taught that he must look in a book for everything. The conscientious teacher who was now trying to separate him from his notion may have been the very one who, perhaps unconsciously, had instilled it; if so, her fault had thus returned to plague her.

The boy or girl who comes to attach a sacredness or a wizardry to the book in itself will naturally believe, after a little, that whether he understands what is in it matters little—and this is the malady of which we have been complaining.

A college teacher of the differential calculus, in a time now happily long past, when a pupil timidly inquired the reason for this or that, was wont to fix the interrogator with his eye and say, "Sir; it is so because the book says so!" Even in more recent days a well-known university teacher, accustomed to use his own text-book, used to say when a student had ventured to vary its classic phraseology, "It can not be expressed better than in the words of the book!" These instances, of course, are taken from the dark ages of education, but even to-day I believe that a false idea of the value of a printed page merely as print—not as the record of a mind, ready to make contact with the mind of a reader—has impressed itself too deeply on the brains of many children at an age when such impressions are apt to be durable. Not that the schools are especially at fault; we have all played our part in this unfortunate business. It might all fade, at length; we all know that many good teachings of our childhood do vanish; why should not the bad ones occasionally follow suit?

But now come in all the well-meaning instructors of the adult—the Chautauquans, the educational extensionists, the lecturers, the correspondence schools, the advisers of reading, the makers of booklists, the devisers of "courses." They deepen the fleeting impression and increase its capacity for harm, while varying slightly the mechanism that produced it. As the child grows into a man, his childish idea that a book will produce a certain effect independently of what it contains is apt to yield a little to reason. The new influences, some of which I have named above, do not attempt directly to combat this dawning intelligence; they utilise it to complete the mental discomfiture of their victims. They admit the necessity of comprehending the contents of the book, but they persuade the reader that such comprehension is easier than it really is. And they often administer specially concocted tabloids that convince one that he knows more than he really does. Thus the unsuspecting adult goes on reading what he does not understand, not now thinking that it does not matter, but falsely persuaded that he has become competent to understand.

Every one of the agencies that I have named aims to do good educational work; every one is competent to do such work; nearly every one does much of it. I am finding fault with them only so far as they succeed in persuading readers that they are better educated than they really are. In this respect such agencies are precisely on a par with the proprietary medicine that is an excellent laxative or sudorific, but is offered also as a cure for tuberculosis or cancer.

I once heard the honoured head of a famous body that does an enormous amount of work of this sort deliver an *apologia*, deserving of all attention, in which he complained that his institution had been falsely accused of superficiality. It was, he said, perfectly honest in what it taught. If its pupils thought that the elementary knowledge they were gaining was comprehensive and thorough, that was their fault—not his. And yet, at that moment, the institution was posing before its pupils as a "university" and using the forms and nomenclature of such a body to strengthen the idea in their minds. We cannot acquit it, or any of the agencies like it, of complicity in the causation of the malady whose symptoms we are discussing.

It is not the fault of the women's clubs that they have fallen into line in such an imposing procession as this. Their formation and work constitute one of the most interesting and important manifestations of the present feminist movement. Their rôle in it is partly social, partly educational; and as they consist of adults, elementary education is of course excluded from their programme. We therefore find them committed, perhaps unconsciously, to the plan of required or recommended reading, in a form that has long been the bane of our educational systems both in school and out.

One of the corner-stones of this system is the idea that the acquisition of information is valuable in itself, no matter what may be the relationship between it and the acquiring mind, or what use of it may be made in the future. According to this idea, if a woman can once get into her head that the Medici were a family and not "a race of people," it matters little that she is unfitted to comprehend why they are worth reading about at all, or that the fact has nothing to do with what she has ever done or is likely to be called upon to do in the future.

That the members of these clubs are willing to pursue knowledge under these hampering conditions is of course a point in their favour, so far as it goes. A desire for knowledge is never to be despised, even when it is not entertained for its own sake. And a secondary desire may often be changed into a primary one, if the task is approached in the right way.

The possibility of such a transformation is a hopeful feature of the present situation.

The reading that is done by women in connection with club work is of several different types. In the simplest organisations, which are reading clubs pure and simple, a group of books, roughly equal in number to the membership, is taken and passed around until each person has read them all. There is no connection between them, and each volume is selected simply on some one's statement that it is a "good book." A step higher is the club where the books are on one general subject, selected by some one who has been asked to prescribe a "course of reading." By easy gradations we arrive at the final stage, where the reading is of the nature of investigation and its outcome is an essay. A subject is decided on at the beginning of the season. The programme committee selects several phases of it and assigns each to a member, who prepares her essay and reads it to the club at one of the stated meetings. In this case the reading to be done in preparation for writing the essay may or may not be guided by the committee. In many cases, where the local public library coöperates actively with the clubs, a list may be made out by the librarian and perhaps printed, with due acknowledgment, in the club's year book. No one can doubt, in looking over typical programmes and lists among the thousands that represent the annual reading of the women's clubs throughout the United States, that a serious and sustained effort is being made to introduce the intellect, as an active factor, into the lives of thousands of women—lives where hitherto it has played little part, whether they are millionaires or nearpaupers, workers or idlers. With this aim there must be full measure of sympathy, but I fear we can commend it only in the back-handed fashion in which a great authority on sociology recently commended the Socialists. "If sympathy with what they are trying to do, as opposed to the way in which they are trying to do it, makes one a Socialist," said the Professor, "then I am a Socialist." Here also we may sympathise with the aim, but the results are largely dependent on the method; and that method is the offspring of ignorance and inefficiency. The results may be summed up in one word—superficiality. I have elsewhere warned readers not to think that this word means simply a slight knowledge of a subject. A slight knowledge is all that most of us possess, or need to possess, about most subjects. I know a little about Montenegro for instance—something of its origin and relationships, its topography, the names and characteristics of a city or two, the racial and other peculiarities of its inhabitants. Yet I should cut a poor figure indeed in an examination on Montenegrin history, geography or government. Is my knowledge "superficial"? It could not properly be so stigmatised unless I should pose as an authority on Montenegro, or unless my opportunities to know about the country had been so great that failure to take advantage of them should argue mental incapacity. The trouble with the reading-lists and programmes of our women's clubs, inherited in some degree from our general educational methods, is that they emphasise their own content and ignore what they do not contain, to such an extent that those who use them remain largely in ignorance of the fact that the former bears a very small proportion indeed to the latter.

It was once my duty to act as private tutor in algebra and geometry to a young man preparing for college. He was bright and industrious, but I found that he was under the impression that when he had gone to the end of his text-books in those two subjects he would have mastered, not only all the algebra and geometry, but all the mathematics, that the world held in store. And when this story has been told in despair to some very intelligent persons they have commented: "Well, there isn't much more, is there?"

The effort of the text-book writer, as well as that of the maker of programmes, lists, and courses, appears to have been to produce what he calls a "well-rounded" effect; in other words, to make the student think that the whole subject—in condensed form perhaps, but still the whole—lies within what he has turned out. Did you ever see a chemistry that gave, or tried to give, an idea of the world of chemical knowledge that environs its board cover? One has to become a Newton before he feels, with that sage, like a child, playing on the sands, with the great, unexplored ocean of knowledge stretching out before him. Most students are rather like ducks in a barnyard puddle, quite sure that they are familiar with the whole world and serene in that knowledge.

Most writers of text-books would indignantly deny that this criticism implies a fault. It is none of their business, they would say, to call attention to what is beyond their scope. So be it. Unfortunately, every one feels in the same way and so the horizon of our women's clubs is that of the puddle instead of the ocean.

It is a most interesting fact in this connection that there exist certain organisations which make a business of furnishing clubwomen with information for their papers. I have heard this service described as a "godsend," to clubs in small places where there are no libraries, or where the libraries are poorly equipped with books and *personnel*. But, if I am correctly informed, the service does not stop with the supply of raw material; it goes on to the finished product, and the perplexed lady who is required to read a paper on "Melchisedek" or on "Popular Errors Regarding the Theory of Groups," may for an adequate fee, or possibly even for an inadequate one, obtain a neatly typewritten manuscript on the subject, ready to read.

This sort of thing is not at all to be wondered at. It has gone on since the dawn of time with college theses, clergymen's sermons, the orations and official papers of statesmen. Whenever a man is confronted with an intellectual task that he dare not shirk, and yet has not the intellect or the interest to perform, the first thing he thinks of is to hire some one to do it for him, and this demand has always been great enough and widespread enough to make it profitable for some one to organise the supply on a commercial basis. What interests us in the present case is the fact that its existence in the woman's club affords an instant clue to the state of mind of many of its members. They have this in common with the plagiarising pupil, clergyman, or statesman—they are called upon to do something in which they have only a secondary interest. The minister who reads a sermon on the text "Thou Shalt Not Steal," and considers that the fact that he has paid five dollars for it will absolve him from the charge of inconsistency, does not—cannot—feel any desire to impress his congregation with a desire for right living—he wants only to hold his job. The university student who, after ascertaining that there is no copyable literature in the Library on "Why I Came to College," pays a classmate a dollar to give this information to the Faculty, cares nothing about the question; but he does care to avoid discipline. So the clubwoman who reads a purchased essay on "Ireland in the Fourteenth Century," has not the slightest interest in the subject; but she does want to remain a member of her club, in good and regular standing. It is the same substitution of adventitious for natural motives and stimuli that works intellectual havoc from the mother's knee up to the Halls of Congress.

When I assert boldly that at the present time the majority of vague and illogical readers are women, and that women's clubs are responsible for much of that kind of reading, I shall doubtless incur the displeasure of the school of feminists who seem bent on minimising the differences between the two sexes. Obvious physical differences they have not been able to explain away, and to deny that corresponding mental differences exist is to shut one's eyes to all the teachings of modern physiology. The mental life is a function, not of the brain alone, but of the whole nervous system of which the brain is but the principal ganglion. Cut off a man's legs, and you have removed something from his mental, as well as from his physical equipment. That men and women should have minds of the same type is a physiological impossibility. A familiar way of stating the difference is to say that in the man's mind reason predominates, in the woman's, intuition. There is doubtless something to be said for this statement of the distinction, but it is objectionable because it is generally interpreted to mean—quite unnecessarily—that a woman's mind is inferior to a man's—a distinction about as foolish as it would be to say the negative electricity is inferior to positive, or cold to heat. The types are in most ways supplementary, and a combination of the two has always been a potent intellectual force—one of the strongest arguments for marriage as an institution. When we try to do the work of the world with either type alone we have generally made a mess of it. And the outcome seems to make it probable that the female type is especially prone to become the prey of fallacies like that which has brought about the present flood of useless, or worse than useless, reading.

I shall doubtless be asked whether I assert that one type of mind belongs always to the man and one to the woman. By no means. I do not even lay emphasis on the necessity of naming the two types "male" and "female." All I say is that the types exist—with those intermediate cases that always bother the classifier—and that the great majority of men possess one type and the great majority of women the other. It is possible that differences of training may have originated or at least emphasised the types; it is possible that future training may obliterate the lines that separate them, but I do not believe it. I am even afraid of trying the experiment, for there is reason to believe that its success in the mental field might react unfavourably on those physical differences on which the future of the race depends. We may have gone too far in this direction already; else why the feverish anxiety of the girls' colleges to prove that their graduates are marrying and bearing children?

The fact is that the problem of the education of the sexes is not yet solved. Educating one sex alone didn't work; neither, I believe, does the present plan of educating both alike, whether in the same institution, or separately.

II—A *Diagnosis*

Reading, like conversation, is, or ought to be, a contact between two minds. The difference is that while one may talk only with his contemporaries and neighbours one may read the words of a writer far distant both in time and space. It is no wonder, perhaps, that the printed word has become a fetish, but fetishes of any kind are not in accordance with the spirit of the age, and their veneration should be discouraged. Reading in which the contact of minds is of secondary importance, or even cuts no figure at all, is meaningless and valueless.

In a previous paper, reasons have been given for believing that reading of this kind is peculiarly prevalent among the members of women's clubs. The value of these organisations is so great, and the services that they have rendered to women, and through them to the general cause of social betterment, are so evident, that it seems well worth while to examine the matter a little more closely, and to complete a diagnosis based on the study of the symptoms that have already presented themselves. As most of the reading done in connection with clubs is in preparation for the writing and reading of papers, we may profitably, perhaps, direct our attention to this phase of the subject.

Most persons will agree, probably, that the average club paper is not notably worth while. It is written by a person not primarily and vitally interested in the subject, and it is read to an assemblage most of whom are similarly devoid of interest—the whole proceeding being more or less perfunctory. Could it be expected that reading done in connection with such a performance should be valuable?

This is worth pondering, because it is a fact that almost all the vital informative literature that is produced at first hand sees the light in connection with clubs and associations—bodies that publish journals, "transactions" or "proceedings" for the especial purpose of printing the productions of their members.

This literature, for the most part, does not come to the notice of the general reader. The ordinary books on the technical subjects of which it treats are not raw material, but a manufactured product—compilations from the original sources. And the pity of it is that very many of them, often the best of them from a purely literary point of view, are so unsatisfactory, viewed from the point of view of accomplishment. They do not do what they set out to do; they are full of misunderstandings, misinterpretations, interpolations and omissions. It is the old story; those who know won't tell and the task is assumed by those who are eminently able to tell, but don't know. The scientific expert despises the public, which is forced to get its information through glib but ignorant expounders. This is a digression, but it may serve to illuminate the situation, which is that the authoritative literature of special subjects sees the light almost wholly in the form of papers, read before clubs and associations. Evidently there is nothing in the mere fact that a paper is to be read before a club, to make it trivial or valueless. Yet how much that is of value to the world first saw the light in a paper read before a woman's club? How much original thought, how much discovery, how much invention, how much inspiration, is put into their writing and emanates from their reading?

There must be a fundamental difference of some kind between the constitution and the methods of these two kinds of clubs. A study of this difference will throw light on the kind of reading that must be done in connection with each and may explain, in great part, why the reading done for women's club-papers is what it is.

A scientific or technical society exists largely for the purpose of informing its members of the original

work that is being done by each of them. When anyone has accomplished such work or has made such
progress that he thinks an account of what he has
done would be interesting, he sends a description of
it to the proper committee, which decides whether it
shall be read and discussed at a meeting, or published
in the Proceedings, or both, or neither. The result
depends on the size of the membership, on its activity,
and on the value of its work. It may be that the programme committee has an embarrassment of riches
from which to select, or that there is poverty instead.
But in no case does it arrange a programme. The
Physical Society, if that is its name and subject, does
not decide that it will devote the meetings of the current season to a consideration of Radio-activity and
assign to specified members the reading of papers on
Radio-active springs, the character of Radium Eman-
ation, and so on. If it did, it would doubtless get precisely the same results that we are complaining of in
the case of the Woman's Club. A man whose specialty is thermodynamics might be told off to prepare a
paper on Radio-active Elements in Rocks—a subject
in which he is not interested. He could have nothing
new nor original to say on the subject and his paper
would be a mere compilation. It would not even be a
good compilation, for his interest and his skill would
lie wholly in another direction. The good results
that the society does get are wholly dependent on the
fact that each writer is full of new information that
he desires, above all things, to communicate to his
fellow-members.

In the preparation of such a paper, one needs, of
course, to read, and often to read widely. Much of
the reading will be done in connection with the work
described, or even before it is begun. No one wishes
to undertake an investigation that has already been
made by someone else, and so the first thing that a

competent investigator does is to survey his field and ascertain what others have accomplished in it. This task is by no means easy, for such information is often hidden in journals and transactions that are difficult to reach, and the published indexes of such material, though wonderfully advanced on the road toward perfection in the past twenty years, have yet far to travel before they reach it. Not only the writer's description of what he has done or ascertained, but the character of the work itself; the direction it takes—the inferences that he draws from it, will be controlled and coloured by what he reads of others' work. And even if he finds it easy to ascertain what has been done and to get at the published accounts and discussions of it, the mass may be so great that he has laid out for him a course of reading that may last many months.

But mark the spirit with which he attacks it! He is at work on something that seems to him supremely worth while. He is labouring to find out truth, to dissipate error, to help his fellow-men to know something or to do something. The impulse to read, and to read much and thoroughly, is so powerful that it may even need judicious repression. The difference between this kind of reading and that done in the preparation of a paper to fill a place in a set programme hardly needs emphasis.

The preparation of papers for professional and technical societies has been dwelt upon at such length, because I see no reason why the impulse to reading that it furnishes cannot also be placed at the disposal of the woman's club; and I shall have some suggestions toward this end in a future article.

Meanwhile, I shall doubtless be told that it is unfair to compare the woman's club, with its didactic aim, and the scientific association of trained and interested investigators. It is true that we have plenty of clubs—some of men alone, some of both sexes—whose object is to listen to interesting and instructive papers on a set subject, often forming part of a pre-arranged programme. These, however, need our attention here only so far as the papers are prepared by members of the club, and in this case they are in precisely the same class as the woman's club. In many cases, however, the paper is merely the excuse for a social gathering, perhaps at a dinner or a luncheon. Of course if the paper or lecture is by an expert invited to give it, the case falls altogether outside of the region that we are exploring.

I am condemning here all clubs, formed for an avowed educational or cultural purpose, that adopt set programmes and assign the subjects to their own members. I am deploring the kind of reading to which this leads, the kind of papers that are prepared in this way, and the kind of thought and action that are the inevitable outcome.

It would seem that the women's clubs now form an immense majority of all organisations of this kind and that there are reasons for warning women that they are specially prone to this kind of mistake.

The diversity of interests of the average man, the wideness of his contacts—the whole tradition of his sex—tends to minimise the injury that may be done to him, intellectually and spiritually, by anything of this kind. The very fact that he is the woman's inferior spiritually, and in many cases, in intellect, also —although probably not at the maximum—relieves him, in great part, of the odium attaching to the error that has been described. Women are becoming keenly alive to the deficiencies of their sex-tradition; they are trying to broaden their intellectual contacts —that is the great modern feminist movement. Some of those who are active in it are making two mistakes —they are ignoring the differences between the sexes and they are trying to substitute revolution for evolution. In this latter error they are in very good company—hardly one of the great and the good has not made it, at some time and in some way. Revolution is always the outcome of a mistake. The mistake may be antecedent and irrevocable, and the revolution therefore necessary, but this is rarely the case. The revolutionist runs a risk common to all who are in a hurry—he may break the object of his attention instead of moving it. When he wants to hand you a dish he hits it with a ball-bat. Taking a reasonable amount of time is better in the long run.

That there is no royal road to knowledge has long been recognised. The trouble with most of us is that we have interpreted this to mean that the acquisition of knowledge must always be a distasteful process. On the contrary, the vivid interest that is the surest guide to knowledge is also the surest smoother of the path. Given the interest that lures the student on, and he will spend years in surmounting rocks and breaking through thorny jungles, realising their difficulties perhaps, but rejoicing the more when those difficulties prove no obstacles.

The fact that the first step toward accomplishment is to create an interest has long been recognised, but attempts have been made too often to do it by devious ways, unrelated to the matter in hand. Students have been made to study history or algebra by offering prizes to the diligent and by threatening the slothful with punishment. More indirect rewards and punishments abound in all our incitements to effort and need not be mentioned here. They may often be effective, but the further removed they are from direct personal interest in the subject, the weaker and the less permanent is the result. You may offer a boy a dollar to learn certain facts in English history, but those facts will not be fixed so well or so lastingly in his mind as those connected with his last year's trip to California, which he remembers easily without offer of reward or threat of punishment.

The interest in the facts gathered by reading in connection with the average club paper is merely the result of a desire to remain in good standing by fulfilling the duties of membership; and these duties may be fulfilled with slight effort and no direct interest, as we have already seen.

If interest were present even at the inception of the programme, something would be gained; but in too many cases it is not. The programme committee must make some kind of a programme, but what it is to be they know little and care less.

Two women recently entered a branch library and asked the librarian, who was busy charging books at the desk, what two American dramatists she considered "foremost." This was followed by the request, "Please tell me the two best plays of each of them." A few minutes later the querists returned and asked the same question about English dramatists, and still later about German, Russian, Italian and Spanish writers of the drama. Each time they eagerly wrote down the information and then retired to the reading-room for a few minutes' consultation.

Finally they propounded a question that was beyond the librarian's knowledge, and then she asked why they wanted to know.

"We are making out the programme for our next year's study course in the Blank Club," was the answer.

"But you mustn't take my opinion as final," protested the scandalised librarian. "You ought to read up everything you can find about dramatists. I may have left out the most important ones."

"This will do nicely," said the club-woman, as she folded her sheets of paper. And it did—whether nicely or not deponent saith not; but it certainly constituted the club programme.

On another occasion a clubwoman entered the library and said with an air of importance, "I want your material on Susanna H. Brown."

The librarian had never heard of Susanna, but experience had taught her modesty and also a certain degree of guile, so she merely said, "What do you want to know about her, particularly?"

"Our club wishes to discuss her contributions to American literature."

Now the Brown family has been active in letters, from Charles Brockden down to Alice, but no one seems to know of Susanna H. The librarian contrived to put off the matter until she could make some investigations of her own, but, all the resources of the central reference room proving unequal to the task, she timidly asked the clubwoman, at her next visit, to solve the problem.

"Oh, we don't know who Susanna H. Brown was; that is why we came to you for information!"

"But where did you find the name?"

"Well, I don't know exactly; but one of our members, in a conversation with some one who knows a lot about literature—I forget just who it was—was told that Susanna H. Brown had rendered noteworthy services to American literature. We've got to find out, for her name is already printed on the programme!"

I don't know what was said of Miss, or Mrs. Brown at the meeting; but my opinion is that this particular item on the programme had to be omitted.

Another lady entered a library abruptly and said, "I want your books on China."

"Do you mean the country of that name? or are you looking up porcelain?"

First perplexity and then dismay spread over the lady's face. "Why, I don't know," she faltered. "The program just said China!"

A university professor was once asked by one of these program committees for a list of references on German folklore—a subject to which it had decided that its club should devote the current season. The list, as furnished, proved rather stiff, and the astonished professor received forthwith the following epistle (quoted from memory):

"DEAR PROFESSOR—

Thank you so much for the folk-lore; but we have changed our minds and have decided to study the Chicago Drainage Canal instead."

This hap-hazard method of programme-making is not confined to club papers, as the following anecdote will show:

An officer of a woman's club entered a library and said that she thought it would be nice to vary the usual literary programme by the introduction of story-telling, and she asked for aid from the library staff. It was a busy season and as the librarian hesitated the clubwoman added hastily that the whole programme need not occupy more than half an hour. "We want the very simplest things, told in a few words, so that it will really be no trouble at all."

Pressed to be more specific, she went on: "Well— no story must take more than three minutes, and we want Little Nell, Louis IX, Moses in the Bulrushes, the Princes in the Tower, Cinderella, Jack and the Bean Stalk, the Holy Night and Louis XI.

"You see that allowing three minutes apiece would bring them all within twenty-four minutes— less than half an hour, just as I said.

"And—oh, yes! we want the storyteller to sit on a platform, and just in front of her we will pose a group of little girls, all in white frocks. Won't that be nice?"

The making of programmes has in many cases been influenced by the fact that some subjects are considered more "high-toned" than others. The drama is at present a particularly high-toned subject. The fine arts are always placed in the first class. Ap parently anything closely related to the personal lives, habits and interests of those concerned is under a ban. The fine arts, for instance, are not recognised as including the patterns of wall-paper or curtains, or the decoration of plates or cups. Copying from one programme to another is a common expedient. The making of these programmes betrays, all through its processes and their inevitable result, lack of original- ity, blind adherence to models, unquestioning imita- tion of something that has gone before. I do not be- lieve these to be sex-characteristics, and there are signs that the sex is growing out of them. If they are not sex characteristics they must be the results of ed- ucation, for ordinary heredity would quickly equalise the sexes in this respect. I have already stated my belief that the physical differences between the sexes are necessarily accompanied by mental differences, and I think it probable that the characteristics noted above, although not proper to sex, spring from the fact that we are expecting like results from the same educational treatment of unlike minds. When we have learned how to vary our treatment of these minds so as to produce like results—in those cases where we want the results to be alike, as in the present instance—we shall have solved the problem of education, so far as it affects sex-differences.

It has long been recognised that whenever woman does show a deviation from standards she is apt to deviate far and erratically. So far, however, she has shown no marked tendency so to deviate in the arts and a very slight one in the sciences. There have been lately some marked instances of her upward deviation in the field of science. In literature, no age has been wanting in great woman writers, though there have been few of them. I look eventually to see woman physicists as eminent as Helmholtz and Kelvin, woman painters as great as Raphael and Velasquez, woman musicians as able as Bach and Beethoven. That we have had none yet I believe to be solely the fault of inadequate education. Of this inadequacy our imitative, arbitrary and uninspiring club programmes are a part—the very fact that our clubwomen pin their faith to programmes of any kind is a consequence of it. The substitution of something else for these programmes, with the accompanying change in the interests and reading of clubwomen, will be one step toward the rationalisation of education—for all processes of this kind are essentially educative.

We need not despair of finding ultimately the exact differences in method which, applied in the education of the sexes, will minimise such of the present mental differences as we desire to obliterate. Problems of this sort are solved usually by the discovery of some automatic process. In this case the key to such a process is the fact that the mental differences between the sexes manifest themselves in differences of interest.

Every parent of boys and girls knows that these differences begin early to show themselves. We have been too prone to disregard them and to substitute a set of imagined differences that do not really exist. We go about the moral training of the boy and the girl in precisely the same way, although their moral points of view and susceptibilities differ in degree and kind; and then we marvel that we do not get precisely similar moral products. But we assume that there is some natural objection to the climbing of trees by girls, while it is all right for boys—an imaginary distinction that has caused tears and heartburnings. We are outgrowing this particular imaginary distinction, and some others like it. Possibly we may also outgrow our systems of co-education, so far as this means the subjection of the male and the female mind to exactly the same processes of training. The training of the sexes in the same institution, with its consequent mental contact between them, has nothing to do with this, necessarily, and has advantages that cannot be overlooked.

Whatever we do in school, our subsequent education, which goes on at least as long as we inhabit this world, must be in and through social contact, men and women together. But if each sex is not true to itself and does not live its own life, the results cannot be satisfactory. Reactions that are sought in an effort made by women to conform their instincts, aspirations and mental processes to those of men will be feeble or perverted, just as they would be if men should seek a similar distortion. The remedy is to let the woman's mind swing into the channel of least resistance, just as the man's always has done. Then the clubs, and the clubwomen, their exercises, their papers and their preparatory reading will all be released from the constraint that is now pinching them and pinning them down and will bud and blossom and grow up to normal and valuable fruition.

We have started with the fact that the reading done by the members of women's clubs, especially in connection with club papers, is often trivial, superficial, devoid of intelligence and lacking in judgment. Treating this as a symptom; we have, I think, traced the cause to a total lack of interest due to arbitrary, perfunctory and unintelligent programme-making. The disease may be diagnosed, I think, as acute programitis and the physician is in a position to consider what therapeutic measures may be indicated. We shall endeavor to prescribe some simple remedies.

III—*The Remedy*

When we have once discovered the cause of a malady, we may proceed in two ways to combat it; either we may destroy the cause or we may render the possible victims immune. To put it a little differently, we may eliminate either of the two elements whose conjunction causes the disease. To grow weeds, there must co-exist their seeds and a favourable soil. They may be exterminated either by killing the seeds or sterilising the soil. Either of these methods may be used in dealing with the disease that prevails among readers, or, if you prefer the other metaphor, with the rank vegetation that has choked the fertile soil of their minds, making any legitimate mental crop impossible. We have seen that the conditions favorable to the disease are a lack of interest and a fallacious idea that there is something inherent in the printed page *per se* that makes its perusal valuable whether the reader is interested or not—somewhat as a charm is supposed to work even when it is in a language that the user does not understand.

We are considering only the form of the disease that affects clubwomen, and this we have diagnosed as *programitis*—the imposition of a set programme of work—which, as an exciting cause, operates on the mental soil prepared by indifference and fetichism to produce the malady from which so many are now suffering.

I think physicians will generally agree that where the exciting cause can be totally removed that method of dealing with the disease is far more effective than any attempt to secure immunity. I believe that in most cases it is so in the present instance.

In other words, my prescription is the abandonment, in nine cases out of ten, of the set programme, and the substitution of something that is interesting primarily to each individual concerned. This is no new doctrine. Listen to William James:

Any object not interesting in itself may become interesting through becoming associated with an object in which an interest already exists. The two associated objects grow, as it were, together: the interesting portion sheds its quality over the whole; and thus things not interesting in their own right borrow an interest which becomes as real and as strong as that of any natively interesting thing. . . . If we could recall for a moment our whole individual history, we should see that our professional ideals and the zeal they inspire are due to nothing but the slow accretion of one mental object to another, traceable backward from point to point till we reach the moment when, in the nursery or in the schoolroom, some little story told, some little object shown, some little operation witnessed, brought the first new object and new interest within our ken by associating it with some one of those primitively there. The interest now suffusing the whole system took its rise in that little event, so insignificant to us now as to be entirely forgotten. As the bees in swarming cling to one another in layers till the few are reached whose feet grapple the bough from which the swarm depends; so with the objects of our thinking—they hang to each other by associated links, but the original source of interest in all of them is the native interest which the earliest one once possessed.

If we are to exorcise this spirit of indifference that has settled down like a miasma upon clubdom we must find James's original germ of interest—the twig upon which our cluster of bees is ultimately to hang. Here we may introduce two axioms: Everyone is deeply interested in something; few are supremely interested in the same thing. I shall not attempt to prove these, and what I shall have to say will be addressed only to those who can accept them without proof. But I am convinced that illustrations will occur at once to everyone. Who has not seen the man or woman, the boy or girl who, apparently stupid, indifferent and able to talk only in monosyllables, is suddenly shocked into interest and volubility by the mere chance mention of some subject of conversation —birds, or religion, or Egyptian antiquities, or dolls, or skating, or Henry the Eighth? There are millions of these electric buttons for galvanising dumb clay into mental and spiritual life, and no one of them is likely to act upon more than a very few in a given company—the theory of chances is against it. That is why no possible programme could be made that would fit more than a very small portion of a given club. We have seen that many club-programmes are made with an irreducible minimum of intelligence; but even a programme committee with superhuman intellect and angelic goodwill could never compass the solution of such a problem as this. Nor will it suffice to abandon the general programme and endeavour to select for each speaker the subject that he would like best to study and expound. No one knows what these subjects are but the owners of the hearts that love them.

We have seen how the scientific and technical societies manage the matter and how well they succeed.

They appoint a committee whose duty it is to receive contributions and to select the worthiest among those presented. The matter then takes care of itself. These people are all interested in something. They are finding out things by experimentation or thought; by induction or deduction. It is the duty and the high pleasure of each to tell his fellows of his discoveries. It is in this way that the individual gives of his best to the race—the triumph of the social instinct over selfishness. As this sort of intellectual profit-sharing becomes more and more common, the reign of the social instinct will extend and strengthen. To do one's part toward such an end ought to be a pleasure, and this is one reason why this course is commended here to the women's clubs.

Everyone, I repeat, is deeply interested in something. I am not talking of idiots; there are no such in women's clubs. I have been telling some odd stories of clubwomen, in which they are represented as doing and saying idiotic things. These stories are all true, and if one should take the time to collect and print others, I do not suppose, as the sacred writer says, "that all the world could contain the books that should be written." Things quite as idiotic as these that I have reported are said and done in every city and every hamlet of these United States every day in the year and every hour in the day—except possibly between three and five A.M., and sometimes even then. Yet those who say and do these things are not idiots. When your friend Brown is telling you his pet anecdote for the thirty-fifth time, or when Smith insists that you listen to a recital of the uninteresting accomplishments of his newly-arrived infant, you may allow your thoughts to wander and make some inane remark, yet you are not an idiot. You are simply not interested. You are using most of your mind in another direction and it is only with what is left of it that you hear Brown or Smith and talk to him. Brown or Smith is not dealing with your personality as a whole, but with a residuum.

And this is what is the matter with the clubwomen who read foolishly and ask foolish questions in libraries. They are residual personalities. Not being at all interested in the matter in hand, they are devoting to it only a minimum part of their brains; and what they do and say is comparable with the act of the perambulating professor, who, absorbed in mathematical calculation, lifted his hat to the cow.

The professor was perhaps pardonable, for his mind was not wandering—it was suffering, on the contrary, from excessive concentration—but it was not concentrated on the cow. In the case of the clubwomen, the rôle of the cow is played by the papers that they are preparing, while, in lieu of the mathematical problems, we have a variety of really absorbing subjects, more or less important, over which their minds are wandering. What we must do is to capture these wandering minds, and this we can accomplish only by enlisting their own knowledge of what interests them.

If you would realise the difference between the mental processes of a mere residue and those of the whole personality when its vigour is concentrated on one subject, listen first to one of those perfunctory essays, culled from a collection of cyclopædias, and then hear a whole woman throw her whole self into something. Hear her candid opinion of some person or thing that has fallen below her standard! Hear her able analysis of the case at law between her family and the neighbours! Hear her make a speech on woman suffrage—I mean when it is really to her the cause of causes; there are those who take it up for other reasons, as the club-women do their papers, with not dissimilar results. In all these cases clearness of presentation, weight of invective, keenness of analysis spring from interest. None of these women, if she has a feminine mind, treats these things as a man would. We men are very apt to complain of the woman's mental processes, for the same reason that narrow "patriots" always suspect and deride the methods of a foreigner, simply because they are strange and we do not understand them. But what we are compelled to think of the results is shown by the fact that when we are truly wise we are apt to seek the advice and counsel of the other sex and to act upon it, even when we cannot fathom the processes by which it was reached.

All the more reason this why the woman should be left to herself and not forced to model her club paper on the mental processes of a man, used with many necessary elisions and sometimes with very bad workmanship, in the construction of the cyclopædia article never intended to be employed for any such purpose.

Perhaps we can never make the ordinary clubwoman talk like Susan B. Anthony, or Anna Shaw, or Beatrice Hale, or Fola La Follette; any more than we can put into the mouth of the ordinary business man the words of Lincoln, or John B. Gough, or Phillips Brooks, or Raymond Robins—but get somehow into the weakest of either sex the impulses, the interests, the energies that once stood or now stand behind the utterances of any one of these great Americans, and see if the result is not something worth while!

An appreciative critic of the first paper in this series, writing in *The Yale Alumni Weekly,* gives it as his opinion that these readers are in the first stage of their education—that of "initial intellectual interest." He says: "Curiosity, then suspicion, come later to grow into individual intellectual judgment."

I wish I could agree that what we have diagnosed as a malady is only an early stage of somthing that is ultimately to develop into matured judgment. But the facts seem clearly to show-that, far from possessing "initial intellectual interest," these readers are practically devoid of any kind of interest whatever, properly speaking. Such as they have is not proper to the subject, but simply due to the fact that they desire to retain their club membership, to fulfil their club duties, and to act in general as other women do in other clubs. To go back to our recent simile, it is precisely the same interest that keeps you listening, or pretending to listen, to a bore, while you are really thinking of something else. If you were free to follow your impulses, you would insult the bore, or throw him downstairs, or retreat precipitately. You are inhibited by your sense of propriety and your recognition of what is due to a fellow-man, no matter how boresome he may be. The clubwoman doubtless has a strong impulse to throw the encyclopædia out of the window, or to insult the librarian (occasionally she does) or even to resign from the club. She is prevented, in like manner, by her sense of propriety, and often, too, we must admit, by a real, though rudimentary, desire for knowledge. But such inhibitions cannot develop into judgment. They are merely negative, while the interest that has a valuable outcome is positive.

Another thing that we shall do well to remember is that no condition or relation one of whose elements or factors is the human mind can ever be properly considered apart from that mind. Shakespeare's plays would seem to be fairly unalterable. Shakespeare is dead and cannot change them, and they have been written down in black and white this many a year. But the real play, so far as it makes any difference to us to-day, is not in the books; or, at least, the book is but one of its elements. It is the effect produced upon the auditor, and of this a very important element is the auditor's mental and spiritual state. Considered from this standpoint, Shakespeare's plays have been changing ever since they were written. Environment, physical and mental, has altered; the language has developed; the plain, ordinary talk of Shakespeare's time now seems to us quaint and odd; every-day allusions have become cryptic. It all "ain't up to date," to quote the Cockney's complaint about it. Probably no one to-day can under any circumstances get the same reaction to a play of Shakespeare as that of his original audience, and probably no one ever will.

Anecdotes possess a sort of centripetal force; tales illustrative of the matter at hand have been flying to me from all parts of the country. From the Pacific Northwest comes this, which seems pertinent just here. A good clubwoman, who had been slaving all day over a paper on Chaucer, finally at its close threw down her pen and exclaimed, "Oh, dear! I wish Chaucer were *dead!*" She had her wish in more senses than the obvious one. Not only has Chaucer's physical body long ago given up its substance to earth and air, but his works have to be translated for most readers of the present day; his language is fast becoming as dead as Latin or Greek. But, worse still, his very spirit was dead, so far as its reaction on her was concerned. Poetry, to you and me, is what we make of it; and what do you suppose our friend from Oregon was making of Chaucer? Our indifference, our failure to react, is thus more far-reaching than its influence on ourselves—it is, in some sense, a sin against the immortal souls of those who have bequeathed their spiritual selves to the world in books. And this sin the clubs are, in more cases than I care to think, forcing deliberately upon their members.

A well-known cartoonist toiled long in early life at some uncongenial task for a pittance. Meanwhile he drew pictures for fun, and one day a journalist, seeing one of his sketches, offered him fifty dollars for it—the salary of many days. "And when," said the cartoonist, "I found I could get more money by playing than by working, I swore I would never work again—and I haven't."

When we can all play—do exactly what we like—and keep ourselves and the world running by it, then the Earthly Paradise will be achieved. But, meanwhile, cannot we realize that these clubwomen will accomplish more if we can direct and control their voluntary activity, backed by their whole mental energy, than when they devote some small part of their minds to an uncongenial task, dictated by a programme committee?

I shall doubtless be reminded that the larger clubs are now generally divided into sections, and that membership in these sections is supposed to be dictated by interest. This is a step in the right direction, but it is an excessively short one. The programme, with all its vicious accompaniments and lamentable results, persists. What I have said and shall say applies as well to an art or a domestic science section as to a club *in toto*.

To bring down the treatment to a definite prescription, let us suppose that the committee in charge of a club's activities, instead of marking out a definite programme for the season, should simply announce that communications on subjects of personal interest to the members, embodying some new and original thought, method, idea, device, or mode of treatment, would be received, and that the best of these would be read and discussed before the club, after which some would appear in print.   No conditions would be stated, but it would be understood that such features as length and style, as well as subject matter, would be considered in selecting the papers to be read. Above all, it would be insisted that no paper should be considered that was merely copied from anything, either in substance or idea.   It is, of course, possible to constitute a paper almost entirely of quotations and yet so to group and discuss these that the paper becomes an original contribution to thought; but mere parrot-like repetition of ascertained facts, or of other people's thoughts, should not be tolerated.

Right here the first obstacle would be encountered.   Club members, accustomed to be assigned for study subjects like "The Metope of the Parthenon" or "The True Significance of Hyperspace," will not easily comprehend that they are really desired to put briefly on paper original ideas about something that they know at first hand.   Mrs. Jones makes better sponge cake than any one in town; the fact is known to all her friends.   If sponge cake is a desirable product, why should not the woman who has discovered the little knack that turns failure into success, and who is proud of her ability and special knowledge, tell her club of it, instead of laboriously copying from a book—or, let us say, from two or three books—some one else's compilation of the facts ascertained at second or third hand by various other writers on "The Character of the Cid"?   Why should not Mrs.

Smith, who was out over night in the blizzard of 1888, recount her experiences, mental as well as physical? Why should not Miss Robinson, who collects coins and differs from the accepted authorities regarding the authenticity of certain of her specimens, tell why and how and all about it? Why should not the member who is crazy about begonias and the one who thinks she saw Uncle Hiram's ghost, and she who has read and re-read George Meredith, seeing beauties in him that no one else ever detected—why should not one and all give their fellows the benefit of the really valuable special knowledge that they have acquired through years of interested thinking and talking and doing?

But there will be trouble, as I have said. The thing, simple as it is, would be too unaccustomed to comprehend. And then a real article in a real cyclopædia by a real writer is Information with a big "I." My little knowledge about making quince jelly, or darning stockings, or driving an auto, or my thoughts about the intellectual differences between Dickens and Thackeray, or my personal theories of conduct, or my reasons for preferring hot-water heat to steam —these are all too trivial to mention; is it possible that you want me to write them down on paper?

It may thus happen that when the committee opens its mail it may find—nothing. What, then? Logically, I should be forced to say: Well, if none of your members is interested enough in anything to have some original information to tell about it, disband your club. What is the use of it? Even three newsboys, when they meet on the street corner, begin at once to interchange ideas. Where are yours?

Possibly this would be too drastic. It might be better to hold a meeting, state the failure, and adjourn for another trial. It might be well to repeat

this several times, in the hope that the fact that absence of original ideas means no proceedings might
soak in and germinate. If this does not work, it might
be possible to fight the devil with fire, by going back
to the programme method so far as to assign definitely to members subjects in which they are known to be
deeply interested. This, in fact, is the second method
of treatment mentioned at the outset, namely, the endeavour to secure immunity where the germ cannot
be exterminated. We shall probably never be able to
rid the world of the *bacillus tuberculosis;* the best we
can do is to keep as clear of it as we can and to
strengthen our powers of resistance to it. So, if we
cannot kill the programme all at once, let us strive
to make it innocuous and to minimise its evil effects
on its victims.

Let us suppose, now, that in one way or another,
it is brought about that every club member who reads
a paper is reporting the result of some personal experience in which her interest is vivid—some discovery, acquisition, method, idea, criticism or appreciation that is the product of her own life and of the
particular, personal way in which she has lived it.

What a result this will have on that woman's
reading—on what she does before she writes her
paper and on what she goes through after it! If her
interest is as vivid as we assume it to be, she will not
be content to recount her own experiences without
comparing them with those of others. And after her
paper has been read and the comment and criticism
of other interested members have been brought out—
of some, perhaps, whose interest she had never before
suspected, then she will feel a fresh impulse to search
for new accounts and to devour them. There is no
longer anything perfunctory about the matter. She
can no longer even trust the labour of looking up her

references to others. She becomes an investigator; she feels something of the joy of those who add to the sum of human knowledge.

And lo! the problem of clubwomen's reading is solved! The wandering mind is captured; the inane residuum is abolished by union with the rest to form a normal, intelligent whole. No more idiotic questions, no more cyclopædia-copying, no more wool-gathering programmes. Is it too much to expect? Alas, we are but mortal!

I trust it has been made sufficiently clear that I think meanly neither of the intellectual ability of women nor of the services of women's clubs. The object of these papers is to give the former an opportunity to assert itself, and the latter a chance to profit by the assertion. The woman's club of the future should be a place where original ideas, fed and directed by interested reading, are exchanged and discussed. Were I writing of men's clubs, I should point out to them the same goal. And then, perhaps, we may look forward to a time when a selected group of men and women may come together and talk of things in which they both, as men and women, are interested.

When this happens, I trust that in the discussion we shall not heed the advice of some modern feminists and forget that we are as God made us. Why should each man talk to a woman "as if she were another man"? I never heard it advised that each woman should talk to each man "as if he were another woman"; but I should resent it if I did. Why shut our eyes to the truth? I trust that I have not been talking to the club-women "as if they were men"; I am sure I have not meant to do so. They are not men; they have their own ways, and those ways should be developed and encouraged. We have had the psychology of race, of the crowd and of the criminal; where is the investigator who has studied the Psychology of Woman? When she (note the pronoun) has arrived, let us make her president of a woman's club.

It is with diffidence that I have outlined any definite procedure, because, after all, the precise manner in which the treatment should be applied will depend, of course, on the club concerned. To prescribe for you most effectively, your physician should be an intimate friend. He should have known you from birth—better still, he should have cared for your father and your grandfather before you. Otherwise, he prescribes for an average man; and you may be very far from the average. The drug that he administers to quiet your nerves may act on your heart and give you the smothers—it might conceivably quiet you permanently. Then the doctor would send to his medical journal a note on "A Curious Case of Umptiol Poisoning," but you would still be dead, even if all his readers should agree with him.

I have no desire to bring about casualties of this kind. Let those who know and love each particular club devote themselves to the task of applying my treatment to it in a way that will involve a minimum shock to its nerves and a minimum amount of interference with its metabolic processes. It will take time. Rome was not built in a day, and a revolution in clubdom is not going to be accomplished over night.

I have prescribed simple remedies—too simple, I am convinced, to be readily adopted. What could be simpler than to advise the extermination of all germ diseases by killing off the germs? Any physician will tell you that this method is the very acme of efficiency; yet, the germs are still with us, and bid fair to spread suffering and death over our planet for many a long year to come. So I am not sanguine that we shall be able all at once to kill off the programmes. All that may be expected is that at some distant day the simplicity and effectiveness of some plan of the sort will begin to commend itself to clubwomen. If, then, some lover of the older literature will point out the fact that, back in 1915, the gloomy era when fighting hordes were spreading blood and carnage over the fair face of Europe, an obscure and humble librarian, in the pages of THE BOOKMAN, pointed out the way to sanity, I shall be well content.

BOOKS FOR TIRED EYES

The most distinctive thing about a book is the possibility that someone may read it. Is this a truism? Evidently not; for the publishers, who print books, and the libraries, which store and distribute them, have never thought it worth their while to collect and record information bearing on this possibility. In the publisher's or the bookseller's advertising announcements, as well as on the catalogue cards stored in the library's trays, the reader may ascertain when and where the book was published, the number of pages, and whether it contains plates or maps; but not a word of the size or style of type in which it is printed. Yet on this depends the ability of the reader to use the book for the purpose for which it was intended. The old-fashioned reader was a mild-mannered gentleman. If he could not read his book because it was printed in outrageously small type, he laid it aside with a sigh, or used a magnifying lens, or persisted in his attempts with the naked eye until eyestrain, with its attendant maladies, was the result. Lately however, the libraries have been waking up, and their readers with them. The utilitarian side of the work is pushed to the front; and the reader is by no means disposed to accept what may be offered him, either in the content of the book or its physical make-up. The modern library must adapt itself to its users, and among other improvements must come an attempt to go as far as possible in making books physiologically readable.

Unfortunately the library cannot control the output of books, and must limit itself to selection. An experiment in such selection is now in progress in the St. Louis Public Library. The visitor to that library will find in its Open Shelf Room a section of shelving marked with the words "Books in large type." To this section are directed all readers who have found it difficult or painful to read the ordinary printed page but who do not desire to wear magnifying lenses. It has not been easy to fill these shelves, for books in large type are few, and hard to secure, despite the fact that artists, printers, and oculists have for years been discussing the proper size, form, and grouping of printed letters from their various standpoints. Perhaps it is time to urge a new view—that of the public librarian, anxious to please his clients and to present literature to them in that physical form which is most easily assimilable and least harmful.

Tired eyes belong, for the most part, to those who have worked them hardest; that is, to readers who have entered upon middle age or have already passed through it. At this age we become conscious that the eye is a delicate instrument—a fact which, however familiar to us in theory, has previously been regarded with aloofness. Now it comes home to us. The length of a sitting, the quality, quantity, and incidence of the light, and above all, the arrangement of the printed page, become matters of vital importance to us. A book with small print, or letters illegibly grouped, or of unrecognizable shapes, becomes as impossible to us as if it were printed in the Chinese character.

It is an unfortunate law of nature that injurious acts appear to us in their true light only after the harm is done. The burnt child dreads the fire after he has been burned—not before. So the fact that the middle-aged man cannot read small, or crooked, or badly grouped type means simply that the harmfulness of these things, which always existed for him, has cumulated throughout a long tale of years until it has obtruded itself upon him in the form of an inhibition. The books that are imperative for the tired eyes of middle age, are equally necessary for those of youth—did youth but know it. Curiously enough, we are accustomed to begin, in teaching the young to read, with very legible type. When the eyes grow stronger, we begin to maltreat them. So it is, also, with the digestive organs, which we first coddle with pap, then treat awhile with pork and cocktails, and then, perforce, entertain with pap of the second and final period. What correspond, in the field of vision, to pork and cocktails, are the vicious specimens of typography offered on all sides to readers—in books, pamphlets, magazines, and newspapers—typography that is slowly but surely ruining the eyesight of those that need it most.

Hitherto, the public librarian has been more concerned with the minds and the morals of his clientele than with that physical organism without which neither mind nor morals would be of much use. It would be easy to pick out on the shelves of almost any public library books that are a physiological scandal, printed in type that it is an outrage to place before any self-respecting reader. I have seen copies of "Tom Jones" that I should be willing to burn, as did a puritanical British library-board of newspaper notoriety. My reasons, however, would be typographic, not moral, and I might want to add a few copies of "The Pilgrim's Progress" and "The Saint's Everlasting Rest," without prejudice to the authors' share in those works, which I admire and respect. Perhaps it is too much to ask for complete typographical expurgation of our libraries. But, at least, readers with tired eyes who do not yet wear, or care to wear, corrective lenses, should be able to find, somewhere on the shelves, a collection of works in relatively harmless print—large and black, clear in outline, simple and distinctive in form, properly grouped and spaced.

The various attempts to standardize type-sizes and to adopt a suitable notation for them have been limited hitherto to the sizes of the type-body and bear only indirectly on the size of the actual letter. More or less arbitrary names— such as minion, bourgeois, brevier, and nonpareil,—were formerly used; but what is called the point-system is now practically universal, although its unit, the "point," is not everywhere the same. Roughly speaking, a point is one-seventy-second of an inch, so that in three-point type, for example, the thickness of the type-body, from the top to the bottom of the letter on its face, is one-twenty-fourth of an inch. But on this type-body the face may be large or small—although of course, it cannot be larger than the body,—and the size of the letters called by precisely the same name in the point notation may vary within pretty wide limits. There is no accepted notation for the size of the letters themselves, and this fact tells, more eloquently than words, that the present sizes of type are standardized and defined for compositors only, not for readers, and still less for scientific students of the effect upon the readers' eyes of different arrangements of the printed page.

What seems to have been the first attempt to define sizes of type suitable for school grades was made fifteen years ago by Mr Edward R. Shaw in his "School Hygiene"; he advocates sizes from eighteen-point in the first year to twelve-point for the fourth. "Principals, teachers, and school superintendents," he says, "should possess a millimetre measure and a magnifying glass, and should subject every book presented for their examination to a test to determine whether the size of the letters and the width of the leading are of such dimensions as will not prove injurious to the eyes of children." To this list, librarians might be well added—not to speak of authors, editors, and publishers. In a subsequent part of his chapter on "Eyesight and Hearing," from which the above sentence is quoted, appears a test of illumination suggested by "The Medical Record" of Strasburg, which may serve as a "horrid example" in some such way as did the drunken brother who accompanied the temperance lecturer. According to this authority, if a pupil is unable to read diamond type —four-and-one-half-point—"at twelve-inch distance and without strain," the illumination is dangerously low. The adult who tries the experiment will be inclined to conclude that whatever the illumination, the proper place for the man who uses diamond type for any purpose is the penitentiary.

The literature upon this general subject, such as it is, is concerned largely with its relations with school hygiene. We are bound to give our children a fair start in life, in conditions of vision as well as in other respects, even if we are careless about ourselves. The topic of "Conservation of Vision," in which, however, type-size played but a small part, was given special attention at the Fourth International Congress of School Hygiene, held in Buffalo in 1913. Investigations on the subject, so far as they affect the child in school, are well summed up in the last chapter of Huey's "Psychology and Pedagogy of Reading." In general, the consensus of opinion of investigators seems to be that the most legible type is that between eleven-point and fourteen-point. Opinion regarding space between lines, due to "leading."

is not quite so harmonious. Some authorities think that it is better to increase the size of the letters; and Huey asserts that an attempt to improve unduly small type by making wide spaces between lines is a mistake.

As to the relative legibility of different type-faces, one of the most exhaustive investigations was that made at Clark University by Miss Barbara E. Roethlin, whose results were published in 1912. This study considers questions of form, style, and grouping, independently of mere size; and the conclusion is that legibility is a product of six factors, of which size is one, the others being form, heaviness of face, width of the margin around the letter, position in the letter-group, and shape and size of adjoining letters. For "tired eyes" the size factor would appear of overwhelming importance except where the other elements make the page fantastically illegible. In Miss Roethlin's tables, based upon a combination of the factors mentioned above, the maximum of legibility almost always coincides with that of size. These experiments seem to have influenced printers, whose organization in Boston has appointed a committee to urge upon the Carnegie Institution the establishment of a department of research to make scientific tests of printing-types in regard to the comparative legibility and the possibility of improving some of their forms. Their effort, so far, has met with no success; but the funds at the disposal of this body could surely be put to no better use.

With regard to the improvement of legibility by alteration of form, it has been recognized by experiments from the outset that the letters of our alphabet, especially the small, or "lower-case" letters, are not equally legible. Many proposals for modifying or changing them have been made, some of them odd or repugnant. It has been suggested, for instance, that the Greek lambda be substituted for our *l*, which in its present form is easily confused with the dotted *i*. Other pairs of letters (*u* and *n*, *o* and *e*, for example) are differentiated with difficulty. The privilege of modifying alphabetic form is one that has been frequently exercised. The origin of the German alphabet and our own, for instance, is the same, and no lower-case letters in any form date further back than the Middle Ages. There could be no well-founded objection to any change, in the interests of legibility, that is not so far-reaching as to make the whole alphabet look foreign and unfamiliar. It may be queried, however, whether the lower-case alphabet had not better be reformed by abolishing it altogether. There would appear to be no good reason for using two alphabets, now one and now the other, according to arbitrary rules, difficult to learn and hard to remember. That the general legibility of books would benefit by doing away with this mediaeval excrescence appears to admit of no doubt, although the proposal may seem somewhat startling to the general reader.

In 1911, a committee was appointed by the British Association for the Advancement of Science "to inquire into the influence of school-books upon eyesight." This committee's report dwells on the fact that the child's eye is still in process of development and needs larger type than the fully developed eye of the adult. In making its recommendation for the standardization of school-book type, which it considers the solution of the difficulty, the committee emphasizes the fact that forms and sizes most legible for isolated letters are not necessarily so for the groups that need to be quickly recognized by the trained reader. It dwells upon the importance of unglazed paper, flexible sewing, clear, bold illustrations, black ink, and true alignment. Condensed or compressed letters are condemned, as are long serifs and hair strokes. On the other hand, very heavy-faced type is almost as objectionable as that with the fine lines, the ideal being a proper balancing of whites and blacks in each letter and group. The size of the type face, as we might expect, is pronounced by the committee "the most important factor in the influence of books upon vision"; it describes its recommended sizes in millimetres—a refinement which, for the purposes of this article, need not be insisted upon. Briefly, the sizes run from thirty-point, for seven-year-old children, to ten-point or eleven-point, for persons more than twelve years old. Except as an inference from this last recommendation, the committee, of course, does not exceed its province by treating of type-sizes for adults; yet it would seem that it considers ten-point as the smallest size fit for anyone. however good his sight. This would bar much of our existing reading matter.

A writer whose efforts in behalf of sane typography have had practical results is Professor Koopman, librarian of Brown University, whose plea has been addressed chiefly to printers. Professor Koopman dwells particularly on the influence of short lines on legibility. The eye must jump from the end of each line back to the beginning of the next, and this jump is shorter and less fatiguing with the shorter line. though it must be oftener performed. Owing largely to his demonstration, "The Printing Art," a trade magazine published in Cambridge, Massachusetts, has changed its make-up from a one-column to a two-column page. It should be noted, however, that a uniform, standard length of line is even more to be desired than a short one. When the eye has become accustomed to one length for its linear leaps, these leaps can be performed with relative ease and can be taken care of subconsciously. When the lengths vary capriciously from one book, or magazine, to another, or even from one page to another, as they so often do, the effort to get accustomed to the new length is more tiring than we realize. Probably this factor, next to the size of type, is most effective in tiring the middle-aged eye, and in keeping it tired. The opinion may be ventured that the reason for our continued toleration of the small type used in the daily newspapers is that their columns are narrow, and still more, that these are everywhere of practically uniform width.

The indifference of publishers to the important feature of the physical make-up of books appears from the fact that in not a single case is it included among the descriptive items in their catalogue entries. Libraries are in precisely the same class of offenders. A reader or a possible purchaser of books is supposed to be interested in the fact that a book is published in Boston, has four hundred and thirty-two pages, and is illustrated, but not at all in its legibility. Neither publishers nor libraries have any way of getting information on the subject, except by going to the books themselves. Occasionally a remainder-catalogue, containing bargains whose charms it is desired to set forth with unusual detail, states that a certain book is in "large type," or even in "fine, large type," but these words are nowhere defined, and the purchaser cannot depend on their accuracy. An edition of Scott, recently advertised extensively as in "large, clear type," proved on examination to be printed in ten-point.

In gathering the large-type collection for the St. Louis Library fourteen-point was decided upon as the standard, which means, of course, types with a face somewhere between the smallest size that is usually found on a fourteen-point body, even if actually on a smaller body, and the largest that this can carry, even if on a larger body. The latter is unusually large, but it would not do to place the standard below fourteen-point, because that would lower the minimum, which is none too large as it is. The first effort was to collect such large-type books, already in the library, as would be likely to interest the general reader. In the collection of nearly 400,000 volumes, it was found by diligent search that only 150 would answer this description. Most octavo volumes of travel are in large type, but only a selected number of these was placed in the collection, to avoid overloading it with this particular class. This statement applies also to some other classes, and to certain types of books, such as some government reports and some scientific monographs, which have no representatives in the group. The next step was to supplement the collection by purchase. All available publishers' catalogues were examined, but after a period of twelve months it was found possible to spend only $65.00 in the purchase of 120 additional books. A circular letter was then sent to ninety-two publishers, explaining the purpose of the collection and asking for information regarding books in fourteen-point type, or larger, issued by them. To these there were received sixty-three answers. In twenty-nine instances, no books in type of this size were issued by the recipients of the circulars. In six cases, the answer included brief lists of from two to twelve titles of large-type books; and in several other cases, the publishers stated that the labor of ascertaining which of their publications are in large type would be prohibitive, as it would involve actual inspection of each and every volume on their lists. In two instances, however, after a second letter, explaining further the aims of the collection, publishers promised to undertake the work. The final result has been that the Library now has over four hundred volumes in the collection. This is surely not an imposing number, but it appears to represent the available resources of a country in which 1,000 publishers are annually issuing 11,000 volumes—to say nothing of the British and Continental output. In the list of the collection and in the entries, the size of the type, the leading, and the size of the book itself are to be distinctly stated. The last-mentioned item is necessary because the use of large type sometimes involves a heavy volume, awkward to hold in the hand.

The collection for adults in the St. Louis Library, as it now exists, may be divided into the following classes, according to the reasons that seem to have prompted the use of large type:

1. Large books printed on a somewhat generous scale and intended to sell at a high price, the size of the type being merely incidental to this plan. These include books of travel, history, or biography in several volumes, somewhat high-priced sets of standard authors, and books intended for gifts.

2. Books containing so little material that large type, thick paper, and wide margins were necessary to make a volume easy to handle and use. These include many short stories of magazine length, which for some inscrutable reason are now often issued in separate form.

3. Books printed in large type for aesthetic reasons. These are few, beauty and artistic form being apparently linked in some way with illegibility by many printers, no matter what the size of the type-face.

The large-type collection is used, not only by

elderly persons, but also in greater number by young persons whose oculists forbid them to read fine print, or who do not desire to wear glasses. The absence of a wide range in the collection drives others away to books that are, doubtless, in many cases bad for their eyes. Some books that have not been popular in the general collection have done well here, while old favorites have not been taken out. Such facts as these mean little with so limited a collection. Until readers awake to the dangers of small print and the comfort of large type there will not be sufficient pressure on our publishers to induce them to put forth more books suitable for tired eyes. It is probably too much to expect that the trade itself will try to push literature whose printed form obeys the rules of ocular hygiene. All that we can reasonably ask is that type-size shall be reported on in catalogues, so that those who want books in large type may know what is obtainable and where to go for it.

It has often been noted that physicians are the only class of professional men whose activities, if properly carried on, tend directly to make the profession unnecessary. Medicine tends more and more to be preventive rather than curative. We must therefore look to the oculists to take the first steps towards lessening the number of their prospective patients by inculcating rational notions about the effects of the printed page on the eye. Teachers, librarians, parents, the press—all can do their part. And when a demand for larger print has thus been created the trade will respond. Meanwhile, libraries should be unremitting in their efforts to ascertain what material in large type already exists, to collect it, and to call attention to it in every legitimate way.

THE MAGIC CASEMENT*

Anyone who talks or writes about the "movies" is likely to be misunderstood. There is little to be said now about the moving picture as a moving picture, unless one wants to discuss its optics or mechanics. The time is past when anyone went to see a moving picture as a curiosity. It was once the eighth wonder of the world; it long ago abdicated that position to join its dispossessed brothers the telephone, the X-ray, the wireless telegraph and the phonograph. What we now go to see is not the moving picture, but what the moving picture shows us; it is no more than a window through which we gaze—the poet's "magic casement" opening (sometimes) "on the foam of perilous seas." We may no more praise or condemn the moving picture for what it shows us than we may praise or condemn a proscenium arch or the glass in a show window.

The critic who thinks that the movies are lowering our tastes, or doing anything else objectionable, as well as he who thinks they are educating the masses, is not of the opinion that the moving pictures are doing these things because they show moving objects on a screen, but because of the character of what is photographed for such exhibition.

Thoughts on the movies, therefore, must be rather thoughts on things that are currently shown us by means of the movies; thoughts also on some of the things that we might see and do not. I have compared the screen above to a proscenium arch and a

* Read before the Town and Gown Club, St. Louis.

show window, but both of these are selective: the screen is as broad as the world. It is especially adapted to show realities; through it one may see the coast of Dalmatia as viewed from a steamer, the habits of animals in the African jungle, or the play of emotion on the faces of an audience at a ball game in Philadelphia. I am pleased to see that more and more of these interesting realities are shown daily in the movie theatres. There has been a determined effort to make them unpopular by calling them "educational," but they seem likely to outlive it. One is educated, of course, by everything that he sees or does, but why rub it in? The boy who thoroughly likes to go sailing will get more out of it than he who goes because he thinks it will be "an educational experience." As one who goes to the movies I confess that I enjoy its realities. Probably they educate me, and I take that with due meekness. Some of these realities I enjoy because they are unfamiliar, like the boiling of the lava lake in the Hawaiian craters and the changing crowds in the streets of Manila; some because they are familiar, like a college foot-ball game or the movement of vessels in the North River at New York.

I like the realities, too, in the dramatic performances that still occupy and probably will continue to occupy, most of the time at a movie theatre. Here I come into conflict with the producer. Like every other adapter he can not cut loose from the old when he essays the new. We no longer wear swords, but we still carry the buttons for the sword belt, and it is only recently that semi-tropic Americans gave up the dress of north-temperate Europe. So the movie producer can not forget the theatre. Now the theatre has some advantages that the movie can never attain —notably the use of speech. The movie, on the other hand, has unlimited freedom of scene and the use of real backgrounds. We do not object to a certain amount of what we call "staginess" on the stage—it is a part of its art; as the pigment is part of that of the painter. We are surrounded by symbols; we are not surprised that costume, gesture and voice are also symbolic instead of purely natural. But in the moving picture play it is, or should be, different. The costume and make-up, the posture and gesture, that seem appropriate in front of a painted house or tree on a back-drop, become so out-of-place as to be repulsive when one sees them in front of a real house and real trees, branches moving in the wind, running water—all the familiar accompaniments of nature. The movie producers, being unable to get away from their stage experience, are failing to grasp their opportunity. Instead of creating a drama of reality to correspond with the real environment that only the movie can offer, they are abandoning the unique advantages of that environment, to a large degree. They build fake cities, they set all their interiors in fake studio rooms, where everything is imitation; even when they let us see a bit of outdoors, it is not what it pretends to be. We have all seen, on the screen, bluffs 200 feet high on the coast of Virginia and palm trees growing in the borough of the Bronx. And they hire stage actors to interpret the stagiest of stage plots in as stagy a way as they know how. I am taking the movie seriously because I like it and because I see that I share that liking with a vast throng of persons with whom it is probably the only thing I have in common—persons separated from me by differences of training and education that would seem to make a common ground of any kind well-nigh impossible. With some persons the fact that the movie is democratic puts it outside the pale at once. Nothing, in their estimation, is worth discussing unless appreciation of it is limited to the few.   Their attitude is that of the mother who said to the nurse: "Go and see what baby is doing, and tell him he musn't." "Let us," they say "find out what people like, and then try to make them like something else." To such I have nothing to say. We ought rather, I believe, to find out the kind of thing that people like and then do our best to see that they get it in the best quality— that it is used in every way possible to pull them out of the mud, instead of rubbing their noses further in.

On the other hand, some capable critics, like Mr. Walter Pritchard Eaton, decry the movies because they are undemocratic—because they are offering a form of entertainment appealing only to the uneducated and thus segregating them from the educated, who presumably all attend the regular theatre, sitting in the parquet at two dollars per. One wonders whether Mr. Eaton has attended a moving-picture theatre since 1903. I believe the movie to be by all odds the most democratic form of intellectual (by which I mean non-physical) entertainment ever offered; and I base my belief on wide observation of audiences in theatres of many different grades. Now this democracy shows itself not only in the composition of audiences but in their manifestations of approval. I do not mean that everyone in an audience always likes the same thing. Some outrageous "slapstick" comedy rejoices one and offends another. A particularly foolish plot may satisfy in one place while it bores in another. But everywhere I find one thing that appeals to everybody—realism. Just as soon as there appears on the screen something that does not know how to pose and is forced by nature to be natural—an animal or a young child, for instance —there are immediate manifestations of interest and delight.

The least "stagy" actors are almost always favorites. Mary Pickford stands at the head. There is not an ounce of staginess in her make-up. She was never particularly successful on the stage. Some of her work seems to me ideal acting for the screen— simple, appealing, absolutely true. Of course she is not always at her best.

To the stage illusions that depend on costume and make-up, the screen is particularly unfriendly. Especially in the "close-ups" the effect is similar to that which one would have if he were standing close to the actor looking directly into his face. It is useless to depend on ordinary make-up under these circumstances. Either it should be of the description used by Sherlock Holmes and other celebrated detectives (we rely on hearsay) which deceives the very elect at close quarters, or else the producer must choose for his characters those that naturally "look the parts." In particular, the lady who, although long past forty, continues to play *ingenue* parts and "gets away with it" on the stage, must get away *from* it, when it comes to the screen. The "close up" tells the sad story at once. The part of a sixteen-year-old girl must be played by a real one. Another concession to realism, you see. And what is true of persons is true of their environment. I have already registered my disapproval of the "Universal City" type of production. It is almost as easy for the expert to pick out the fake Russian village or the pasteboard Virginia courthouse as it is for him to spot the wrinkles in the countenance of the school girl who left school in 1892. Next to a fake environment the patchwork scene enrages one—the railway that is double-track with 90-pound rails in one scene and single-track with streaks of rust in the next; the train that is hauled in quick succession by locomotives of the Mogul type, the Atlantic and the wood-burning vintage of 1868. There is here an impudent assumption in the producer, of a lack of intelligence in his audience, that is quite maddening. The same lack of correspondence appears between different parts of the same street, and between the outside and inside of houses. I am told by friends that I am quite unreasonable in the extent to which I carry my demands for realism in the movies. "What would you have?" they ask. I would have a producing company that should advertise, "We have no studio" and use only real backgrounds—the actual localities represented. "Do you mean to tell me," my friend goes on, "that you would carry your company to Spain whenever the scene of their play is laid in that country? The expense would be prohibitive." I most certainly should not, and this because of the very realism that I am advocating. Plays laid in Spain should be acted not only in Spain but by Spaniards. The most objectionable kind of fake is that in which Americans are made to do duty for Spaniards, Hindus or Japanese when their appearance, action and bearing clearly indicate that they were born and brought up in Skowhegan, Maine or Crawfordsville, Indiana. I have seen Mary Pickford in "Madame Butterfly", and I testify sadly that not even she can succeed here. No; if we want Spanish plays let us use those made on Spanish soil. Let us have free interchange of films between all film-producing countries. All the change required would be translating the captions, or better still, plays might be produced that require no captions. This might mean the total reorganization of the movie-play business in this country—a revolution which I should view with equanimity. Speaking of captions, here again the average producer appears to agree with Walter Pritchard Eaton that he is catering only to the uneducated. The writers of most captions seem, indeed, to have abandoned formal instruction in the primary school. Why should not a movie caption be good literature? Some of them are. The Cabiria captions were fine: though I do not admire that masterpiece. I am told that D'Annunzio composed them with care, and equal care was evidently used in the translation. The captions of the George Ade fables are uniformly good, and there are other notable exceptions. Other places where knowledge of language is required are inadequately taken care of. Letters from eminent persons make one want to hide under the chairs. These persons usually sign themselves "Duke of Gandolfo" or "Secretary of State Smith." Are grammar school graduates difficult to get, or high-priced? I beg you to observe that here again lack of realism is my objection.

But divers friends interpose the remark that the movies are already too realistic. "They leave nothing to the imagination." If this were so, it were a grievous fault—at any rate in so far as the moving-picture play aims at being an art-form. All good art leaves something to the imagination. As a matter of fact, however, the movie is the exact complement of the spoken play as read from a book. Here we have the words in full, the scene and action being left to the imagination except as briefly sketched in the stage direction. In the movie we have scene and action in full, the words being left to the imagination except as briefly indicated in the captions. Where captions are very full the form may perhaps be said to be complementary to the novel, where besides the words we are given a written description of scene and action that is often full of detail. The movie leaves just as much to the imagination as the novel, but what is so left is different in the two cases. Do I think that everyone in a movie audience makes use of his privilege to imagine what the actors are saying? No; neither does the novel-reader always image the scene and action. This does not depend on ignorance or the reverse, but on imaging power. Exceptional visual and auditive imaging power are rarely present in the same individual. I happen to have the former. I automatically see everything of which I read in a novel, and when the descriptions are not detailed, this gets me into trouble. On a second reading my imaged background may be different and when the earlier one asserts itself there is a conflict that I can compare only to hearing two tunes played at once. Persons having already good visual imaging power should develop their auditive imaging power by going to the movies and hearing what the actors say; these with deficient visual imagery should read novels and see the scenery. But to say that the movies allow no scope for the imagination is absurd. As I said at the outset, the movie play is just a play seen through the medium of a moving picture. It is like seeing a drama near enough to note the slightest play of feature and at the same time so far away that the actors can not be heard—somewhat like seeing a distant play through a fine telescope. The action should therefore differ in no respect from what would be proper if the words were intended to be heard. Doubtless this imposes a special duty upon both the author of the scenario and the producer, and they do not always respond to it. Action is introduced that fails to be intelligible without the words, and to clear it up the actors are made to use pantomime. Pantomime is an interesting and valuable form of dramatic art, but it is essentially symbolic and stagy and has, I believe, no place in the moving picture play as we have developed it. If owing to the faulty construction of the play, or a lack of skill on the part of producer or actors, all sorts of gestures and grimaces become necessary that would not be required if the words were heard, the production can not be considered good. Sometimes, of course, words are *seen;* though not heard. The story of the deaf mutes who read the lips of the movie actors, and detected remarks not at all in consonance with the action of the play, is doubtless familiar. It crops up in various places and is as ubiquitous as Washington's Headquarters. It is good enough to be true, but I have never run it to earth yet. Even those of us who are not deaf-mutes, however, may detect an exclamation now and then and it gives great force to the action, though I doubt whether it is quite legitimate in a purely picture-play.

I beg leave to doubt whether realism is fostered by a method of production said to be in vogue among first rate producers; namely keeping actors in ignorance of the play and directing the action as it goes on.

"Come in now, Mr. Smith; sit in that chair; cross your legs; light a cigar; register perplexity; you hear a sound; jump to your feet"—and so on. This may save the producer trouble, but it reduces the actors to marionettes; it is not thus that masterpieces are turned out.

Is there any chance of a movie masterpiece, anyway? Yes, but not in the direction that most producers see it. What Vachell Lindsay calls "Splendor" in the movies is an interesting and striking feature of them—the moving of masses of people amid great architectural construction—sieges, triumphs, battles, mobs— but all this is akin to scenery. Its movements are like those of the trees or the surf. One can not make a play entirely of scenery, though the contrary seems to be the view of some managers, even on the stage of the regular theatre. So far, the individual acting and plot construction in the great spectacular movies has been poor. It was notably so, it seems to me in the Birth of a Nation and not much better in Cabiria. Judith of Bethulia (after T. B. Aldrich) is the best acted "splendor" play that I have seen. Masterpieces are coming not through spending millions on supes, and "real" temples, and forts; but rather by writing a scenario particularly adapted to film-production, hiring and training actors that know how to act for the camera, preferably those without bad stage habits to unlearn, cutting out all unreal scenery, costume and make-up and keeping everything as simple and as close to the actual as possible. The best movie play I ever saw was in a ten-cent theatre in St. Louis. It was a dramatization of Frank Norris's "McTeague." I have never seen it advertised anywhere, and I never heard of the actors, before or since. But most of it was fine, sincere work, and seeing it made me feel that there is a future for the movie play.

One trouble is that up to date, neither producers nor actors nor the most intelligent and best educated part of the audience take the movies seriously. Here is one of the marvels of modern times; something that has captured the public as it never was captured before. And yet most of us look at it as a huge joke, or as something intended to entertain the populace, at which we, too are graciously pleased to be amused. It might mend matters if we could have every day in some reputable paper a column of readable serious stuff about the current movie plays—real criticism, not simply the producer's "blurb."

Possibly, too, a partnership between the legitimate stage and the movie may be possible and I shall devote to a somewhat wild scheme of this sort the few pages that remain to me. To begin with, the freedom enjoyed by the Elizabethan dramatists from the limitations imposed by realistic scenery has not been sufficiently insisted upon as an element in their art. Theirs was a true *drame libre,* having its analogies with the present attempts of the vers-librists to free poetry from its restrictions of rhyme and metre. But while the tendency of poetry has always been away from its restrictions, the *mise-en-scene* in the drama has continually, with the attempts to make it conform to nature, tightened its throttling bands on the real vitality of the stage.

Those who periodically wonder why the dramatists of the Elizabethan age—the greatest productive period in the history of the English stage—no longer hold the stage, with the exception of Shakespeare, and who lament that even Shakespeare is yielding his traditional place, have apparently given little thought to this loss of freedom as a contributing cause. While the writers of *vers libre* have so far freed themselves that some of them have ceased to write poetry at all, it is a question whether the scenic freedom of the old dramatists may not have played such a vital part in the development of their art, that they owed to it at least some of their pre-eminence.

Shakespeare's plays, as Shakespeare wrote them, read better than they act. Hundreds of Shakespeare-lovers have reached this conclusion, and many more have reached it than have dared to put it into words. The reason is, it seems to me, that we can not, on the modern stage, enact the plays of Shakespeare as he intended them to be acted—as he really wrote them.

If we compare an acting edition of any of the plays with the text as presented by any good editor, this becomes increasingly clear. Shakespeare in his original garb, is simply impossible for the modern stage.

The fact that the Elizabethan plays were given against an imaginary back-ground enabled the playwright to disregard the old, hampering unity of place more thoroughly than has ever been possible since his time. His ability to do so, was the result not of any reasoned determination to set his plays without "scenery," but simply of environment. As the scenic art progressed, the backgrounds became more and more realistic and less and less imaginary. The imagination of the audience, however, has always been more or less requisite to the appreciation of drama, as of any other art. No stage tree or house has ever been close enough to its original to deceive the onlooker. He always knows that they are imitations, intended only to aid the imagination, and his imagination has always been obliged to do its part. In Shakespeare's time the imagination did all the work; and as imaginary houses and trees have no weight, the services of the scene-shifter were not required to remove them and to substitute others. The scene could be shifted at once from a battlefield in Flanders to a palace in London and after the briefest of dialogues it could change again to a street in Genoa—all without inconveniencing anyone or necessitating a halt in the presentation of the drama. Any reflective reader of Shakespeare will agree, I think, that this ability to shift scenes, which after all, is only that which the novelist or poet has always possessed and still possesses, enables the dramatist to impart a breadth of view that was impossible under the ideas of unity that governed the drama of the Ancients. Greek tragedy was drama in concentration, a tabloid of intense power—a brilliant light focussed on a single spot of passion or exaltation. The Elizabethan drama is a view of life; and life does not focus, it is diffuse—a congeries of episodes, successive or simultaneous—something not re-producible by the ancient dramatic methods.

To-day, while we have not gone back to the terrific force of the Greek unified presentation, we have lost this breadth. We strive for it, but we can no longer reach it because of the growth of an idea that realism in *mise-en-scéne* is absolutely necessary. Of course this idea has been injurious to the drama in more ways than the one that we are now considering. The notable reform in stage settings associated with the names of Gordon Craig, Granville Barker, Urban, Hume and others, arises from a conviction that *mise-en-scéne* should inspire and reflect a mood—should furnish an atmosphere, rather than attempt to reproduce realistic details. To a certain extent these reforms also operate to simplify stage settings and hence to make a little more possible the quick transitions and the play of viewpoint which I regard as one of the glories of the Elizabethan drama. This simplification, however, is very far from a return to the absolute simplicity of the Elizabethan setting. Moreover, it is doubtful whether the temper of the modern audience is favorable to a great change in this direction. We live in an age of realistic detail and we must yield to the current, while using it, so far as possible, to gain our ends.

This being the case, it is certainly interesting to find that, entirely without the aid or consent of those who have at heart the interests of the drama, a new dramatic form has grown up which caters to the utmost to the modern desire for realistic detail—far beyond the dreams of ordinary stage settings—and at the same time makes possible the quick transitions

that are the glory of the Elizabethan drama. Here,
of course, is where we make connection with the moving picture, whose fascinating realism and freedom
from the taint of the footlights have perhaps been
sufficiently insisted upon in what has been already
said. In the moving picture, with the possibility of
realistic backgrounds such as no skill, no money, no
opportunity could build up on the ordinary stage—
distant prospects, marvels of architecture, waving
trees and moving animals—comes the ability of passing from one environment to another, on the other
side of the globe perhaps, in the twinkling of an eye.
The transitions of the Elizabethan stage sink into in-
significance beside the possibilities of the moving-
picture screen. Such an alternation as is now common in the film play, where two characters, talking
to each other over the telephone, are seen in quick
succession, would be impossible on the ordinary
stage. The Elizabethan auditor, if his imagination
were vivid and ready, might picture such a background of castle or palace or rocky coast as no pho-
tographer could produce; but even such imagination
takes time to get under way, whereas the screen-
picture gets to the brain through the retina instantly.

It is worth our while, I think, to consider whether
this kind of scenery, rich in detail, but immaterial
and therefore devoid of weight, could not be used in
connection with the ordinary drama. There are obstacles, but they do not appear insuperable. The
ordinary moving-picture, of course, is much smaller
than the back drop of a large stage. Its enlargement
is merely a matter of optical apparatus. Wings must
be reduced in number and provided each with its own
projection-machine, or replaced with drops similarly
provided. Exits and entrances must be managed
somewhat differently than with ordinary scenery.

All this is surely not beyond the power of modern stagecraft, which has already surmounted such obstacles and accomplished such wonders. The projection, it is unnecessary to say, must be from behind, not from before, to avoid throwing the actors' shadows on the scenery. There must still, of course, be lighting from the front, and the shadow problem still exists, but no more than it does with ordinary scenery. Its solution lies in diffusing the light. No spotlight could be used, and its enforced absence would be one of the incidental blessings of the moving scene.

The advantages of this moving-picture scenery would be many and obvious. Prominent among them of course are fidelity to nature and richness of detail. The one, however, on which I desire to lay stress here is the flexibility in change of scene that we have lost with the introduction of heavy material "scenery" on our stages. This flexibility would be regained without the necessity of discarding scenery altogether and going back to the Elizabethan reliance on the imagination of the audience.

Of course, moving scenery would not be required or desired in all dramatic productions—only in those where realistic detail combined with perfect flexibility and rapidity of change in scene seems to be indicated. The scenery should of course be colored, and while we are waiting for the commercial trichroic picture with absolutely true values, we may get along very well with the di-chroic ones, such as those turned out with the so-called Kinemacolor process. Those who saw the wonderful screen reproduction of the Indian durbar, several years ago, will realize the possibilities.

And more than all else, may we not hope that these new backgrounds may react on the players who perform their parts in front of them? Not necessarily; for we have seen that it does not always do so in the present movie play. But I am confident that the change will come. Little by little the necessities of the case are developing actors who act naturally. One may pose in a canoe on a painted rapid; but how can he do so in the real water course, where every attitude, every play of the muscles must be adapted to the real propulsion of the boat?

In short, the movie may ultimately require its presenters to be real, and so may come a school of realism in acting that may have its uses on the legitimate stage also.

Who will be the first manager to experiment with this new adjunct to the art of the stage?

A WORD TO BELIEVERS*

People may be divided into a great many different classes according to their attitude toward belief and beliefs—toward the meaning and value of belief in general—toward their own beliefs and those of their neighbors. We have the man who does not know what "belief" means, and who does not care; the man whose idea of its meaning is perverse and wrong; the man who thinks his own beliefs are important and those of his neighbors are unimportant; the man who thinks it proper to base belief on certain considerations and not on others—the man, for instance, who will say he believes that two plus two equals four, but can not believe in the existence of God because the grounds for such belief can not be stated in the same mathematical symbols. These are only a few of the classes that might be defined, using this interesting basis of classification. But before we can take up the question of instruction in the church's beliefs, about which I have been asked to address you this evening, we must recognize the existence of these classes, and possibly the fact that you yourselves are not all in accord in the way in which you look at the subject.

What I shall say is largely personal and you must not look upon me as representing anybody or anything. I may even fail to agree with some of the instruction that you have received in this interesting and valuable course. But I do speak, of course, as one who loves our church and as a loyal and I hope a thoughtful layman.

* Address at the closing session of the Church School of Religious Instruction, St. Louis.

First, what is belief? We surely give the word a wide range of values. A man says that he believes in his own existence, which the philosopher Descartes said was the most sure thing in the world—"*Cogito, ergo sum.*" He also says that he believes it will rain to-morrow. What can there be in common between these two acts of faith? Between a certainty and a fifty per cent chance, or less? This—that a man is always willing to act on his beliefs; if not, they are not beliefs within the meaning of this address. If you believe it will rain, you take an umbrella. Your doing so is quite independent of the grounds for your belief. There may really be very little chance of its raining; but it is your belief that causes your action, no matter whether it is justified or not. You could not act more decisively if you were acting on the certainty of your own existence. It is this willingness to act that unifies our beliefs—that gives them value. If I heard a man declare his belief that a fierce wild animal was on his track, and if I then saw him calmly lie down and go to sleep on the trail, I should know that he was either insane or a liar.

I have intimated above that belief may or may not be based on mathematical certainty. Fill up a basket with black and white pebbles and then draw out one. Let us create a situation that shall make it imperative for a person to declare whether a black or a white pebble will be drawn. For instance, suppose the event to be controlled by an oriental despot who has given orders to strike off the man's head if he announces the wrong color. Of course, if he has seen that only white pebbles went into the basket he says boldly "White." That is certainty. But suppose he saw one black pebble in the mass. Does he any the less say "White"? That one black pebble represents a tiny doubt; does it affect the direction of his enforced action? Suppose there were two black pebbles; or a handful. Suppose nearly half the pebbles were black? Would that make the slightest difference about what he would do? If you judge a man's belief by what he does, as I think you should do, that belief may admit of a good deal of doubt before it is nullified. Are your beliefs all based on mathematical certainties? I hope not; for then they must be few indeed.

That many of our fellow men have a wrong conception of belief is a very sad fact. The idea that it must be based on a mathematical demonstration of certainty, or even that it must be free from doubt is surely not Christian. Our prayers and our hymns are full of the contrary. We are beset not only by "fightings" but by "fears"—"within; without;" by "many a conflict, many a doubt"; we pray to be delivered from this same doubt. The whole body of Christian doctrine is permeated with the idea that the true believer is likely to be beset by doubts of all kinds, and that it is his duty, despite all this, to believe.

And yet there are many who will not call themselves Christians so long as they can not construct a rigid demonstration of every Christian doctrine. There are many thoughtful men who call themselves Agnostics just because they can not be mathematically sure of religious truth. Some of these men are better Christians than many that are so named. That they hold aloof from Christian fellowship is due to their mistaken notion of the nature of belief. The more is the pity. Now let us go back for a moment to our basket of pebbles. We have seen that the action of the guesser is based to some extent on his knowledge of the contents of the basket. In other words, he has grounds for the belief by which his act

is conditioned. Persons may act without grounds;
it may be necessary for them so to do. Even in this
case there may be a sort of blind substitute for belief.
A man, pursued by a bear, comes to a fork in the road.
He knows nothing about either branch; one may lead
to safety and one to a jungle. But he has to choose,
and choose at once; and his choice represents his bid
for safety. There is plenty of action of this sort in
the world; if we would avoid the necessity for it we
must do a little preliminary investigation; and if we
can not find definitely where the roads lead, we may
at least hit upon some idea of which is the safest.

But with all our investigation we shall find that
we must rely in the end on our trust in some person;
either ourselves or someone else. Even the certainty
of the mathematical formula depends on our confidence in the sanity of our own mental processes.
The man who sees the basket filled with white pebbles
must trust the accuracy of his eyesight. If he relies
for his information on what someone else told him, he
must trust not only that other's eyesight, but his
memory, his veracity, his friendliness. And yet one
may be far safer in trusting another than in relying
on his own unaided powers. *Securus judicat orbis
terrarum,* says the old Latin. "The world's judgment is safe." We have learned to modify this, for
we have seen world judgments that are manifestly incorrect. The world thought the earth was flat. It
thought there were witches, and it burned them.
Here individuals simply followed one another like
sheep; and all, like sheep, went astray. But where
there is a real, independent judgment on the part of
each member of a group, and all agree, that is better
proof of its correctness than most individual investigations could furnish. My watch, of the best
make and carefully regulated, indicates five o'clock,

but if I meet five friends, each of whom tells me, independently, that it is six, I conclude that my watch is wrong. There was never a more careful scientific investigation than that by which a French physicist thought he had established the existence of what he called the "N ray"—examined its properties and measured its constants. He read paper after paper before learned bodies as his research progressed. He challenged the interest of his brother scientists on three continents. And yet he was entirely wrong: there never was any "N ray." The man had deceived himself. The failure of hundreds to see as he did weighed more than his positive testimony that he saw what he thought he saw. Here as elsewhere our view of what may be the truth is based on trust. If you trust the French physicist, you will still believe in the "N ray." Creeds we are told, are outworn, and yet we are confronted, from birth to death, with situations that imperiously require action of some sort. Every act that responds must be based on belief of some kind. Creeds are only expressions of belief. The kind of Creed that *is* outworn (and this is doubtless what intelligent persons mean when they make this statement) is the parrot creed, the form of words without meaning, the statement of belief without any grounds behind it or any action in front of it. For this the modern churchman has no use.

And if he desires to avoid the parrot creed, he must surely inform himself regarding the meaning of its articles and the grounds on which they are held. More; he must satisfy himself of the particular meaning that they have for him and the personal grounds on which he is to hold them. This is the reason why such a course as that which you complete to-night is necessary and valuable. I have heard instruction of this kind deprecated as likely to bring disturbing elements into the mind.   One may doubtless change from belief to skepticism by too much searching.   It used to be a standing joke in Yale College, when I was a student there, that a well-known professor, reputed to be an Atheist, had been perfectly orthodox until he had heard President Porter's lectures on the "Evidences of Christianity."   But seriously, this objection is but another phase of the fallacy at which we have already glanced—that doubts are fatal to belief.   I am certain that the professor in question might have examined in detail every one of President Porter's "Evidences," and found them wanting, only to discover clearer and stronger grounds of belief elsewhere—in his mere confidence in others, perhaps. Or he might have turned pragmatist and believed in Christianity because it "worked"—a valid reason in this case doubtless, but not always to be depended on ; because the Father of Lies sometimes makes things "work" himself—at least temporarily.

But if examining into the grounds of his belief makes a man honestly give up that belief, then I bid him God-speed.   I may weep for him, but I cannot help believing that he stands better with his Maker for being honest with himself than if he had gone on with his parrot belief that meant absolutely nothing. I can not feel that the Aztecs who were baptized by the followers of Cortes were any more believers in Christianity after the ceremony than they were before.   It seems to me, however that a Christian, examining faithfully the grounds of his belief, will usually have that belief strengthened, and that a churchman, examining the doctrines of the church will be similarly upheld.

Not that church instruction should be one-sided. The teaching that tends to make us believe that every intelligent man thinks as we do reacts against itself.

It is like the unfortunate temperance teaching that represents the liking for wine as always acquired. When the pupil comes to taste wine and finds that he likes it at once, he concludes that the whole body of instruction in the physiology of alcohol is false and acts accordingly. When a boy is taught that there is nothing of value beyond his own church, or nothing of value outside of Christianity, he will think less of his church, and less of Christianity when he finds intelligent, upright, lovable outsiders. I look back with horror on some of the books, piously prepared under the auspices of the S. P. C. K. in London, that I used to take home from Sunday School. In them we were told that a good man outside the church was worse than a bad man in it. If that was not the teaching in the book, it was at least the form in which it took lodgment in my boyish brain. Thank God it never found permanent foothold there. Instead, I hold in my memory the Eastern story of God's rebuke to Abraham when he expelled the Fire Worshipper from his tent. "Could you not bear with him for one hour? Lo! I have borne with him these forty years!"

I have always thought that a knowledge of what our neighbors believe is an excellent balance-wheel to our own beliefs and that our own beliefs, so balanced, will be saner and more restrained. It would be well, I think, if we could have a survey of the world's religions, setting down in parallel columns all the faiths of mankind. If this is too great a task we might begin with a survey of Christianity, set down in the same way. I believe that the results of such a survey might surprise us, showing, as I think it would do, the many fundamentals that we hold in common and the trivial nature of some of the barriers that appear to separate us.

In your course, just completed, you have had such a survey, I doubt not, of the beliefs of our own beloved church. Where her divines have differed, you have had the varying opinions spread before you. You have not been told that the mind of every churchman has always been a replica of the mind of every other churchman. Personally, I feel grateful that this has not been the case. As I say my creed and begin "I believe in God, the Father Almighty," I realize that the aspect of even such a basic belief as this, is the same in no two minds; that it shifts from land to land and from age to age. I know that God, as he is, is past human knowledge and that until we see Him face to face we can not all mean just the same thing when we repeat this article of belief. But I realize also that this is not due to the mutability of the Almighty but to man's variability. The Gods of St. Jerome, of Thomas Carlyle and of William James are different; but that is because these men had different types of minds. Behind their human ideas stands God himself—"the same yesterday, to-day and forever." So we may go through the creed; so we may study, as you have been doing, the beliefs of the church. Everywhere we see the evidences of the working, upon fallible human minds of a dim appreciation of something beyond full human knowledge—

> "That one far-off divine event
> Toward which the Whole Creation moves."

We have a wonderful church, my friends. It is a church to live with; a church to be proud of. Those who miss what we are privileged to enjoy are missing something from the fulness of life. We have not broken with the historic continuity of the Christian faith: there is no chasm, filled with wreckage, between us and the fathers of the church. Above all we have enshrined our beliefs in a marvellous liturgy, which is ever old and ever new, and which had the good fortune to be put into English at a day when the force of expression in our Mother tongue was peculiarly virile, yet peculiarly lovely. I know of nothing in the whole range of English literature that will compare with the collects as contained in our Book of Common Prayer, for beauty, for form, for condensation and for force. They are a string of pearls. And indeed, what I have said of them applies to the whole book. When I see Committees of well-meaning divines trying to tamper with it, I shudder as I might if I witnessed the attempt of a guild of modern sculptors to improve the Venus of Milo by chipping off a bit here and adding something there. Good reasons exist for changes, doubtless; but I feel that we have here a work of art, of divine art; and art is one of God's ways of reaching the human heart. We are proud that we have not discarded it from our church buildings, from our altars, from the music of our choirs. Let us treat tenderly our great book of Common Prayer, like that other great masterpiece of divine literary art, the King James version of the Bible. There are plenty of better translations; there is not one that has the same magic of words to fire the imagination and melt the heart.

These are all trite things to say to churchmen: I have tried, on occasion, to say them to non-churchmen, but they do not seem to respond. There are those who rejoice in their break with historic continuity, who look upon a written form of service with horror. It is well, as I have said, for us to realize that our friends hold these opinions. One can not strengthen his muscles in a tug of war unless some one is pulling the other way. The savor of religion, like that of life itself, is in its contrasts. I thank God that we have them even within our own Communion.

We are high-church and low-church and broad-church. We burn incense and we wear Geneva gowns. This diversity is not to be condemned. What is to be deprecated is the feeling among some of us that the diversity should give place to uniformity—to uniformity of their own kind, of course. To me, this would be a calamity. Let us continue to make room in our church for individuality. God never intended men to be pressed down in one mold of sameness. In the last analysis, each of us has his own religious beliefs. The doctrines of our church, or of any church are but a composite portrait of these beliefs. But when one takes such a portrait throughout all lands and in all time, and the features keep true, one can not help regarding them as the divine lineaments.

This is how I would have you regard the beliefs of our church, as you have studied them throughout this course—as our particular composite photograph of the face of God, as He has impressed it on the hearts and minds of each one of us. I commend this view to those who have no reverence for beliefs, particularly when they are formulated as creeds. These persons mean that they have no regard for group beliefs but only for those of the individual. Each has his own beliefs, and he must have confidence in them, for they are the grounds on which he acts, if he is a normal man. Even the faith of an Agnostic is based on a very positive belief. As for me, I feel that the churchman goes one step beyond him: he even doubts Doubt. Said Socrates: "I know nothing except this one thing, that I know nothing. The rest of you are ignorant even of this." Socrates was a great man. If he had been greater still, he might have said something like this: "I freely acknowledge that a mathematical formula can not satisfy all the cases that we discuss. But neither can it be stated mathematically that they are all unknowable.   I am not even sure that I know nothing." Surely, under these circumstances, we may give over looking for mathematical demonstrations and believe a few things on our own account—that our children love us—that our eyes do not deceive us; that the soul lives on; that God rules all. We may put our faith in what our own church teaches us, even as a child trusts his father though he can not construct a single syllogism that will increase that trust.

This does not mean that we shall not benefit by examining the articles of our faith; by learning what they are, what they mean and what others have thought of them. The churchman must combine, in his mental habits, all that is best of the Conservative and the Radical. While holding fast that which is good he must keep an open mind toward every change that may serve to bring him nearer to the truth or give him a clearer vision of it.

How we can insure this better than by such an institution as the Church School for Religious Instruction I am sure I do not see. May God guide it and aid it in its work!

INDEX

Magazines, Support of, 68
Magical remedies, 233
Magnet, Definition of, 87
Make-up in motion pictures, 317
Malemployment, 229
Maxwell Jas. Clerk, 115
Mayflower, The, 183
Medical Record, Strasburg, 305
Meetings in libraries, 147
Memory, Latent, 74
Meredith, Geo., 110
Mexican commission, 194
Military associations, 48
Mill, John Stuart, 243, 244
Mind, Male and female types, 272
Moderation, Lack of in America, 235
Mohammedanism, 219
Molecular theory, 115
Moon's motion, 84
Morals, Eclecticism in, 216
Morgan, J. P., 169
Motives of library users, 11
Moving pictures, 313
Municipal ownership and operation, 154
Music, American, 218

N-ray, 333
Narrative, earliest literary form, 37
National Academy of Fine Arts, 57
National Academy of Science, 52
National Education Association, 50; Address before, 145
Nautical Almanac, 80
New country, What is? 182
New England Society, 179
New York, Free Circulating Library, 19
New York, Library support in, 200; West side readers, 42
New York Public Library, 11, 30, 220
Newcomb, Simon, Sketch of, 79
Newspapers, 36
Newton, Isaac, 83
Non-partisanship of library, 250
Norris, Frank, 322

Omar Khayyam, 108
Open shelves, 104; Origin of, 225
Optic, Oliver, 174
Ostwald, Wilhelm, 114

Pacifism, 157
Pageant of St. Louis, 188
Pantomime in the motion picture, 320
Papers, Ready-made, for clubs, 270; scientific, 275
Pater, Walter, 168
Paulist fathers, 220
Pauperization, intellectual, 68
Pendleton, A. M., quoted, 140
Perry, Bliss, quoted, 211

Pharmacy, School of, address to, 229
Philadelphia Free Library, Address at, 67
Philosophy, an interesting subject, 133, 138; in America, 220
Phonograph, Uses of, 94
Physics made interesting, 138
Pickford, Mary, 247; 317
Planck, Max, 113, 120
Planets, Orbits of, 83
Players' Club, N.Y., 51
Pocahontas, 183
Poincaré, Henri, 113, 120
"Poison labels" for books, 96
Porter, Noah, 334
Posse, International, 159
Possessive case, Use of, 19
Pragmatism in America, 221
Prayer Book as literature, 337
Prescott, William H., 95
Press, Slight influence of, 13
Pride, Personal and group, 185
Princeton University, 219
Printing Art, magazine, 308
Programitis, club disease, 286
Programmes, Club, 268, 280, 295
Public as library owners, 205
Public Library, 169; eclecticism of, 221; people's share in, 197
Publicity, Library, 140
Publisher, Function of, 67
Puritanism, 219

Quanta, 121; hypothesis of, 113

Race-record, Library as a, 74
Radio-activity, 231
Rayleigh's Law, 120
Readers, Do they read? 3
Reading, mechanism of, 91; skill in, 135
Realism in education, 246; in motion pictures, 314
Recall, earliest form of, 213
Records, varieties of, 94
Recreation through books, 99
Religion in America, 219
Renewal, Preservation by, 97
Repetition a test of art, 166
Reprinting, Use of, 98
Re-reading, Art of, 163
Residual personality, 290
Resonators, 121
Revolution, American, notions of, 180; versus evolution, 279
Revue Scientifique, 113
Roethlin, Barbara E., 306
Roman Catholic Church, 220
Roman viewpoint in history, 181
Rome, decadence of, 227
Rousiers, Paul de., quoted, 55, 56, 57

St. Louis Academy of Science, paper before, 113
St. Louis, library tax in, 200
St. Louis Public Library, 140, 254, 302; meetings in, 150